It Works

"As followers of Jesus our primary calling is to love God first, our neighbors second, and to bear the fruit of the Spirit. This book will not only deepen your relationship with God and open you up to fresh ways of experiencing his transforming grace, but it will also help you develop a greater awareness of others and enable you to live a life of active worship."

—**Charles Hewlett**, National Leader,
Baptist Churches of New Zealand

"The Halsteads are nothing short of modern-day prophets and mystics, and their voices are greatly valued in the over-industrialized and utilitarian West. Drawing together a range of voices to speak to the effective and affective results of spiritual practices, they offer a breath of fresh air to our stale environment, they press pause on the noise of the world, and they call each of us to linger longer than we otherwise might in God's presence—however strange and uncomfortable that may be. Stories are offered here that have the power to shape our imagination, actions, and practices, all with the intent to hear God more clearly and become more like him in our daily lives. Perhaps 'tonic for the soul' would have been a suitable subtitle."

—**Myk Habets**, Head of School of Theology,
Laidlaw College, Auckland, New Zealand

"While the agent of our transformation into Christ's image is the Spirit, we are invited to partner with the living God in this process. *It Works* brims over with stories of these partnerships and how they are lived out in creative, embodied, and encultured practices. If you have ever struggled with intentional spiritual practices, I encourage you to read this book. You will discover just how life-giving partnering through these practices can be."

—**Christa L. McKirland**, Dean of Faculty,
Carey Baptist College, New Zealand

"*Ehara taku toa i te toa takitahi, engari he toa takitini*. This Māori proverb speaks to the strength of the collective. It so beautifully describes the treasure of this collaborative work. The acknowledgement, in this book, of land (*whenua*) and place resounds significantly to me as an indigenous person of New Zealand. Our *whenua* is where transformative spiritual practices are engaged, and our Creator God draws close. This is a rich and thought-provoking work from Philip Halstead and Angelika Halstead. *Tēnā kōrua*, I acknowledge you."

—**Luke Kaa-Morgan**, *Te Pouaraki* (Māori leader), Carey Baptist College, New Zealand

It Works

Stories of Transformative Spiritual Practices

Edited by
Philip John Halstead
and **Angelika Halstead**

WIPF & STOCK · Eugene, Oregon

IT WORKS
Stories of Transformative Spiritual Practices

Copyright © 2025 Wipf and Stock Publishers. All rights reserved. Except for brief quotations in critical publications or reviews, no part of this book may be reproduced in any manner without prior written permission from the publisher. Write: Permissions, Wipf and Stock Publishers, 199 W. 8th Ave., Suite 3, Eugene, OR 97401.

Wipf & Stock
An Imprint of Wipf and Stock Publishers
199 W. 8th Ave., Suite 3
Eugene, OR 97401

www.wipfandstock.com

PAPERBACK ISBN: 979-8-3852-4767-7
HARDCOVER ISBN: 979-8-3852-4768-4
EBOOK ISBN: 979-8-3852-4769-1

VERSION NUMBER 07/14/25

Unless otherwise marked, Scriptures are taken from the Holy Bible, New International Version®, NIV®. Copyright © 2011 by Biblica, Inc.™ Used by permission of Zondervan. All rights reserved worldwide. www.zondervan.com.

Scripture quotations marked ESV are from The ESV® Bible (The Holy Bible, English Standard Version®), © 2001 by Crossway, a publishing ministry of Good News Publishers. Used by permission. All rights reserved.

Scripture quotations marked MSG are taken from The Message, copyright © 2018 by Eugene H. Peterson. Used by permission of NavPress. All rights reserved. Represented by Tyndale House Publishers.

Scripture quotations marked NLT are taken from the Holy Bible, New Living Translation, copyright © 2015 by Tyndale House Foundation. Used by permission of Tyndale House Publishers, Carol Stream, Illinois 60188. All rights reserved.

Scripture quotations marked NRSV are from New Revised Standard Version Bible, copyright © 1989 National Council of the Churches of Christ in the United States of America. Used by permission. All rights reserved worldwide.

Scripture quotations marked NRSVUE are taken from the New Revised Standard Version Updated Edition. Copyright © 2021 National Council of Churches of Christ in the United States of America. Used by permission. All rights reserved worldwide.

Scripture quotations marked NTFE are from The New Testament for Everyone, 3rd ed. Copyright © 2019 by Nicholas Thomas Wright. The Society for Promoting Christian Knowledge. All rights reserved. Published by Zondervan, 2023, Grand Rapids, Michigan. www.zondervan.com.

Scripture quotations marked TLB are taken from The Living Bible, copyright © 1971 by Tyndale House Foundation. Used by permission of Tyndale House Publishers, Carol Stream, Illinois 60188. All rights reserved.

Scripture quotations marked TPT are from The Passion Translation®. Copyright © 2020 by Passion & Fire Ministries, Inc. Used by permission. All rights reserved. ThePassionTranslation.com.

Scripture quotations marked KJV or from the Māori translation are in the public domain.

Contents

Introduction | xi
 —Philip Halstead and Angelika Halstead

Prologue: Transformation Through Spiritual
 Practices: How Does It Work? | 1
 —Angelika Halstead

Part 1: Transformed Through the Power of Words and Scripture

1 Spiritual Exercises of Ignatius of Loyola | 23
 —Alan Jamieson

2 Lectio Divina: The Practice of Living in Scripture | 33
 —John Tucker

3 Replacing Worldliness via Remembering the Word | 50
 —Tim Collins

4 Reading the Bible Missionally | 60
 —George M. Wieland

Part 2: Transformed Through Returning to the Wild Earth and the Beauty of Creation

5 An Unexpected Journey: Hiking as a Spiritual Practice | 73
 —Santhosh George

6 Fostering a Contemplative Gaze Toward Creation | 85
 —Katrina Tulip

7   Contemplative Gardening: A Spiritual Practice
    That Prevents and Heals Burnout | 103
    —Angelika Halstead

Part 3: Transformed Through Principles and Radical Ways of Being

8   Counting Down Our Days | 121
    —Philip Halstead

9   The Joy of Having Less | 131
    —Jaimee van Gemerden

Part 4: Transformed Through Love and Living in Community

10 Catching Up with a Brother: The Intimacy of Fellowship | 143
    —Simon Moetara

11 Encountering God in the Whenua (The Land) | 154
    —Manakinui Te Kahu and Philip Halstead

12 But *How* Do We "Taste and See That the Lord Is Good?" Feasting as Spiritual Practice | 168
    —Michael J. Rhodes

Part 5: Transformed Through Prayer and Conversations with God

13 Karakia and Īnoi | 187
    —Lyndon Drake

14 Experiencing More of God | 198
    —Mick Duncan

15 Journaling Conversations with God | 207
    —Robyn Mellar-Smith

16 Prophetic Listening and Discernment: A Practical Introduction to Hearing God's Voice | 216
    —Tim Palmer

17 Prayer: A Near-Death Experience | 232
    —Sam Burrows

Part 6: Transformed Through the Arts

18   Practicing a Visual Spirituality: Fueling Your Eyes
        When Your Faith Depends on It | 245
    —Mike Crudge

19   The Sacred Art of Dancing | 255
    —Jenny De Leon

Index | 267

Introduction

Philip Halstead and Angelika Halstead

Hungry for God

Have you longed to draw closer to God but not known how to do so? Is your present relationship with the divine feeling flat?[1] Are you looking for fresh spiritual practices to enliven your devotional life? Would you like to have a resource up your sleeve to offer folks who wish to connect more deeply with God? If you responded with a yes to any of these questions, this book is for you.

While many fine books have been written on the topic of spiritual practices,[2] this one is unique. It portrays nineteen people's stories of searching for meaningful spiritual practices and how they engage with them.[3]

Some of the spiritual practices discussed in the book are original. One reason for their freshness is God's inside knowledge of every writer and God's desire to connect with each one of them (and all of us) in a uniquely personal way. A second is that every author penned their accounts whilst residing in Aotearoa (New Zealand). Given the country's striking landscapes and its vast surrounding oceans, it is not surprising

---

1. For an interesting discussion on the concept of boredom and spiritual practices see Strawn and Gioielli, "Spiritual Practices Are Boring."

2. See, for example, Blythe, *50 Ways to Pray*; Calhoun, *Spiritual Disciplines Handbook*; and Foster, *Celebration of Discipline*.

3. We prefer the term *spiritual practices* to *spiritual disciplines* and *spiritual exercises* because the phrase *spiritual practices*, for some folks, encourages trying with no expectation of perfection, whereas the labels *spiritual disciplines* and *spiritual exercises*, for some people, have connotations of dourness, drudgery, and oppression. Having said that, for ease of reading we do interchange the terms on occasions.

that land and sea feature in some of the narratives. Sheila Pritchard describes this dynamic well: "Of course my spirit and God's Spirit have a chance to meet when I am close to the work of his hands."[4] A third plausible explanation for the newness of three of the practices is that their authors are Māori. Māori are the indigenous people of Aotearoa, and te reo Māori, often just "te reo," (which features in their chapters) is their mother tongue. We have experienced that te ao Māori(the Māori worldview) has much to teach the likes of us. It "is an interconnected framework that emphasises the harmony between humans and the environment" and hapori (community) "is at the heart of te ao Māori. Values like manaakitanga (hospitality) and whanaungatanga (kinship) emphasise the importance of nurturing relationships and supporting one another."[5] For those of us who are not so familiar with these rich perspectives, the spiritual practices discussed by Simon Moetara (chapter 10), Manakinui Te Kahu (chapter 11), and Lyndon Drake (chapter 13) may be of especial benefit.

Of course, none of the above is to discount the import of tried and proven spiritual practices; after all, spiritual exercises have a long, rich, and proven pedigree.[6] Jesus practiced "the three most important disciplines of Judaism"—namely, alms giving, prayer, and fasting from food for spiritual purposes.[7] And if you were to study the life of any biblical luminary, saint, or godly person you know, you would invariably discover a range of spiritual practices that these folks employ.

The book also illustrates how spiritual practices help to transform people's lives. In our view, spiritual journeys are supposed to be transformative and purge us of our egocentric ways. Spiritual practices promote these changes and lead us to truth; truth in turn is a springboard to freedom; freedom leads us to love; and love empowers us to be cocreators with Christ and set the world ablaze with love. This will be further explained in the following chapter which describes the process of transformation in more detail.

So, what exactly are spiritual practices and how can they be employed? John Mark Comer contends that they are "disciplines based on the lifestyle of Jesus that create time and space for us to access the

4. Pritchard, *On the Journey*, 17.

5. New Zealand Association of Resource Management, "Te Ao Māori" (italics added).

6. Forster, "Disciplines, Spiritual," 311.

7. Forster, "Disciplines, Spiritual," 311.

presence and power of the Spirit and, in doing so, be transformed from the inside out."[8] Comer continues,

> What drills are to basketball . . . the practices are to becoming a person of love. We do what we can do—read Scripture, pray, practice Sabbath, eat a meal with community—to be formed into people who can *eventually* do what we *currently* cannot do: live and love like Jesus.[9]

Adele Ahlberg Calhoun paints a similar picture. She states that spiritual practices "put us in a place where we can begin to notice God and respond to his word to us." They "give the Holy Spirit space to brood over our souls" and to birth "the ever-fresh Christ-life within."[10] Whilst our engagement in these disciplines does not necessarily obligate God to act, they prepare us for his movements and Calhoun argues that "unless we open ourselves to [God] through spiritual practices, we will miss his coming altogether."[11]

Joshua Jipp underscores these points in more technical language:

> If sharing in the life of God through the person of Christ is humanity's supreme good—an eschatological reality that nevertheless has been inaugurated *now* through humanity's relation to Christ and the Spirit—one must learn about the specific practices that facilitate growth toward humanity's telos. Any account of human flourishing, in other words, must set forth the mechanisms. Disciplines, habits, and exercises that facilitate this growth through offering a practical account of what to do and how to live.[12]

The transformational changes that we are talking about within these pages do not occur overnight. Neither do they materialize by magic, alchemy, or embodying the latest fad. Perseverance with at least one or even several practices is needed to experience change and greater connection with God. Paul's exhortation to Timothy to train himself in godliness (1 Tim 4:7) underscores this requisite. This is why Comer says, "There are no accidental saints."[13]

---

8. Comer, *Practicing the Way*, 177.
9. Comer, *Practicing the Way*, 178.
10. Calhoun, *Spiritual Disciplines Handbook*, 19.
11. Calhoun, *Spiritual Disciplines Handbook*, 19.
12. Jipp, *Pauline Theology*, 201.
13. Comer, *Practicing the Way*, 80.

When Annas the high priest and numerous other dignitaries noticed "the courage of Peter and John" as they preached the gospel, they "realized that they were unschooled, ordinary men, they were astonished and they took note that these men had been *with* Jesus" (Acts 4:13; italics added). We need to be *with* Jesus to be transformed by Jesus and to get to know him better. We need to be *with* Jesus to be emboldened and empowered by him to preach with authority and heal the infirm in his name (Acts 3:1–10). Spiritual practices are a primary means of facilitating this sense of *withness* and profound connection to Jesus.

How to Read This Book

There are several ways that you can engage with this book. You may, for instance, read it from cover to cover. You might pick a spiritual practice after surveying the table of contents and identifying one that resonates with you. Or you may choose to read the introductory words that precede each of the nineteen narratives to determine which practice to try. The key is to start somewhere and trial one to create movement and momentum.

The Layout of This Book

Angelika Halstead's chapter "Transformation Through Spiritual Practices" follows these preliminary pages. It explains how the psycho-spiritual nature of transformation occurs. As you digest this rich fare, you will observe a shift in Angelika's story from linear to more cyclical and inclusive approaches, from cerebral to experiential learning, and from individual to collective ways of being. Interestingly, Angelika likens this path to that of finding her authentic self, or the way home, or the place where God resides.

The ensuing nineteen narratives have been clustered under six categories:

1. Transformed Through the Power of Words and Scripture

Words are powerful whether you write, read, speak, or listen to them. A word in season can change the trajectory of a life. Words inspire, comfort, encourage, exhort, heal, and transform us. Words can also release stress- and anxiety-inducing hormones like cortisol as well as feel-good hormones such as dopamine and endorphins. What we think of and meditate on influences our bodies, souls, and spirits, and shapes our characters and realities.

Scripture intensifies these realities. We know that Scripture is "God-breathed" and "useful for teaching, rebuking, correcting and training in righteousness, so that the servant of God may be thoroughly equipped for every good work" (2 Tim 3:16–17). However, if the word of God is not making its way from our heads to our hearts, from abstract concepts to practical actions, its value and efficacy are greatly undermined. It may end up having no more impact than reading a good novel or the news. Since engaging with God's word is essential for our spiritual growth, transformational journeys, and effective service, this first cluster of spiritual practices show us a number of ways to engage effectively with biblical texts.

In chapter 1, Alan Jamieson introduces us to the "Spiritual Exercises of Ignatius of Loyola" that are designed to slow us down in our reading of Scripture, so that we might move from a place of merely reading the words to a place where we allow them to read our lives. By using not just our rational thinking but also our imaginations and senses, we place ourselves into the context of the Scripture and allow our hearts to be moved, our emotions to be stirred, and our God-given desires to arise. We do this with the intention of responding to God's promptings and call in our lives.

John Tucker unpacks a second Ignatian exercise—"Lectio Divina: The Practice of Living in Scripture"—in chapter 2. This approach understands Scripture as a meeting place for a personal encounter with the divine. Our reading of the Bible turns into a dialogue with God where we listen deeply to the voice of God and respond to what we hear with our hearts. Over time, this beautiful practice expands our capacity to sense God's presence in our daily lives and activities.

In chapter 3, Tim Collins discusses the spiritual exercise of Scripture memory. Tim shows us how the verses we commit to memory can take up residence within us, rewire our brains (think neuroplasticity), and transform our thoughts, emotions, and behaviors. Bible verses learned by heart can also be accessed in times of need and thereby offer us comfort, guidance, and encouragement for our paths.

George Wieland invites us in chapter 4 to dig deeply into the word of God by "Reading the Bible Missionally." This profound way of engaging with Scripture signifies a purposeful movement and is an important theme in the narrative of the Bible and the life of the church. We are not only called to know God and deepen our relationship with him, but also to make him known to others.

2. Transformed Through Returning to the Wild Earth and the Beauty of Creation

Have you ever been surprised by the beauty found in nature? Has your soul ever been coaxed to the land of wonder by a luminous moment where heaven and earth seemed to be one? The perfection of a rainbow, a sunrise, the play of the waves along a sandy beach, fragrant pine trees, wild blueberries, or the lightness of a bird's feather pirouetting on the autumn breeze are all invitations to linger at the thresholds where the unknown and divine await us. The authors of the next three chapters know about the beauty of nature. They have felt its call and how it invites us beyond ourselves into a world that is teeming with possibilities and sacred encounters.

In chapter 5, Santhosh George shares his experience of hiking as a transformative spiritual practice that moves him from places of restriction to states where he feels more whole, expansive, unified, compassionate, curious, and open to God. Experiencing these extraordinary rewards may only be a hike away for you!

The spiritual practice of contemplative nature gazing is the focus of chapter 6. Therein, Katrina Tulip describes how she receives solace and inspiration through her escapades in the cathedral of the great outdoors. It is in nature where she meets the One who can never be fully known, claimed, controlled, or even predicted. As she goes on her contemplative walks and allows God to find her, she discovers new dimensions of his inexhaustible qualities that inspire and transform her life.

The focus of chapter 7 is succinctly summarized in its title—"Contemplative Gardening: A Spiritual Practice that Prevents and Heals Burnout." Angelika Halstead describes in these pages the five stages of her own burnout experience and shares how her daily practice of visiting the sanctuary of her garden and tending to her plants brought healing and restoration to her body and soul. A garden can teach us many things and applying its lessons can change the way we approach other areas of our lives and our relationships with God.

3. Transformed Through Principles and Radical Ways of Being

One of the many benefits of spiritual practices is that they help to clear away clutter that impedes our view of God and thereby enable us to see God and the eternal more accurately. The next two chapters illustrate this dynamic graphically.

In chapter 8, Philip Halstead depicts the practice of "Counting Down Our Days" and how this simple exercise of reminding himself every day that he is mortal has revolutionized his life in a good way. The practice engenders playfulness, aids decision-making, brings clarity and focus, and orders priorities. What is more, it takes less than one minute per day.

Many of us are familiar with the phrase "less is more."[14] In "The Joy of Having Less" Jaimee van Gemerden introduces us to the vivifying practices of simplicity and asceticism within a range of Christian spiritualities and shows us how we can become more by consuming less. These disciplines are based on the teachings of Jesus and lead to the transformation of our desires and a new way of engaging with God and the world around us. Moving away from lifestyles of domination and exploitation to principles of reciprocity and regeneration not only change us but also our surroundings and the future of this planet.

4. Transformed Through Love and Living in Community

The chapters in this fourth cluster affirm that we are relational beings, created by love and for love. Our need to belong and our desire to love and be loved are deeply ingrained into our innermost beings. Love is like a portal that opens our minds and hearts to the breadth and depth of communion, acceptance, and inclusion.

Proverbs 27:9 (TPT) states, "Sweet friendships refresh the soul and awaken our hearts with joy, for good friends are like the anointing oil that yields the fragrant incense of God's presence." In chapter 10, Simon Moetara describes the spiritual practice of "Catching Up with a Brother: The Intimacy of Fellowship." For Simon, this involves going to a friend in times of need. Sometimes the two men will converse. On other occasions, they may eat a steak, watch a movie, or simply *be* in one another's presence. Every time Simon engages in the spiritual practice of going to

---

14. The phrase "less is more" is widely attributed to Ludwig Mies van der Rohe, a pioneer of modern architecture and minimalism. See Van der Lubbe, "Less Is More."

a trusted brother, he comes alive, feels loved, and knows that he belongs. Unsurprisingly, it also supports the metamorphosis in both men.

Manakinui Te Kahu and Philip Halstead's chapter 11 is titled "Encountering God in the Whenua (The Land)." In it, Manakinui describes his regular practice of travelling to his family's whenua to meet with God. The ten-hour drive to the family land is part of this pilgrimage. It entails leaving his day-to-day life behind and adopting a heart of expectancy for God to speak. As Manakinui draws close to God, God in turn draws close to him (Jas 4:8–10 TLB).

In chapter 12, Michael Rhodes spotlights the biblical claim that communal feasts play a pivotal role in spiritual formation. They include food and beverages that differ in quantity or quality from our normal food practices and, more often than not, ritual elements. If you seek closer intimacy with God and you like food, this chapter may well transform your life.

5. Transformed Through Prayer and Conversations with God

Expectedly, the topic of prayer comprises a major section in this book. This is not surprising, because the very way we communicate with God is prayer. There are many forms prayer can take, including spoken, written, or silent methods. It may encompass the reciting of specific texts or taking part in customs that assist us to practice the presence of God and/or listening to God. Prayer changes us. It also fosters a sense of connection and decreases isolation, loneliness, and fear.

Having established the importance and benefits of prayer, Lyndon Drake commences our conversation on the topic of prayer by addressing the question when to pray. He does this by introducing us to the spiritual practice of liturgical morning and evening prayers. Morning prayers prepare us for the day and ready us to find God, beauty, and wonder in the ordinary. Evening prayers assist us to review our day, thank God for his faithfulness, release the burdens of the day, and thus lighten our load. These liturgical prayers provide a bright light that carries us through dark hours and a container that is large enough to hold our vulnerability, frailty, and unbelief.

In chapter 14, Mick Duncan leads us on an extraordinary journey. From his beginnings in the hippie drug counterculture to a place where Jesus is as close as he can be, Mick's prayer journey of almost fifty years educates, challenges, inspires, and dazzles us. As you read this chapter you are reminded that all things are possible in Jesus and through prayer.

Imagine you could ask God any question and God would respond with a clear and comprehensible answer. Suppose you could write to God about absolutely anything, and God in turn would interact with you and offer you his perspectives. Robyn Mellar-Smith describes this very process in chapter 15, titled "Journaling Conversations with God," and shares some of her experiences.

Relatedly, Tim Palmer teaches us about listening to God's voice in his inspiring chapter, "Prophetic Listening and Discernment: A Practical Introduction to Hearing God's Voice." He leads us through a series of four exercises in prophetic listening that encourages believers of all ages to develop the spiritual practice of listening to God. Tim also explores the important topic of discernment as people move from an individual focus on listening prayer toward a collective practice.

Chapter 17 is titled "Prayer: A Near-Death Experience." Sam Burrows shares his experience of spiritual awakening during the COVID lockdowns which resulted in the revolution of his prayer life. By following a morning routine of reading a short passage of Scripture, spending some time in contemplation, and praying for various people, his attitude toward God, others, and the unfolding of each day was radically transformed. Sam describes a path that goes beyond traditional forms of prayer and allows God to become what we most desire. Intrigued?

6. Transformed Through the Arts

Dallas Willard argues that "to withhold our bodies from religion is to exclude religion from our lives. Our life is a bodily life, even though that life is one that can be fulfilled solely in union with God."[15] The authors of the book's last two chapters concur.

In "Practicing a Visual Spirituality," chapter 18, Mike Crudge shares his faith journey and discovery of a spiritual practice that aligns with his learning style and personality. As a person who strongly responds to visual images, Mike seeks in the world around him signs of God's presence and character. He believes that art transcends language and feeds the imagination. Visual images with their beauty and enchantment create moments of awe and wonder. They communicate what words fail to convey and move us to liminal spaces. It is here where we transcend our current limitations and see glimpses of God and God's wonder-full world.

---

15. Willard, *Spirit of the Disciplines*, 31.

We finish this book with a chapter on dancing because this practice, like no other spiritual practice, engages every part of our beings—our bodies, souls, and spirits. Jenny De Leon has dedicated her whole life to choreographing and dancing in preparation for the time when she can dance face-to-face before her Lord and Maker. The sacred art of dancing has not just been a form of physical movement for Jenny but a means of connecting with God with her entire being and aligning herself to his character and will. As she dances, she yields to God's presence and force at work within her. With every movement of her body, she surrenders both her ego and willfulness so that God's love and wisdom can move through her unhindered.

After nineteen stories we present our offering to you, the reader, with the prayer that one or more of the spiritual practices described in this book will contribute to your personal transformation and increase your intimacy with the author of your life.

Bibliography

Blythe, Teresa A. *50 Ways to Pray: Practices from Many Traditions and Times.* Nashville: Abingdon, 2006.

Calhoun, Adele Ahlberg. *Spiritual Disciplines Handbook: Practices That Transform Us.* Downers Grove, IL: InterVarsity, 2005.

Comer, John Mark. *Practicing the Way: Be with Jesus, Become like Him, Do as He Did.* Colorado Springs: WaterBrook, 2024.

Forster, Roger T. "Disciplines, Spiritual." In *New Dictionary of Christian Ethics and Pastoral Theology,* edited by David J. Atkinson and David F. Field, 311–12. Downers Grove, IL: InterVarsity, 1995.

Foster, Richard J. *Celebration of Discipline: The Path to Spiritual Growth.* San Francisco: HarperSanFrancisco, 1998.

Jipp, Joshua W. *Pauline Theology as a Way of Life: A Vision of Human Flourishing in Christ.* Grand Rapids: Baker Academic, 2023.

New Zealand Association of Resource Management. "Te Ao Māori." https://nzarm.org.nz/resources/knowledge-hub/te-ao-maori.

Pritchard, Sheila. *On the Journey: A Collection of Columns from the Popular Series in Reality Magazine.* Auckland, NZ: Impetus, 2000.

Strawn, Brad D., and Chris D. Gioielli. "Spiritual Practices Are Boring: A Psychoanalytic Understanding of Spiritual Ennui." *Pastoral Psychology* 69 (2020) 509–22. https://link.springer.com/article/10.1007/s11089-020-00926-1.

Van der Lubbe, Tom. "Less Is More: What Organizations Can Learn from Mies van der Rohe." Corporate Rebels, Oct. 10, 2020. https://www.corporate-rebels.com/blog/mies-van-der-rohe.

Willard, Dallas. *The Spirit of the Disciplines: Understanding How God Changes Lives.* New York: HarperOne, 1998.

Prologue

Transformation Through Spiritual Practices

How Does It Work?

Angelika Halstead

In this foundational chapter I will first describe what has influenced my own spiritual practices and how these practices have developed and changed throughout the years. This chapter then further highlights the purpose of spiritual practices and describes how they affect not just our spiritual development but also lead to psycho-spiritual growth and transformation. These considerations are informed by Carl Jung's concept of the human self with its conscious and unconscious domains and by the idea that spiritual practices encourage an inward, upward, and outward motion.

In 2005, I completed my studies as a spiritual director. After a twenty-year career in education I said yes to a vocation as a spiritual director and counselor. Since then, I have had the privilege of accompanying many individuals on their spiritual journeys. And what a joy it has been to support others who were eager to develop their spiritual lives further. Many of these precious people longed for a deeper and more intimate connection with God. They wanted to know God's character, get glimpses of their own souls, and discern how God is inviting them to live, love, and be in the world around them. I have greatly appreciated my directees' willingness to change and strong commitment to spiritual growth.

In the ensuing years, I noticed that the persons who consulted me were looking for bigger patterns and larger possibilities than their current ones. They did not want to be driven by the cultural trends and norms of their time. Rather than accepting the status quo and accommodating a worldview based on power, prestige, and possession, they longed for their story to unfold differently. These folks searched for alternative ways of living, new vistas, and more transcendent perspectives. Although they had a strong desire to deepen their faith, they did not know what practical steps to undertake to reach the next phase of their spiritual growth and evolution. Some of them had engaged in well-known spiritual practices but discontinued them because they could not understand how these exercises would impact their spiritual formation or transform their relationship to God, others, and the different aspects of their unique and wondrous beings.

Being more attuned to God, hearing and responding to his voice, and reaching higher levels of consciousness and psycho-spiritual transformation was what these spiritual seekers wanted to learn more about. They asked questions like, "How do we grow in our capacity to love God?" "How do we cultivate more compassion for others and for our own longings, desires, and the choices we have made?" Phil and I wanted to respond to these people's quests, and this is how the idea for this book emerged.

This book also tries to respond to the complex issues we face in our epoch. In a time where many of us suffer under information fatigue we need activities that help us cultivate a sound mind. There is a high level of chaos in the world, and we are all exposed to numerous stress points that consistently push us to our limits. Many of us have heavy hearts and lose hope and motivation to fight the systems of this world. There is war, destruction, hatred, and little care for life, the planet, and the thriving of human and other beings. All of this can be overwhelming and sometimes our nervous system does not feel equipped or strong enough to cope with the onslaught of terrible news from all corners of the globe. How do we respond to this situation and this destructive era with love, wisdom, and goodwill? How do we move away from denial and despair even as the conflict and the division in our world and society threaten us?

In these challenging times, more than ever before, we need spiritual practices that ground us deeply in our relationship with God, ourselves, others, and the natural world around us. We need practices that sustain our inner strength, and give us a profound sense of purpose, and connectedness; practices that combat the bitterness, fear, disappointment, and toxicity of our century. Our souls desire to be recharged with love, mercy, vision, anticipation, and equanimity. This time calls for a regular spiritual practice that teaches us spiritual resilience and equips us to live good lives of defiant joy.

Imagining a better future starts by finding it within ourselves. Engaging in a meaningful regular spiritual practice will help us firstly to care for our own spiritual health and growth. As we nourish our faith, we feel resourced to help others tend their inner flame, spirituality, and devoutness. Together we can then change the world.

Stages of Faith and Spiritual Practices

I am writing this chapter at the age of sixty-five. Having grown up in a Christian family and followed Jesus all my life I call myself a seasoned spiritual seeker and a person who has always been looking for new ways to deepen my faith. My experience shows that an intentional and consistent commitment to spiritual practices greatly impacts our spiritual development and maturation. I have therefore faithfully engaged in such practices. I grew up in a fundamentalist church, then immersed myself into the charismatic renewal. This was followed by the inner healing movement and later the contemplative tradition. As I reflect on the different stages of my spiritual journey, I notice a tripartite connection between first, my psychological development; second, the particular spiritual practices I engaged with; and third, the church communities or faith traditions I was part of in each given season. Let me explain this further.

In the early stage of my faith while living in Germany, I attended a fundamentalist church that focused on nonnegotiable concepts and the literal meaning of the Bible, Jesus's resurrection, the atonement, evangelism, and the imminent physical second coming of Jesus. Reading and studying the Bible by paying attention to the text's original, historical and literary contexts, learning Scriptures by heart, allowing God to search my heart and convict me of my wrongdoings through the Scriptures I read, and praying for my friends' salvation were daily practices during this season. Learning and obeying the principles and rules of a Christian life, building a sound foundation and biblical understanding, and finding my place in a church community paralleled my psychological development.

My life was focused on success, security, and containment or, as Richard Rohr calls it, on creating a proper container and answering "the first essential questions: 'What makes me significant?' 'How can I support myself?' and 'Who will go with me?'"[1]

In my thirties I was drawn to the charismatic renewal movement which emphasizes the availability of the gifts of the Holy Spirit described in 1 Cor 12:1–11 and the need for a personal relationship with God through Jesus Christ. Singing God's praises, praying in tongues, engaging in spiritual warfare prayers, listening to God's voice and writing down what I perceived God was saying shaped my devotional times in this season. Parallel to this development in my faith journey was my experience of leaving my home country, the narrow valleys of the Black Forest and a very ordered and predictable lifestyle, and of immigrating to New Zealand. Living in a new country gave me an opportunity to depart from more traditional forms of Christianity and venture into new unknown areas.

The next phase of my spiritual journey was influenced by the inner healing movement, which is purported to have started with Agnes Sanford.[2] This Christ-centered prayer approach invites the Holy Spirit into areas of brokenness, grief, or woundedness, and is geared toward the healing of memories and emotions. When I was introduced to this healing ministry, I was encouraged to engage in personal prayer, forgiveness, and repentance. Lies that had operated as self-protecting schemes were rejected and replaced with biblical truths, and painful memories were processed by inviting God's presence into these places and asking him to pour his healing love into the wounded parts of my being. For me this was quite a soul-searching and painful yet very fruitful season. Parental wounds, generational sins, boundary and self-esteem issues, and my fear of abandonment were addressed and worked through. It was a journey that took me from my head to my heart and into deeper levels of my subconscious mind. Some of the spiritual practices that I employed here included journaling to get in touch with my emotions, confession, visualizing God's healing touch, exercising more transparency and trust in my key relationships, and spending time in God's loving gaze and presence.

In my late forties, my search for authentic, personal knowledge of the truth and for transformative dimensions brought me in touch with

---

1. Rohr, *Falling Upward*, 1.
2. Renovaré, "Agnes Sanford."

contemplative Christianity. I accepted this tradition's invitation toward silence, solitude, and stillness and built regular moments for contemplation and silent retreats into my daily, weekly, and monthly timetable. In my devotional times I followed an Ignatian approach where I used my senses and imagination to place myself into a biblical text to experience the story more holistically and become part of it. (Alan Jamieson expands on the Ignatian approach to prayer in chapter 1.) Over the next period, I also engaged in centering prayer, seeking God in nature, gratefulness practices, the examen,[3] and a daily practice of listening to God to better connect with myself and divine love. Contemplative spirituality is not about adding more to our lives but rather about simplifying our days so that we can focus on the journey home to the place within where God dwells.

In my fifties I became acutely aware that I, like many others, am motivated by the primal needs for safety and security, affection and esteem, and power and control, which are woven into our central nervous system and deeply rooted in our physical bodies. Thomas Keating, an American Catholic monk and priest who developed the contemplative practice of centering prayer confirms this by saying, "Our issues are in our tissues."[4] I learned that we cannot become free from or move beyond these attachments on our own, or by sheer willpower, or intellectual insight. We need a profound revelation of God's love and his transformative work within us to free us.

In my work as a spiritual director and therapist, I have always been interested in the intersection of psychology and spirituality.[5] My own life has been shaped by an irresistible passion for exploration and the longing for continuous becoming and greater consciousness that expresses itself in new and more complex ways. I have been fascinated by what I call "sacred moments," those mysterious "peak experiences" that often lead to new insights, breakthroughs, and change.[6] A desire for such moments and an interest in the journey and process of transformation has been with me for a very long time.

In recent years I have observed that sacred moments relate to states beyond ego and that spiritual practices, such as contemplation and

---

3. The examen is a five-step spiritual exercise that helps us to notice God's activities in our lives. See, for example, Calhoun, *Spiritual Disciplines Handbook*, 52–55.

4. Keating, quoted in Begeman et al., *Welcoming Prayer*, 14.

5. This and the following three paragraphs are adapted from my unpublished PhD dissertation. See Halstead, "Writing Your Way Home," 2.

6. Maslow, *Religions, Values, and Peak-Experiences*, 59–68.

meditation, train our egos to collaborate with God. I feel drawn past the "threshold (*limen*, in Latin)" of rational thinking and into the sacred space that anthropologists call liminality. It is the place where "we are betwixt and between the familiar and the completely unknown,"[7] a place where "the transformation of consciousness, perspective, and heart" takes place.[8]

This liminal space for me is like a waiting room. It is filled with anticipation. Entering this space can be life giving but it can also be unsettling and induce a type of inner crisis; however, this can make us receptive and prepare us for the needed transition. For change to happen, for new vistas to be seen, we need to move out of our comfort zone or "business as usual" and relinquish control. We need to be willing to have our current beliefs deconstructed and open ourselves up to a new point of view, "to another world, that is much bigger and more inclusive, that both relativizes and reenchants this world that we take as normative."[9] Our hope is that the practices introduced in this book will take you to this other world.

Moving Inward

Moving inward, upward, and outward through spiritual practices is what the chapters in this book invite you to do. These three movements combine the psychological, spiritual, and generative aspects that are essential for spiritual growth and transformation. Some of the practices introduced in this book interweave all three movements, others focus on one or two of them.

The inward journey invites you to become present to yourself, take stock of your life and circumstances, and get in touch with your emotions and inner workings. It embraces rather than ignores our inner reality and invites us to pause frequently and notice the deeper workings of our minds. Paying attention to our thoughts, feelings, body sensations, and inner realities can open new pathways for our personal and spiritual growth.

Many of us carry emotional baggage from previous life experiences. This is stored in our neural pathway system and our bodies. The collection of both our positive and painful memories is present in the conscious and unconscious domains of our beings. It influences or colors our

---

7. Rohr, "Liminal Space," para. 2.
8. Rohr, *Everything Belongs*, 48.
9. Rohr, *Everything Belongs*, 5.

perceptions of life, ourselves, others, and God. People who are unaware of these emotional and physical residues usually project their unsorted and unacknowledged material onto other people or God. Spiritual practices that help us to pause and notice our conscious, semi-conscious, and unconscious thoughts and emotional patterns can offer us important insights into how our internal landscape, perspectives, and perceptions have been shaped by our past experiences.

As we move inward and reflect on our desires and experiences, as well as the choices we have made, we gain insights into our automatic reactions and patterns. We are then able to choose more conscious responses and make wiser choices. Spiritual practices that help us to move into these interior places might bring up emotional responses and disturbances that, although first unpleasant, will gradually lead to new levels of awareness and growth. Inviting a dialogue between our conscious and unconscious domain can remove barriers toward transformation and growth. It can also help our understanding of who we truly are and thus lead to an ever-deepening relationship to ourselves, others, and God.

Socrates famously said, "The unexamined life is not worth living."[10] The inward movement in our spiritual practices encourages us to examine our lives in the presence of our loving God. As we pay attention to what arises in our hearts, revisit and name our human experiences, and look at our experiences through God's eyes, we discover his perspectives and holy invitations. This activity keeps a sense of wonder alive. It engages us in thinking about what makes life worth living and how we might in the future live with more love and less fear.

We do not undertake the inward journey on our own but in communion with God and sometimes by turning to trusted others. David prays in Ps 139:23, "Search me, God, and know my heart; test me and know my anxious thoughts." When we pray this prayer God will bring to our awareness what we need to know about our inner landscape. As we present our anxious thoughts before God and process our wounds as well as the thoughts and emotions connected with them, we invite a greater level of order and peace into our interiority. Practices that focus on this inner journey help to identify and heal that which hinders us from being connected to our deepest and most authentic self, which is the self that God communes with.

---

10. Plato, *Apology* 38a5–6.

There are parts of us that we wrestle with and need to soften by meeting them with compassion. It is often in the seasons of our life when we feel especially vulnerable, overwhelmed, and stretched thin that we dig a little deeper within ourselves to find the loving presence of the divine spark within us. When we are hospitable to the inner workings of our heart and learn to process our thoughts and emotions, we feel more equipped to meet life as it comes to us. We then live with a greater level of openness, connectedness, freedom, and equanimity. The call of hospitality is so important in these turbulent times. As we meet the wounded parts within ourselves with love, compassion, and care we become equipped to offer hospitality to others and can make room for the lament, grief, and weeping that comes with witnessing the violence and loss of life. May we encourage you to try out some of the spiritual practices in this book that invite you to connect with the parts within you that need healing and your attention. Follow these inner invitations and dare to go within and practice your way into a renewed way of being.

Moving Upward

Unsurprisingly, moving upward takes us beyond our limited understanding of our personal or cultural stories and images of God. It widens our horizons and opens us to new insights and inspirations. James 4:8 (ESV) states, "Draw near to God, and he will draw near to you." The great aim here is that we do not settle for a Christian life in isolation or at a distance from God, but rather that we fellowship with him. Drawing near to God has to do with directing our attention into the presence of God, allowing his gaze to remind us of our belovedness, grounding our whole being in his goodness and love, and allowing him to become the anchor of our soul and reality—making God our North Pole.

All relationships are built on an investment of time. The more time we spend with Jesus and seek to know and understand him, the more we will become like him and are familiar with his ways. Pioneers and experts in relationship science, John and Julie Gottman, have invented the concept of *love maps* which describe the cognitive space in your brain that is allocated to a particular person.[11] These maps entail all the information that you have collected about the other person's history, concerns, personality, preferences, and reality. Similarly, most spiritual practices

---

11. Gottman and Gottman, *Gottman Love Map Exercise*.

mentioned in this book move us upward into God's presence and into a deeper, more intimate, and connected relationship with him.

As I write this chapter, I reflect on the summer holiday we have just returned from. We spent ten days in Papamoa at a beautiful New Zealand beach relaxing in the sun and swimming in the ocean. Both of these activities are like soaking in the presence of God. Enjoying the sunshine and taking the beautiful warmth of the sun into our bodies compares to resting in the presence of God and receiving the goodness of the Holy Spirit. When we immerse ourselves in water while swimming in the sea, every part of us gets wet and all we come in touch with afterward will be saturated. Similarly, our spending time in God's presence affects all areas of our lives and the world around us. I do not know about you, but spending time with God seems much easier when I am less busy and more relaxed.

In our modern life our thoughts are often filled with chatter, worry, and distraction. How can we connect with God in a deep and personal way when our minds are so busy and preoccupied? How can we eradicate spiritual poverty when we constantly distract ourselves with social media and activities that stop us from entering the silence where we hear the whispers of the Holy Spirit? Jesus shows us the way. He often withdrew to solitary places to spend quality time with his Father. Like many of us, Jesus longed for peace and quiet and understood the need of his inner life for contemplation.

I am wondering if Jesus was longing to rest in the compassionate, understanding, loving gaze of his Father, the place where he felt fully seen, heard, and understood, the place where he got restored on a neurobiological and spiritual level. I am also wondering if he, like me, used these times to attune to God in a way where he felt deeply beloved and profoundly free. What is evident is that these special times with his Father greatly influenced his ministry and service. Jesus says, "I tell you the truth, the Son can do nothing by himself. He does only what he sees the Father doing. Whatever the Father does, the Son also does" (John 5:19 NLT). May we learn from Jesus, and after times of moving inward and upward feel refreshed and ready to venture out into the world and serve our God in whatever way we are called to.

Moving Outward

As followers of Jesus, we are sent into the world to be agents of positive change. We are called to be salt and light and fully immerse ourselves in the places and work we inhabit. Our spiritual practices prepare us to be more alive in the world, to participate in our communities, and to be active for the common good. Finding longer moments of solitude in the day might be difficult for parents of little children. However, even if it is only five minutes, having a regular devotional time with God and engaging in spiritual practices will give us the strength, courage, and vitality for meaningful times in our work, other holy assignments such as bringing up children, and social action. This might also include participating in the restoration of God's beloved creation, standing up for injustices, challenging political and cultural ideas, speaking truth to power, or assisting in other humanitarian efforts and actions.

When we feel deeply grounded in our faith and well resourced through our spiritual practices, we can face the challenges of this world knowing that, although we have pain now, we will see Jesus again and our heart will rejoice and no one can take our joy from us (John 16:22 NRSVUE). There is a quality to this joy that flows out of our times with God. It is a defiant joy that we can experience and express even amid all chaos and suffering. It is a joy that has a prophetic edge to it. It is a joy that does not meet the challenges and trials of life with disappointment, bitterness, fear, or negativity but rather reframes them. Our times with God and the resulting joy help us to create a story of spiritual resilience, and a story of potential filled with vision, anticipation, mercy, love, and equanimity. It is a joy that can both mourn the losses and sadness of our time and imagine that although we walk through the valley of the shadow of death we hold on to God's presence and the fact that something beautiful can be born and that love will always win.

Regular spiritual practices present intentional actions that over time form a habit that leads to the transformation of our character and a different quality of life. These habits open our eyes to the reality of God's love, keep us aligned with his will and calling for our lives, and thus determine our future and destiny. Spiritual practices are therefore not an optional secondary pathway but more like an animating, inspiring, life-giving, and life-changing center of everything.

There are short-term effects and long-term benefits connected with spiritual practices. Hal Elrod describes in his book *The Miracle Morning* six practices to engage with before 8:00 a.m. that will long-term transform the reader's life. He uses the acronym SAVERS to introduce these lifesaving practices and encourages the reader to practice Silence, Affirmations, Visualization, Exercise, Reading, and Scribing.[12] Similarly, the spiritual practices described here in this book will prompt insight, soften entrenched patterns, deepen character, and positively influence your well-being. They will help you to discover the abundance of God's nourishing gifts, such as inner peace, hope, love, strength, resilience, gratitude, and joy, which respond to your soul's true hungers and, over time, transform you.

Many of the practices described in this book interrupt our ordinary way of thinking or processing information and create a new level of awareness or way of seeing. A single moment of illumination or lucid seeing can cleave our heart, open our mind, and free us from illusions. We are suddenly able to perceive God's movements and activities and focus on the good, the true, and the beautiful in everything. Our mind goes quiet, and an inner window opens providing entrance to a world beyond our normal vision. The ordinary becomes sacred and the common miraculous in those moments of heightened awareness. I wonder if you are familiar with the magic that sometimes transpires?

These illuminating moments that often happen when we engage in spiritual practices arrest our discursive and thinking mind. Furthermore, they change our sense of time and get us in touch with what is eternal. American psychologist Abraham Maslow used the term *being psychology* (*B-psychology*) as opposed to *deprivation psychology* (*D-psychology*) to describe the shift in our awareness that often occurs during spiritual practices. During moments of B-psychology we have a different sense of time and space, and experience feelings of wholeness, harmony, freedom from interior conflicts, and a sense of deep connection to God, others, nature, and ourselves.[13]

The Pathway Home

This book invites you to engage in a regular and meaningful spiritual practice to advance your transformational journey and find your way home to the place of your most authentic self from which you commune

12. Elrod, *Miracle Morning*, xxi.
13. Maslow, *Religions, Values, and Peak-Experiences*, 106.

with God. Included are nineteen writers' presentations of transformative spiritual practices that have grown out of their individual journeys with God. This book also responds to questions such as: What are the stages and the goals of transformation? What kind of change is possible? What would enable this change to happen? How can psychological and spiritual work complement and support each other on this transformational path? I would like to offer now some foundational thoughts to this inquiry.

Mystics, saints, and sages have described transformation as the quest for union with God and as a progression beyond the self. It is a movement toward the sacred and transcendent that ultimately leads to unitive consciousness and thus overcomes all divisions, dichotomies, and dualisms of the world. On this transformational journey we connect more deeply with God as the source of all life, goodness, and love, and with our own inner wisdom, deepest self, and most authentic being.

Through the literature I have read, the stories of others I have listened to, and my own experiences, I have come to believe that there is a home or a place where God dwells within us at the center of our being (1 Cor 3:16). Merton describes this home as a place that is "untouched by sin and by illusion, a point of pure truth, a point or spark which belongs entirely to God . . . and is inaccessible to the fantasies of our own mind."[14] We begin our lives with our own unique, divine DNA, this inner destiny, or absolute core, that knows who we are. Some people call it the divine indwelling, or the Holy Spirit within us. Throughout our life this *imago Dei* begs to be allowed and to show itself more fully. Home for Merton equates to the true self, while a Zen master might call it "the face we had before we were born."[15] The language spoken here is love, and in our original "unwoundedness," or innocence, we are open to receiving and giving love to God, others, and ourselves and living in a state of full connection. Transformational journeys will always lead us home.

Sadly, as we grow up we learn to think of ourselves as separate. We often experience the world as an unsafe place and thus learn the language of fear and consequently spend many years building this separate, egoic, or small self. We get attached to its labels and habits and carefully position ego boundaries around it to protect this social construct and creation of our mind. Interestingly, spiritual teachers like Jesus, the Buddha, the "Teresas" (Ávila, Lisieux, and Calcutta), as well as the mystical

---

14. Merton, *Conjectures of a Guilty Bystander*, 158.
15. Merton, quoted in Rohr, *Everything Belongs*, 77.

poets Hafiz, Kabir, and Rumi, all talk about the need to lose ourselves in order to find ourselves (Mark 8:35). They encourage us to let go of our small, relative, provisional, passing, or manufactured self with its rigid ego boundaries and open ourselves up to the divine and the language and culture of love. Immersed in love we become free of fear and over time our whole being gets transformed into what we behold. We find peace, contentment, and authenticity. Here we are at home and know that love is the ultimate reality.

Maslow, who is considered a founding father of both humanistic and transpersonal psychology, believed that spirituality is innate and that ultimately all human development is a spiritual realization. He argues that we are naturally inclined to press toward good values, such as serenity, kindness, courage, honesty, love, unselfishness, and goodness. The highest ideas that we strive for include the following values: wholeness, perfection, completion, justice, aliveness, richness, simplicity, beauty, goodness, uniqueness, effortlessness, playfulness, truth, and self-sufficiency. These values are not mutually exclusive, separate, or distinct, but rather interrelated "facets of Being."[16]

Many Scriptures in the Bible talk about transformation. We are encouraged to not be conformed to this world but be transformed by the renewal of our mind because then we will be able to test and approve what God's will is—his good, pleasing, and perfect will (Rom 12:2). When we consider nature, we understand that nothing is static. Everything changes, grows, evolves, and unfolds. Similarly, our understanding of God evolves and deepens, and our psychological, spiritual, and moral development surely advances as well. Jesus believed in transformation and change. One of the first public words he spoke was later translated into the Greek verb *metanoeite*, which literally means "change one's mind."[17] It infers going beyond what we know and equates to radical transmutation and transformation at the deepest seat of consciousness itself.

The transformation Jesus talked about leads to a primal change of worldview, or of perceiving and processing information (see Matt 4:17 and Mark 1:15). Instead of letting the culture and paradigms around us shape our storyline of human history we are invited to reframe and redirect the way we think and live according to the gospel. This reprogramming and resulting transformation will enable us to approach the lives

---

16. Maslow, *Toward a Psychology of Being*, 93.
17. Danker et al., *Greek-English Lexicon*, 640.

we lead and the work we do with openheartedness. We will then perceive and recognize God within ourselves, in others, and in all things.

As I reflect on my life, I realize that my spiritual development paralleled my psychological growth and maturation and that both are very closely intertwined. Similarly, I have come to understand that my knowledge and understanding of God are closely connected to my self-knowledge. It is difficult to determine which precedes or gives birth to the other. There have been times in my past when I overspiritualized everything and lost touch with my humanity, and there have been times when I got lost in self-absorption and lived as a sleepwalker on autopilot in a state of mindlessness where God felt very distant. I then learned about the gift of consciousness and that paying attention and practicing presence is the doorway to the transcendent. The cultivation of awareness and presence is an important part of my spiritual practice now and has helped me to experience oneness, truth, and goodness.

My own journey of psycho-spiritual growth and transformation can be defined as "the trajectory of life from innocent beginning, through inevitable brokenness, to putting everything together, through ripening into union—with self, God, the world, and others."[18] It can also be described as the aligning of my heart and mind or the journey from the head to the heart which although literally is a short distance can be the longest and hardest journey anyone ever takes. Depth psychologist David Benner writes that "ultimately, all spiritual practices center on helping the mind enter and take residence in the heart. Like a bird going back to its nest at the close of the day, the mind winds up all its activities as it settles into its home in the heart."[19] But what do we mean by the heart or, in other words, the landscape of our soul?

Psychiatrist Carl Gustav Jung has greatly influenced my understanding of the psyche—which I define as the soul, mind, spirit—and the journey toward spiritual growth and transformation. Jung believed that the transformative journey is at the heart of all religions and that by meeting our innermost being, we also meet and unite with God. This path encourages us to understand our primary purpose which, according to Jung, is to fulfil our deep, innate potential and thus become a true individual who contributes meaningfully to the world.[20]

---

18. Rohr, *Spring Within Us*, 15.
19. Benner, *Human Being and Becoming*, 92.
20. Stein, *Jung's Map of the Soul*, 171.

The landscape of the soul includes conscious and unconscious realms. Although we naturally spend most of our time in the conscious realm, Jung invites us to explore and integrate the subtle, unconscious, and transpersonal aspects of our human experience. These unconscious parts include blueprints and ruling paradigms that often show up in our dreams and behaviors. Our rational mind often dismisses these patterns; however, they can present significant blockages on our spiritual path. If we pay attention to messages revealed from the subconscious mind, and welcome, love, and integrate the various parts of our psyche, we can create a greater level of healing, wholeness, and union with God.

In Jung's understanding of the human self, most of our energy centers around our consciousness, which describes what we know, think, have experienced, and consider to be our reality and identity. Between consciousness and personal unconsciousness, or shadow, is a line called the ego. Our ego can act like a permeable membrane allowing interaction between conscious and unconscious realms or like a rigid boundary line. Our ego greatly influences what is happening in our consciousness and is motivated by our desire and need for safety and security, for control and power, and for affection and esteem. In the bottom half of the circle, we find the deep unconscious, or collective unconscious, which Jung views as the seat of our soul. This part represents our deepest, truest, most authentic, original being and is the place where the Holy Spirit dwells and where we commune with God. It is the place from which the Self emerges, which transcends our comprehension and can be best understood as the "God within us." This Self has an internal drive toward wholeness and transformation and demands conversation between the conscious and unconscious to work through contradictions and personal failures.[21]

Depending on our upbringing, past experiences, and the level of healing that has occurred throughout our life, our ego is either secure, healthy, and flexible or unhealthy, insecure, and rigid. A childhood where the child felt affirmed, seen, heard, and understood, as well as unconditionally loved, contributes to the development of a confident and strong ego and identity. Conversely, parenting that is dysfunctional, oppressive, abusive, invasive, or neglectful contributes to the development of a weak or undeveloped ego. Since our ego's function is to maintain a stable self-image and sense of control, which are both needed for our survival and protection, our ego is naturally highly defended and self-protective and tries to avoid

---

21. Ulanov and Dueck, *Living God and Our Living Psyche*, 20–22.

humiliation. Our ego is eager to define itself "in terms of comparing, competing, analyzing, critiquing, judging, labelling, and positioning."[22]

Jung saw the building of a healthy ego structure with a strong sense of identity and security as an important task of the first half of our lives. The focus in the second half of our lives is the decentering of one's ego and the loosening of the ego's hold on our awareness and identity so that we can enter the transformative field. It is here in the unconscious realm, or the place of our true and authentic self, where we find a deeper source of purpose through a unitive encounter with God and the experience of God's action within.

Below the ego line is the personal unconscious or shadow self which includes aspects that are hidden and denied or have been consistently disowned. The shadow aspects are often repressed and projected onto others or God, and Jung suggested that in order to achieve self-knowledge the shadow parts have to be acknowledged as "present and real" and as important parts of our being.[23] Transformation requires serious shadow work and invites a process of rediscovering and re-owning these aspects of ourselves. Opening to the multiple dimensions of our shadow, befriending and integrating them, is part of the journey toward spiritual awakening, wholeness, and personal growth.

Understanding the process of psycho-spiritual transformation has greatly enhanced my spiritual life. It has increased my motivation to engage in regular spiritual practices and my understanding of how they create change in my psyche, character, and way of being. I hope these insights will also impact and enrich your spiritual life.

As you read through the different chapters in this book you will discover spiritual practices, such as the study of holy Scriptures, that engage your consciousness, build a solid theological foundation, and encourage you to serve. Other practices aim to soften and quiet our noisy ego so that we can enter deeper layers of our unconscious being. We calm the mental chatter and overactive mind to enter our inner quiet space. It is here where we find possibilities for healing and where our self unfolds and collaborates with God and the process of growth. Practices that include times in nature often lead us to holy moments of awe and wonder. When we are awestruck, we transcend our egoic mind and limited understanding and connect with our deeper self. It is in these moments that our eyes

---

22. Rohr, "Letting Go of the Pain-Body," para. 2.
23. Jung, *Essential Jung*, 91–92.

are opened to the reflection of God in the human, in the animal, and in the entire natural world. Some of the practices in this book help us to work with our shadows and cleanse the lenses of our heart. Freed of illusions and with a sharpened perception of what is real we become pure in heart and can see God (Matt 5:8) more clearly and unite with him.

Transformation: Choosing a Different Operating System

Cynthia Bourgeault equates the false self to our egoic mind and the true self to our deeper self and the mind of the heart. She sees the false self as a part of ourselves that is wounded, defended, boundaried, and neurotic. It is concerned with the desire for security and survival, esteem and affection, power and control. On the other hand, it is also a part that constructs a lot of our energy and helps with decision making. Bourgeault therefore suggests that we should honor, respect, and embrace this part of our being. In comparison, the true self is the part of us that feels more real than anything else. It wants to connect with the divine and find its unique giftedness, calling or vocation, and place in this world. It is naturally open and spacious, and can be likened to our home, soul, and essential self.[24]

Our egoic mind or "egoic operating system,"[25] traps us in the search for our true self and holds us in the finite world. For transformation to occur we therefore need a different operating system of perception, namely a "God Positioning System" (GPS). This GPS changes the way we look at the world and puts our mind into our heart. It is open-minded, inquisitive, and non-dualistic in nature. Additionally, it has subtle, subconscious, transpersonal faculties. These include psychic and extrasensory abilities, aesthetic qualities, and intuition. The GPS goes beyond the limited analytic system. Its boundaries are fluid, and it has a more cosmic perspective with a strong drive for unity and connectedness. This operating system is in our heart and operates on love and relationality with the divine. The heart, according to Bourgeault, is an organ of spiritual perception that functions best when it is not clouded by the vision and attachments of the egoic mind. The spiritual practices in this book encourage you to move from your false to your true self, from your head or your

---

24. Bourgeault, "Session Two: Journey Towards."
25. Bourgeault, *Wisdom Jesus*, 33.

mental ego to your heart, and from a life based on an egoic operating system to a life directed by a God Positioning System.

Engaging in spiritual practices can be a very solitary and lonely experience and contrary to our fundamental human need for connection. This book responds to this need and invites you to enter the community of these writers. As you read these chapters try to find a companion for your journey by connecting to the stories these people share. Each author describes one unique spiritual practice that they have found helpful because it matches their personality, stage of faith, learning and thinking style, culture, and age. The practices mentioned here have emerged from their own lived experiences. It is our hope that as you read through these chapters you will enter a dialogue with these writers and, together with them, find the way to a new spiritual practice that enhances your personal faith and enriches your life. Richard Rohr said that "transformed people transform people."[26] May your inward, upward, and outward journey find expressions where your heart's gladness meets the world's hunger and God gets glorified.[27]

Bibliography

Begeman, Pamela et al. *The Welcoming Prayer: Consent on the Go, a 40-Day Praxis*. West Milford, NJ: Contemplative Outreach, 2018.
Benner, David G. *Human Being and Becoming: Living the Adventure of Life and Love*. Grand Rapids: Brazos, 2016.
Bourgeault, Cynthia. "Session Two: Journey Towards the True Self." Paper presented at the New Zealand Christian Counselling Association Conference: True Self and Clinical Practice, Auckland, NZ, 2015.
―――. *The Wisdom Jesus: Transforming Heart and Mind—A New Perspective on Christ and His Message*. Boston: Shambhala, 2008.
Buechner, Frederick. *Wishful Thinking: A Theological ABC*. Rev ed. New York: Harper Collins, 1993.
Calhoun, Adele Ahlberg. *Spiritual Disciplines Handbook: Practices That Transform Us*. Downers Grove, IL: InterVarsity, 2005.
Danker, Frederick W., et al. *Greek-English Lexicon of the New Testament and Other Early Christian Literature*. 3rd ed. Chicago: Chicago University Press, 2000.
Elrod, Hal. *The Miracle Morning: The 6 Habits That Will Transform Your Life Before 8AM*. London: Hodder & Stoughton, 2016.
Gottman, John M., and Julie Gottman. *The Gottman Love Map Exercise*. Seattle: Gottman Institute, 2017. https://newpathcentre.ca/wp-content/uploads/2020/09/build-love-maps-love-map-exercise.pdf.

26. Rohr, "Wounded Healers," para. 1.
27. Adapted from Frederick Buechner, *Wishful Thinking*, 119.

Halstead, Angelika. "Writing Your Way Home: An Organic Inquiry into Psycho-Spiritual Growth and Transformation Through Therapeutic Writing." PhD diss., University of Auckland, 2019.
Jung, Carl Gustav. *The Essential Jung*. Edited by Anthony Storr. Princeton: Princeton University Press, 1983.
Maslow, Abraham H. *Religions, Values, and Peak-Experiences*. Columbus: Ohio State University Press, 1964.
———. *Toward a Psychology of Being*. 3rd ed. New York: Wiley & Sons, 1998.
Merton, Thomas. *Conjectures of a Guilty Bystander*. New York: Image, 1968.
Plato. *Apology*. In *Four Texts on Socrates: Plato's* Euthyphro, Apology, *and* Crito *and Aristophanes'* Clouds, translated by Thomas G. West and Grace Starry West, 63–98. Rev. ed. Ithaca, NY: Cornell University Press, 1984.
Renovaré. "Agnes Sanford." https://renovare.org/people/agnes-sanford.
Rohr, Richard. "Becoming Whole." Center for Action and Contemplation, Oct. 11, 2015. https://cac.org/daily-meditations/becoming-whole-2015-10-11/.
———. *Everything Belongs: The Gift of Contemplative Prayer*. New York: Crossroad, 2014.
———. *Falling Upward: A Spirituality for the Two Halves of Life*. San Francisco: Jossey-Bass, 2011.
———. "Letting Go of the Pain-Body." Center for Action and Contemplation, Oct. 19, 2015. https://cac.org/daily-meditations/letting-go-pain-body-2015-10-19/.
———. "Liminal Space." Center for Action and Contemplation, July 7, 2016. https://cac.org/daily-meditations/liminal-space-2016-07-07/.
———. *A Spring Within Us: A Book of Daily Meditations*. Albuquerque: CAC, 2016.
———. "Wounded Healers." Center for Action and Contemplation, Oct. 26, 2018. https://cac.org/daily-meditations/wounded-healers-2018-10-26/.
Stein, Murray. *Jung's Map of the Soul: An Introduction*. Chicago: Open Court, 1998.
Ulanov, Ann Belford, and Alvin Dueck. *The Living God and Our Living Psyche: What Christians Can Learn from Carl Jung*. Grand Rapids: Eerdmans, 2008.

Part 1

Transformed Through the Power of Words and Scripture

1

Spiritual Exercises of Ignatius of Loyola

Alan Jamieson

Our response to Jesus might not be to "leave our nets and boats" and follow him in a literal sense, but it might be the setting aside of some focused time each day to engage with his word. God loves to communicate with us through words and has spoken to seekers of the truth throughout the centuries through Scripture, the spoken word, sermons, and the incarnate Word. Spiritually minded people read the word of God for different reasons and often find that it offers them a very tangible and intimate way of knowing God more deeply on this side of heaven. Reading Scripture regularly can open our minds to valuable truths or guidance outside of our current comprehension, and to the source of love and God beyond us. We also read the Bible because the very practice changes us and helps us to become more like Jesus. This does not usually happen immediately, but as we faithfully spend time in God's word and meditate over it day by day, month by month, and year to year, what we read and imbibe will transform us.

The spiritual exercises of Saint Ignatius that Alan Jamieson introduces us to in this chapter invite us into an intimate and holistic encounter with God. We use our imagination and all of our senses here to place ourselves in the context of the Scripture reading, we allow our hearts to be moved and our emotions to be stirred, and we welcome God-given desires that might arise.

The exercises are greatly transformative and will help anyone who engages with them to think and act more like Jesus. So, let us join Alan on his journey of discovering these exercises, learn how they have impacted his life, and accept his invitation.

THE SPIRITUAL PRACTICES OF Ignatius of Loyola, a sixteenth-century Spanish Catholic priest, offer the participant a slow, deliberate immersion in prayer and Scripture. Created, refined, and taught by Ignatius, the founder of the Society of Jesus (The Jesuits), the spiritual exercises continue through to this day to offer deep and life-changing refreshment to those seeking to know God more.

Finding a Statue

When my wife and I walked the Camino de Santiago, there was one place I wanted to visit. It was a statue marking the site of a life-shattering moment in the life of one of my spiritual gurus. This man's life and teachings had so transformed my faith, I wanted to stand on that spot and see that statue. The big day came when we were only four days into an eight-hundred-kilometer pilgrimage that would take us over a month, and I had booked us a room with a private bathroom. No dormitory full of snorers tonight. We would have a hot shower and fresh linen. Fortunately for us, when we opened the door to our modest room, we found a pile of someone else's possessions. The apologetic hotelier immediately upgraded us to a deluxe suite. We popped blisters, massaged sore feet, and enjoyed a hot shower before heading out to find my statue.

Unlike most visitors to Pamplona, we were not looking to walk the castle walls or photograph the large bronze sculpture of the bulls running the streets. I was searching for a statute of four men and a dog. Aided very little by our walker's guidebook, we guessed we were close when we stopped at a bar for a cold drink and directions. One of the staff spoke English but neither staff nor local patrons knew of the statue. There was a park three or four blocks down the street that had a statue—try that, the English-speaking bartender said.

He was right. There was the statue of Ignatius of Loyola on the spot where he was shot by a cannonball when, as a soldier, he was defending the city from French attack in 1521.[1] The gravely wounded Ignatius is the central figure of the statue, and the three other men are carrying him off the battlefield to safety. Safety for Ignatius meant a journey of many days as he was carried home by admiring enemy soldiers. He needed two major surgeries, without anesthetic or antibiotics, to repair and straighten his leg and then six months of slow recovery. During his long period of bed rest, Ignatius wanted books of romance and the gallantry of knights in court and battle. He could not get enough of them. When the romance books ran out, he was given a book on the lives of saints and martyrs. As he read, Ignatius noticed something significant: when he thought of romantic interludes or dueling knights, he felt energized, but the excitement soon dissipated. In contrast, when he read about the lives of the saints he was energized and the sense of hopefulness, purpose, and engagement lingered. Ignatius wrote of this experience, speaking of himself in the third person: "When he thought of worldly matters, he found much delight; but after growing weary and dismissing them, he found that he was dry and unhappy. But when he thought of imitating the saints in all the austerities they practiced, he not only found consolation in these thoughts, but even after they had left him, he remained happy and joyful."[2]

Over time Ignatius became increasingly aware of these thoughts and their effects and linked them to the work of God in his life. He became a deeply committed follower of Jesus and leader of a movement known as The Society of Jesus. Today this group is called the Jesuits and is the largest order of the Catholic Church. Ignatius's spiritual exercises were at the heart of his journey, and the cornerstone for those who came to follow Jesus in his charism.

Finding My Way In

I first heard about the spiritual exercises of Ignatius from my friend and mentor James Fowler, who wrote about the influence of them in his own life. James invited me to study with him when he was professor of theology and human development and arguably the world's leading academic in the area. Importantly for me, James was a man of deep personal faith,

---

1. O'Brien, *Ignatian Adventure*, 6.
2. Ignatius, quoted in O'Brien, *Ignatian Adventure*, 6–7.

conviction, and desire to follow Jesus. He shared in his writing about a period in his life when his own faith felt dry and empty. He went to a spiritual director saying, "I need some help. My own prayer life and my living with the Scriptures is all dried up. I'm in trouble." The spiritual director introduced James to the prayer technique underlying the spiritual exercises of Ignatius and it helped him immensely.[3]

I began doing the spiritual exercises myself when my spiritual director at the time—a nun with a long history of spiritual direction—suggested them as a method for going deeper in my prayer life. She knew someone who led people through the exercises and thought it might be worth me talking to him. It certainly was.

On August 24, 2009, Father Gerard and I began the spiritual exercises. It was undoubtedly the spiritual adventure of a lifetime and began a practice I have carried on, and which now carries me. Father Gerard explained to me how Ignatius came to faith, all that he gave up, and his deep commitment to Jesus. He explained how Ignatius recorded his spiritual insights and how he drew on these later when people asked him to guide their own spiritual journeys. In time Ignatius collated these insights as the spiritual exercises, a pathway of prayer that he would continue to refine until his death in 1556. By then The Society of Jesus had grown from eleven friends Ignatius led through the exercises into over a thousand followers from Brazil, throughout Europe, and stretching to Japan.

Gerard introduced me to a new way of prayer, based in a deep imaginative reflection in Scripture. As groundwork, Gerard encouraged me to sit with a short passage, recognizing I was in God's direct gaze of love, and to sink deeply into the passage asking God to guide my heart and thoughts. Gerard urged me to place myself in the scene I was reading, and use my senses to see, hear, and taste all that was going on. He guided me to increase my times of prayer until I could sit with a passage for an hour and then record what I felt, saw, and experienced in a notebook.[4] In my notes, which remained private, I was to list the questions to Jesus raised during my experience of Scripture, along with my sense of Jesus's responses. Ignatius called this conversation between oneself and Jesus the

---

3. Fowler, *Life Maps*, 161. For James's own account of this experience, see 161–63.

4. This time frame is taken from Ignatius, *Spiritual Exercises*, Annotation 19, which states: "A person taken up with public affairs or necessary business, and who is educated or intelligent, can set aside for the Exercises an hour and a half a day." I have since realized that many people recommend thirty to forty minutes of prayer a day. But staying true to Ignatius's original text, Gerard never offered that choice to me.

colloquy. Little did I know this conversation would become an important part of my daily prayer.

Finding a Rhythm

Once I had developed this rhythm of prayer and journaling, which took several weeks, Gerard said I was ready to begin. It had been important to till the soil of my soul to be ready for the seeds of the exercises to take root. By then I was anticipating the journey ahead and excited to get into it. Gerard told me doing the exercises as he prescribed them would take around eight to nine months as I had committed to a daily hour of prayer followed by time to write up my reflections and conversation with Jesus. It is a tough regime and demands a deep commitment to invest this time, fully focused, each day.

Exercises is the right word for this practice. At the time it felt akin to a gym routine. I would have to be there every day and meet with my trainer once a week to adjust to the program. That is exactly what Ignatius intended. In his book on the exercises Ignatius wrote, "For just as strolling, walking and running are exercises for the body, so 'spiritual exercises' is the name given to every way of preparing and making ourselves ready to get rid of all disordered affections so that, once rid of them, one might seek and find the divine will."[5]

Gerard explained that I could complete the exercises in thirty days but that would require a considerable time commitment to pray not just once, but five times a day. This can be done in a retreat space where the journey of prayer is your exclusive focus. As someone with family and work commitments, I did not have the ability to disappear for thirty days, so the slower approach was better. Ignatius intended the exercises to be for everyone and knew that retreating for a month would not be possible for people with jobs, businesses, families, and other such commitments. So, he devised a way to do them in ordinary life.

Finding Jesus

Another spiritual director, William Barry, described the theological framing of the exercises thus:

---

5. Ignatius, *Spiritual Exercises*, Annotation 1.

> Ignatius presupposes that at every moment of our existence God is communicating to us who God is, is trying to draw us into an awareness, a consciousness of the reality of who we are in God's sight. Whether we are aware of it or not, at every moment of our existence we are encountering God, Father, Son and Holy Spirit, who is trying to catch our attention, trying to draw us into a reciprocal conscious relationship.[6]

Before we began, Gerard also explained the flow of the exercises. They are divided into four sections that, if completed over a month, take around a week each. Done in ordinary life, each of the four sections takes two months. These sections intentionally build on each other, drawing the person doing the exercises into a deeper intimacy and connection with Jesus. That is the explicit purpose of the exercises—to grow in our union with God.

In the first section we are invited to meet ourselves in a deeper awareness of ourselves, as people loved deeply and uniquely by God. But also as sinful people whose desires are muddled and whose attachments limit our desire for God. We become aware of our unique story, opportunities, and experiences as someone needing conversion, recognizing the patterns of unhelpful attachments and sin in our lives. Through this, God's unconditional love, invitation to freedom, and gracious gaze holds us.

In the second section, held in God's love and faithfulness, we meet Jesus and journey with him through his life as recorded in the Gospels. We hear afresh his teaching and join the disciples traveling with Jesus. Our prayer is to know Jesus more intimately so we can love him more. As we meet Jesus in the Gospel descriptions and disciples' encounters, we see Jesus's vision and ways more clearly as they become more intimately ours too.

In the third section, we focus on the last few days of Jesus's life. His trial, desertion, suffering, crucifixion, and death. We are invited to stay with the Jesus we have come to love deeply while he is wrongfully trialed, unjustly persecuted, brutally beaten, and scornfully crucified. It was hard for me to stay engaged with the pain, suffering, and death. At times I did not want to go back to the reading or allow myself to be immersed in another round of such struggle, injustice, and unending horror. It was the prayer of watching—powerless, with nothing to offer, no way to comfort Jesus in this harrowing cruelty and senseless death. It was a tough series of prayer times that dragged me more deeply into the powerlessness, futility, and pain of suffering and death.

---

6. Barry, *Finding God in All Things*, 14–15.

In the fourth and final section, we, like the women of Scripture, meet the risen Lord and our pain is transformed to joy. There is still much for Jesus to teach us as he calls us to serve him in the world. We are called personally to love and serve in very concrete and specific ways. We find that Jesus addressed his commission to us (Matt 28:16–20), to us the Spirit is given (Acts 2:1–12), and that he calls us to a community of deep commitment and countercultural living (Acts 2:42–47; 4:32–37).

On the Sunday before I was to begin the spiritual exercises, I remember being in church and having a deep sense of excitement and anticipation for the adventure that was about to begin. Gerard had suggested I not read ahead in the exercises but simply focus on each day and let the adventure unfold in God's own way. This is not how I do things. Typically, I hit Google and read about new things in increasing detail until I have the measure of it. Then I read critiques until I know all about it. But Gerard was inviting me to stand under this five-hundred-year-old prayer tradition and let it unfold; to live into it rather than seek to control it by reading ahead or rushing to the next step.[7] I would meet Gerard briefly, early each Monday morning, for the next nine months. He would listen to what had happened for me in the previous week of prayer and set readings for the week ahead.

Finding My Way

Gerard gave me my first reading from Isa 48:6b–8a:

> From now on I will tell you of new things, of hidden things unknown to you. They are created now, and not long ago; you have not heard of them before today. So you cannot say, "Yes I knew of them." You have neither heard nor understood; from of old your ear has not been opened.

I felt that I was already being guided and my guide, the Holy Spirit or Gerard or both, knew what I was like and was inviting me into something new, precious, and deeply life giving. I was gripped, enticed, expectant.

I woke up the next morning full of anticipation for a new reading and found it was the same passage as the previous day. Little did I know

---

7. Ignatius wrote the spiritual exercises for the person guiding someone through them. They are intended for the coach (or spiritual director) and not the person doing the exercises themselves. As such they have tips for coaching that are to be molded to the unique needs and journey of each person.

that I was being introduced to one of the great lessons of the spiritual exercises, repetition. Some passages need to be savored for longer and coming back for a second or even third reflection raises new insights that deepen the experience and sense of personal engagement with what Jesus is saying. This was true for me as I reread that second day. I thought I had already sucked every ounce of meaning and feeling from those two verses but there was more there. When I look back now on the notes from that second day, I see how much excitement and hope I garnered from the subsequent reading.

As the weeks rolled on, I was introduced to many unique aspects of the exercises, such as Ignatius's "Principle and Foundation" (the purpose of our life in God), the importance of what he called indifference, the colloquy, doing the "Examen" at the end of each day, and dealing with boredom and dryness in times of prayer. I learned about discerning my moods and the movements of my soul, recognizing and dealing with times of consolation and desolation, the examen of conscience, and contemplating God's love.

Gerard would give me a one- or two-page handout for the week ahead. On it were the daily readings for the next seven days and some notes and guidelines. Week by week it was an unfolding surprise, with just the broadest outline of what lay ahead. In retrospect, that was a helpful rhythm for me. Rereading the exercises later, I found them dry and more akin to an instruction manual than a spiritual classic. It reminded me of when I was a teenager and found a book titled *Teach Yourself Judo*. The techniques were all there, but Judo is learned in the dojo with an instructor. No amount of head knowledge teaches you to roll safely or prepares you for what it is like to be thrown or strangled by your opponent.

The daily readings led me to John chapter 4 and Jacob's well. That old, deep, dependable well that had served a community for centuries and was now the source of clean, refreshing water. My reflections flowed like that water as I sensed God's renewal; I was slowly carried into this five-hundred-year-old prayer tradition that is deep and safe and leads to the life-giving water of Jesus. God opened something new. While the flow of the readings was linear, I experienced the flow of the prayer times as more of a spiral, deepening as I received gifts and renewed my desires.

I was engaging daily with Scripture but alongside that I experienced a deepening of my everyday encounters, feelings, hopes, and fears. I was connecting with Jesus's lived experience and allowing it to be woven into the present experiences of my life and prayer. As Kevin O'Brien says,

"The genius and beauty of the Exercises is that we learn to weave our own life narrative into the life story of Jesus Christ in such a way that both become more vivid and interconnected."[8]

Finding Subtle Shifts—Transformation

Through this long journey I found I was being changed. I experienced a deep sense of being grounded and held in God's loving gaze in ways that transformed how I experienced and lived my days. The exercises were leading me, as Ignatius imagined, into a deeper personal connection with Jesus and his lived reality in ways that helped me live my own. In small ways I was experiencing a similar transformation to Ignatius. Kevin O'Brien describes Ignatius's transformation, saying:

> Over the years, the young knight's desire for power, prestige, and privilege had been transformed—by God's grace—into a desire for a life of prayer, service, and simplicity. Gradually, Ignatius grew in his awareness of God's deep love not just for the world generally but for himself personally. He experienced this love as a profoundly intimate call by Christ to follow him, a call that filled Ignatius with a passionate zeal to serve God to help souls.[9]

It is hard to name one ingredient of Ignatius's spiritual exercises that was most important for me. On reflection it opened new layers to my faith, to reading Scripture and to prayer, and I came to see my desire for more as a gift from God, that God loved to meet me in. A few years later I would start attending Ignatian silent retreats, do a five-day course on Ignatius's writings, and then train as a spiritual director in the Ignatian tradition. As I have journeyed through each of these layers of connection, my awareness of and love for Jesus continue to open. Now I long to go back to Spain to do a six-week immersion course in Ignatian spirituality and visit a cave—a cave where Ignatius met, not a cannonball, but God.

For now, a decade on from beginning the spiritual exercises, they remain one of the most significant and shaping aspects of my faith and life. Today I choose to pray through Scripture following Ignatius's approach and I see my spiritual home as Ignatian. This is a faith expression, a prayer life, and a way of encountering Jesus, God's call in my life, and the daily intimacy of the Holy Spirit. Back in 2009 I did not know that within a

8. O'Brien, *Ignatian Adventure*, 4.
9. O'Brien, *Ignatian Adventure*, 11.

few months of finishing the exercises the Canterbury earthquakes would begin. For the next several years those quakes would reshape the church I pastored and the lives of family, friends, staff, and church members.

Because I had journeyed through the exercises, I was better prepared to wait patiently, to sit with suffering, to accept I had nothing to say and could not change the realities of my life or the lives of others; but I could stay and be present. I could lead from a deeper place. I could pray. I knew God was intimately involved in my life and all that was unfolding around me. That was an enormous gift for me personally and I believe it quietly shaped my leading and pastoring in ways that, I hope, helped others.

An Invitation

For those of you who are interested in investigating Ignatius's spiritual exercises, I suggest you start by finding a spiritual director who can introduce you to, and guide you through, the exercises. Undertaking this journey with an experienced guide will help you to prepare well and, importantly, to stay the course. For those interested in learning more about the tradition, I recommend reading *The Jesuit Guide to (Almost) Everything: A Spirituality for Real Life* by James Martin. An amazing transformative adventure awaits you.

Bibliography

Barry, William A. *Finding God in All Things: A Companion to the Spiritual Exercises of St. Ignatius*. Notre Dame: Ave Maria, 1991.

Fowler, James, and Sam Keen. *Life Maps: Conversations on the Journey of Faith*. Edited by Jerome Berryman. Waco, TX: W Publishing, 1985.

Ignatius of Loyola. *The Spiritual Exercises of Saint Ignatius of Loyola: A Translation and Commentary*. Translated by George E. Ganss. Chicago: Loyola, 1992.

Martin, James. *The Jesuit Guide to (Almost) Everything: A Spirituality for Real Life*. San Francisco: HarperOne, 2012.

O'Brien, Kevin. *The Ignatian Adventure: Experiencing the Spiritual Exercises of Saint Ignatius in Daily Life*. Chicago: Loyola, 2011.

2

Lectio Divina
The Practice of Living in Scripture

John Tucker

In our busy and fast-paced world it can be challenging to find time for daily Bible reading. Although we know that there are great benefits for our faith development, as well as our mental, social, emotional, and physical life, not many people incorporate Bible reading into their daily routine. So, how can we regain our passion for these sacred texts? How can we read the words of Scripture in such a way that we hear the living Word and experience his transforming power? John Tucker responds to these questions by introducing us to lectio divina, *an ancient contemplative practice of reading and praying the Bible.*

Lectio divina, which means sacred or divine reading, understands Scripture as a meeting place for a personal encounter with the divine. In this chapter, John considers the central place of the Bible in relation to spiritual formation. He discusses the obstacles to meaningful engagement with Scripture, and he explores lectio divina, *an ancient yet innovative pattern for living in Scripture. If you want to incorporate more Scripture into your prayer life, move beyond the words you read, hear the transforming voice of God, and be formed into the image of the Son of God,* lectio divina *might be where you should start.*

IF YOU WERE MAROONED on a desert island and could have only one book with you, what book would you choose? Somebody once asked this question of G. K. Chesterton. Given his reputation as one of the most erudite Christian writers in the first half of the twentieth century, you might naturally expect his response to have been the Bible. But that was not his reply. Instead, Chesterton chose *Thompson's Guide to Practical Ship Building*.[1] I guess it makes sense. If you were trapped on an island, you would want a book that could help you get home, a book that could show you how to be saved. The truth is we are trapped. We are trapped, as Eugene Peterson put it, on an I-land, where we are constantly deceived into patterns of thought and behavior that lead to death.[2] We need a book that will get us home, a book that can lead us to life. That is why, throughout history, followers of Jesus have given themselves to the practice of reading Scripture. Listening to Scripture is one of the ancient practices at the very heart of Christian spirituality. In this chapter, we will consider the central place of the Bible in relation to spiritual formation. We will discuss the serious obstacles to meaningful engagement with Scripture. And we will explore one ancient yet innovative pattern for living in Scripture.

The Priority of Reading Scripture

I recently attended the funeral of a ninety-six-year-old widow. By the end of her life, her face was lined with heavy wrinkles. Her spine was bent with debilitating arthritis. Her mind had been devoured by dementia. But she was beautiful. She was generous, gracious, grateful, gentle, humble, patient, kind, good, and faithful. She was my mother. And she was a disciple of Jesus. I am a follower of Jesus today largely because of her. As a teenager I thought to myself, "If Jesus is anything like mum, I want to know him; I want to walk with him."

How did my mother become like that? As a kid I remember seeing her listen attentively to the word of God every day. I would often wake up early, around 5:30 a.m., to find mum at the little kitchen table reading her Bible with some Scripture Union notes. At 6:00 a.m. she would wake dad with a cup of tea and two biscuits. While he sat up in bed reading his Bible, mum would jump on the Exercycle in the living room and sing her way through fourteen kilometers of hymns from an old hymn book.

---

1. Ortberg, *Life You've Always Wanted*, 192.
2. Peterson, *Working the Angles*, 22.

Then at 6:30 a.m. mum would join dad and, sitting up in bed together, they would share what they had read, and turn it into prayer.

Why did they do this? They believed the Bible is not just a book. It contains the Spirit-breathed word of God (2 Tim 3:16). And they believed that this word is living and active (Heb 4:12). It has enormous creative power. How did God make the world? Through words. God just had to say, "Let there be light," and there was light (Gen 1:3). This creative speaking was not a once-and-for-all event. Throughout the Old Testament we read of a God who continues to create by the power of his word. In Isa 55:10–11 God says:

> As the rain and the snow come down from heaven, and do not return to it without watering the earth and making it bud and flourish, so that it yields seed for the sower and bread for the eater, so is my word that goes out from my mouth: It will not return to me empty, but will accomplish what I desire and achieve the purpose for which I sent it.

This pattern continues through the New Testament. How did Jesus work his miracles? Often just by speaking. The Roman centurion said to Jesus, "Just say the word, and my servant will be healed" (Matt 8:8). Jesus needs only say the word, and something happens. He says, "Be clean," and a leper is clean (Matt 8:3). "Be still," and the sea is calm (Mark 4:39). "Be silent, and come out of him" and demons flee (Mark 1:25–26 ESV). "Little girl, get up," and a dead child rises to new life (Mark 5:41–42 NLT). The word of God has enormous creative power. As Darrell Johnson says, "The word of God not only informs, it performs, it transforms. The word of God makes things happen."[3]

That is why, throughout Scripture, God consistently urges his people to listen to his word, to live in his word, to feed on his word. Their welfare depends on it. In Deuteronomy, God says to his people, "Israel, hear the decrees and laws I am about to teach you. Follow them so that you may live" (Deut 4:1). In the Psalms, God declares blessing on the person "whose delight is in the law of the Lord, and who meditates on his law day and night" (Ps 1:2). Through the prophet Isaiah, God appeals to his people: "Listen, listen to me, and eat what is good, and you will delight in the richest of fare. Give ear and come to me; listen, that you may live" (Isa 55:2–3).

---

3. Johnson, *Glory of Preaching*, 25.

The greatest prophet of all, Jesus, insists that we can only bear fruit as his disciples if we abide in him and his words abide in us (John 15:1–8). Quoting the Old Testament, Jesus declares that people do "not live on bread alone but on every word that comes from the mouth of the LORD" (Matt 4:4; Deut 8:3). The people of God are nourished and strengthened by the word of God just as a human body is nourished and strengthened by bread. There is a pertinent scene in the book of Revelation where the apostle John sees a mighty angel coming down from heaven holding a scroll containing the word of God. And a voice from heaven says to John, "Take it and eat it" (Rev 10:9). If we are to be sustained in our faith and grow in Christ, we must feed on his word to us in Scripture. As David Wells says,

> Christian faith . . . is about listening, listening to the Word of God. . . . He draws near through his Word, he lifts the fallen, he feeds the hungry, he corrects the wandering, he rebukes the self-sufficient, and everywhere there is found the sweet fragrance of his grace where he has spoken through his Word and ministered by his Spirit.[4]

The Problem with Reading Scripture

If this is true—that listening to Scripture is critical to Christian faith and life—why do so few Christians read or listen to Scripture? According to the Bible Society of New Zealand, only 37 percent of Christians read their Bible on a weekly basis.[5] The majority of Kiwi believers very rarely read their Bibles. Why? There are several reasons for this relative disinterest in Scripture among New Zealand Christians.

The first is cultural. The communications revolution has undermined confidence in words. With the rise of visual media, the image has triumphed, and the word has been humiliated.[6] As Os Guinness writes,

> We are part of the generation in which the image has triumphed over the word, when the visual is dominant over the verbal and where entertainment drowns out exposition. We may go so far

---

4. Wells, *Above All Earthly Pow'rs*, 175–76.
5. New Zealand Bible Society, *New Zealanders and the Bible*.
6. Ellul, *Humiliation of the Word*.

as to claim that we live in an age of the image which is also the age of the anti-word and which potentially is the age of the lie.[7]

This extraordinary revolution in technology has been matched by an equally dramatic revolution in epistemology, that branch of philosophy concerned with knowledge. Philosophical pluralism has undermined our confidence in Scripture as the authoritative, Spirit-breathed, word of God. Fred Craddock articulated this development well in his seminal work, *As One Without Authority*: "Rarely, if ever, in the history of the church have so many firm periods slumped into commas and so many triumphant exclamation marks curled into question marks."[8]

This has, in turn, been accompanied by something of a revolution in pastoral leadership. In the New Testament, pastoral ministry was essentially a ministry of the word. "While one hesitates to go so far as to call [preaching] the one central activity of the apostolic ministry, clearly it was far more than simply one ministerial function among many."[9] Taking their cue from Scripture, the Protestant Reformers believed that the pastor was a *minister verbi divini*, or a servant of the word of God. In the modern western church, however, and particularly in evangelical and charismatic circles, ministers have been encouraged to see themselves less as preachers or servants of the word, and more as business leaders, organizational executives, or entrepreneurs.[10]

Consequently, as Michael Ross observes, "A profound confusion exists in many pastors' minds about the purpose and place of preaching in the ministry."[11] They do not invest much time and energy in their preaching and in their development as preachers. They do not prepare as carefully as they might. They do not linger prayerfully and patiently in a passage of Scripture until they are gripped by a word worth sharing. As a result, their preaching becomes stale, predictable, boring, and thin. And people's confidence in preaching—and in the Bible—withers.

This brings us to the heart of the problem. As Lynne Baab suggests, many people do not read the Scriptures because they simply do not expect to hear a word from the Lord when they do. They have difficulty

---

7. Guinness, quoted in Adam, *Hearing God's Words*, 139.
8. Craddock, *As One Without Authority*, 11.
9. Old, *Biblical Period*, 166.
10. Quicke, *360-Degree Preaching*, 41.
11. Ross, *Preaching for Revitalization*, 62.

experiencing God's presence and hearing God's voice through the Bible.[12] They read Scripture and hear nothing—nothing that might resemble the life-giving word of God. Why is that? Why is it that we can sometimes read the Bible and hear nothing?

Once, when he was being tested by a biblical scholar, Jesus replied, "What is written in the Law? . . . *How* do you read it?" (Luke 10:26; italics added). *How* we read the Bible is critical to *what* we hear and experience. As the parable of the soils reminds us, not all reading or hearing of God's word is fruitful or productive. Often, we find that the words we read, like the seeds in Jesus's parable that fall along the path, or on rocky ground, haven't really taken root in our lives (Matt 13:19–21). This raises a critical question. How do you read the word in such a way that it does take root and bear fruit in your life? How do you read the written word in order to hear the living Word, and be transformed into his likeness?

A Pattern for Reading Scripture

One ancient pattern for reading and living Scripture that many people have found helpful is *lectio divina*. It dates back to the monastic world of the early church, but it was a twelfth-century monk, Guigo the Second, who developed the classic formulation with its four elements. These are: (1) *lectio* (reading), (2) *meditatio* (meditating), (3) *oratio* (praying), and (4) *contemplatio* (living). Guigo describes the process in this way: "Reading, as it were, puts food whole into the mouth, meditation chews it and breaks it up, prayer extracts its flavor, contemplation is the sweetness itself which gladdens and refreshes."[13]

Elsewhere, Guigo describes the steps as four rungs on a ladder. But the stages are not always sequential. They are more like the strands of a rope than steps on a ladder. In recent years, this pattern has become popular in some evangelical and charismatic traditions. There is, however, much confusion about how to practice each of these four elements. So, let us consider each of them in turn.

---

12. Baab, *Power of Listening*, 90–91.
13. Guigo II, *Ladder of Monks*, 69.

1. Lectio

The first stage or strand in the pattern is to simply read a passage of Scripture. But how should you read it?

Eugene Peterson lists three reasons for our failure to really listen and receive when we read. First, he points to a remarkable invention—the development of moveable type and the printing press changed the way we engage with Scripture. Prior to the invention of the printing press, when Scripture was read, it was ordinarily read aloud. Reading was an oral act. Since then, we have tended to read the Bible, rather than listen to the Bible. But, as Peterson says, "reading and listening involve different senses. In listening we use our ears; in reading we use our eyes. We listen to the sound of a voice; we read marks on paper."[14]

Second, Peterson criticizes our education system. In our modern schooling system, we "are taught to read for the factual, the useful, the relevant. . . . We are habituated to looking for information when we read rather than being in relationship with a person who once spoke and then wrote so that we could listen to what was said. . . . If we read [the Scriptures] impersonally with an information-gathering mind, we misread them."[15] Whenever we read the Bible, we are not primarily collecting information; we are listening for a voice.

Third, there is what Peterson calls our "faulty job-description." We live today in a consumer culture. Our primary social identity is as a consumer. We see ourselves as customers. Consequently, Peterson observes, "when we [pastors] sit down to read the Scriptures we already have an end product in view: we want to find something useful for people's lives, to meet their expectations on us as pastors who deliver the goods."[16] However, if we routinely treat the Bible as just a tool to be used, we will find "the tool builds up calluses on our hearts."[17]

In light of this analysis, if we want to hear God speak when we read the Bible, it will help if we read it *aloud*. Use your ears, not just your eyes. Remember, we are not primarily scanning for information, we are listening for a voice, waiting for an encounter with the living Word. It also helps if we read the text *slowly*. Do not gulp it down quickly with your cereal at breakfast. Read it slowly. Listen for that one word or phrase that

---

14. Peterson, *Working the Angles*, 88.
15. Peterson, *Working the Angles*, 94–95.
16. Peterson, *Working the Angles*, 98.
17. Peterson, *Eat This Book*, 92.

captures your attention. As Jeanne Marie Guyon once said, "If you read quickly, it will benefit you little. You will be like a bee that merely skims the surface of a flower."[18] The goal in our reading is to "become as the bee who penetrates into the depths of the flower. You plunge deeply within to remove its deepest nectar."[19]

2. Meditatio

According to Scripture, blessed is the one who does not just read God's word, or hear God's word, but who meditates on God's word (Ps 1:2). How do we do that? There are many ways to meditate on Scripture. First, when you read a passage focus on whatever attracts your attention. Ask questions like: Why has this phrase caught my attention? How does it make me feel? Why does it appeal to me, or trouble me?

Second, think about context. Peterson writes that "meditation moves from looking at the words of the text to entering the world of the text."[20] It is seeing Scripture "as a connected, coherent whole, not a collection of inspired bits and pieces. . . . No text can be understood out of its entire context. The most 'entire' context is Jesus. . . . Meditation discerns the connections and listens for the harmonies that come together in Jesus."[21] Meditation asks, "What does this written word reveal about the living Word?"

Third, engage your imagination. It is through our imagination that we can enter the text—and find the text entering us. As Horace Bushnell said, "God gave [humans] imagination, that He might have a door to enter by."[22] So, engage your imagination when reading the Bible. Utilize your senses. Boyd-MacMillan recommends reading the passage through five times, asking a different question each time: What can you see? What can you hear? What can you smell? What can you touch? What can you taste?[23]

If your passage is a narrative, try composing or recreating the biblical scene in your imagination by engaging your five senses. Say your text is the story of Jesus feeding the five thousand (Mark 6:30–44). Do

---

18. Guyon, quoted in Foster and Smith, *Devotional Classics*, 321.
19. Guyon, quoted in Foster and Smith, *Devotional Classics*, 321.
20. Peterson, *Eat This Book*, 99.
21. Peterson, *Eat This Book*, 99–102.
22. Wiersbe, *Preaching and Teaching with Imagination*, 60.
23. Boyd-MacMillan, *Explosive Preaching*, 122.

you see the crowds scattered "like sheep without a shepherd" (v. 34) on the remote Galilean hills? Do you see them sitting down in groups of hundreds and fifties on the green grass? Do you feel the hunger in your stomach as Jesus's sermon stretches late into the afternoon? Imagine the scene in your mind.

Once you have established the scene in your imagination, choose a character in the story—maybe Peter, or one of the other disciples, or someone in the crowd. Then, from that perspective, run the story in your imagination. Do you see the deep compassion on Jesus's face when he looks out on the crowd? Can you hear Jesus when he says, "*You* give them something to eat" (v. 37; italics added)? When Jesus takes the bread, gives thanks, breaks it, and distributes it, what thoughts or memories does it evoke? As you approach the hungry crowd with just a handful of bread and fish, what goes through your mind?[24]

Some people wonder what place imagination and emotion can have when it comes to handling Scripture. Lynne Baab observes that, for the last hundred years or so, Christian churches in the West have been deeply influenced by a rational approach to faith and practice that underplays the role of our emotion and imagination and senses. It is this clinical historical-critical approach to the Bible that can dissect the living body of Scripture into what Hans Urs von Balthaser calls "a dead heap of flesh, blood and bones."[25] Jesus insisted that we are to love the Lord with all our heart, soul, strength, and mind (Luke 10:27). Biblical meditation brings our whole being before the living Word, including our imagination.[26]

So, focus on what attracts your attention. Locate the passage in its wider context. Engage your imagination. But there is one more important, and largely forgotten, way to meditate on Scripture, and that is to talk to yourself about what you have read. In his classic *The Saints' Everlasting Rest*, the seventeenth-century Puritan pastor Richard Baxter argues that meditation is the practice by which we digest the truth of Scripture in order to nourish and refresh our souls. And the critical step by which we do that he called soliloquy, the practice of speaking to yourself.

We speak to ourselves all the time, whether we know it or not. And what we say to ourselves has a profound impact on our mental, emotional

---

24. I am referring here to the practice of Ignatian Gospel Contemplation. For excellent treatment of this practice, particularly in regards to preaching, see New, *Live, Listen, Tell*; and *Imaginative Preaching*.

25. Balthasar, *Seeing the Form*, 168–69.

26. Baab, *Joy Together*, 105–6.

and spiritual state. Centuries before the development of modern psychology, Baxter recognized the power of this self-talk. He encourages us to intentionally change the conversation by talking to ourselves about the truth of Scripture. He urges us to preach to ourselves about what we have read, to plead the case with our own souls. This, he says, is the key that "opens the door between the head and the heart."[27] It is, in other words, the means in which we move divine truth from our heads to our hearts. It is the great instrument for stirring up our affections. And it is thoroughly biblical:

> Soliloquy has been the practise of God's people in all times. Observe, for example, how David pleaded with his soul and argued it into a holy confidence and comfort in Psalms 42 and 43: "Why are you cast down, oh my soul, and why are you in turmoil within me? Hope in God, for I will yet praise him, who is the health of my countenance and my God" (Ps 43:5). We see soliloquy also in Psalm 103:1–2, "Bless the Lord, oh my soul, and all that is within me, . . . and forget not all his benefits." So this is no new path I persuade you to tread but one that the saints have always used in their meditation.[28]

As Baxter says, this practice of talking to ourselves is an ancient practice, with a long history among the people of God. Today, however, it can feel strange and novel. But in my experience, it can be transformative. So how do we do it? We speak to ourselves the same way good parents appeal to their children. We use the very method ministers use when preaching to their congregations. We reason with our own hearts. We make a case for the truth and the goodness of what we have read. We call on the assistance of our senses by comparing the claims of the word with our experiences in the world—that which we see and hear and touch and taste and smell.

What might this look like? Imagine you are meditating on the words of Phil 4:4–7:

> Rejoice in the Lord always. I will say it again: Rejoice! Let your gentleness be evident to all. The Lord is near. Do not be anxious about anything, but in every situation, by prayer and petition, with thanksgiving, present your requests to God. And the peace of God, which transcends all understanding, will guard your hearts and your minds in Christ Jesus.

---

27. Baxter, *Saints' Everlasting Rest*, 130.
28. Baxter, *Saints' Everlasting Rest*, 149–50.

This is how I might preach these words to myself: "Rejoice in the Lord always." Yes, John, you are facing some challenging situations right now. They are stealing your peace, eroding your joy. But look to Jesus. Rejoice in him. Delight in him. This is the key that will throw open the prison door. Think about who he is. He is "the Lord." He is the King of creation. By his powerful word he created the universe and sustains every living thing. With a word he can still a storm. With a word, he can raise the dead. He is the Lord. He sits on the throne. He is high and lifted up.

But not only that. He is also "near." He is close. He is with you. Your Lord is not just powerful. He is present. He is the One who said, "Surely I am with you always, to the very end of the age" (Matt 28:20). He is the One who says, "Never will I leave you; never will I forsake you" (Heb 13:5; Deut 31:6). This Lord is your shepherd, John. He promises to provide for you. He promises to protect you. He promises to guide you in the right paths for his name's sake (Ps 23:3). He is near to you, and he is near to the situation you are facing.

So, when you think about this situation—these circumstances that are making you anxious—remember and rejoice in the Lord. Do it now! "Always" means now. Rejoice in him, John. Rejoice in his control; rejoice in his care. Rejoice in his power and wisdom and knowledge and love for you—and for those about whom you are worried.

"Let your gentleness be evident to all." John, because of who Jesus is, you do not need to force things. Be gentle with those around you. Be gentle with your family. Be gentle with your colleagues. And "do not be anxious about anything." "Anything" includes this situation! Instead of worrying, pray about these matters. The Lord is saying to you that "in every situation, by prayer and petition" you are to present your requests to him; he wants you to "cast all your anxiety on him because he cares for you" (1 Pet 5:7). With God, all things are possible (Matt 19:26). So John, like a little child approaching their father for help, approach your Lord. Ask, in his name, and it will be given to you. Jesus promises that everyone who asks receives (Luke 11:9).

And when you are praying, do it "with thanksgiving." Thank God for what he is already doing. Thank God for the way his Spirit is always at work, even when you do not see it. Thank God for the way he goes ahead of you. Thank God for the ways in which he has answered your requests in the past. And thank God for what he will do in response to your prayers, knowing that he will only give you what he knows to be "good, pleasing and perfect" (Rom 12:2).

The promise is that "the peace of God, which transcends all understanding, will guard you heart and mind in Christ Jesus." So, John, cast all your anxiety on him. Do it now. Pour your heart out to him in prayer. Talk through with him your list of worries, your different needs. Run to him now, like you used to run to your father when you needed help. He will welcome you, and you will be freed from the anxieties that are burdening you like a heavy tramping pack filled with rocks.

Do you get the idea? According to Richard Baxter, this work of meditation—this reasoning with ourselves, or preaching to ourselves—is so important that he calls it the "great duty of a heavenly life."[29]

3. Oratio

So *lectio divina* involves, first, careful and attentive reading of Scripture, and second, thoughtful and imaginative meditation on Scripture. The third essential strand is honest prayer in response to what we have read and thought. Peterson writes that "God does not make speeches; he enters conversations and we are partners to the conversation."[30] It is as we respond in prayer to what we have heard and move from talking to ourselves to talking to God that we enter a conversation, and experience a life-changing encounter with the living Word. Denis Donoghue once wrote,

> We often assume that the problem of interpreting words is a matter of knowing what they mean and linking meanings together in some reasonable order in our minds. But it's not quite like that. The problem is to decide at any moment what our relation to the words should be, even when we know what they mean.[31]

The way to determine that is through prayer, to move from talking to ourselves to talking to God. So how do we do that? How do we pray Scripture? Look at the Psalms. As the songbook, or prayer book, of the people of God, they are our primary guide to the life of prayer:

> They argue and complain, they lament and they praise, they deny and declaim, they think and they sing. On one page they accuse God of betraying and abandoning them and on the next they turned cartwheels of hallelujahs. Sometimes we suppose that the proper posture of response to God as we read the Bible

---

29. Baxter, *Saints' Everlasting Rest*, 108.
30. Peterson, *Eat This Book*, 107.
31. Donoghue, *Ferocious Alphabets*, 14.

> is to be curled up in a wingback chair before a cozy fire, docile and well-mannered. Some of us are taught to think that reading the Bible means sitting in God's classroom and that prayer is politely raising our hand when we have a question about what he is teaching us in his Deuteronomy lecture. The Psalms, our prayer text within the biblical text, show us something quite different: prayer is *engaging* God, an engaging that is seldom accomplished by a murmured greeting and a conventional handshake. The engagement, at least in its initial stages, is more like a quarrel than a greeting, more like a wrestling match than a warm embrace.[32]

In other words, the Psalms teach us that in prayer, anything goes. "Virtually everything human is appropriate as material for prayer: reflections and observations, fear and anger, guilt and sin, questions and doubts, needs and desires, praise and gratitude, suffering and death. Nothing human is excluded." Peterson concludes: "The Psalms are an extended refutation that prayer is 'being nice' before God. No—prayer is an offering of ourselves, just as we are."[33] When responding to what you have read, pray from your heart. It might be adoration or thanksgiving. It might be confession or repentance, or lament. It might be petition or intercession, questions or critique. Any kind of prayer is appropriate, as long as it is honest.

This strand of *lectio divina* is critical. Julian Green recalls the biblical story about the manna in the wilderness (Exod 16:13–20). To feed the Israelites, God rained down bread from heaven. The people were to go out each day and gather just enough manna for that day. No one was to keep any of it until the morning. They were to eat it all. Some, however, did try to store up manna. But the manna that was not consumed, began to rot and smell. Green comments, "Perhaps this means that all spiritual reading which is not consumed—by prayer and by works—ends by causing a sort of rotting inside us. You die with a head full of fine sayings and a perfectly empty heart."[34]

4. Contemplatio

This brings us to the fourth and final strand in *lectio divina*: contemplation. According to Peterson, "Contemplation means living what we read,

---

32. Peterson, *Eat This Book*, 104–5.
33. Peterson, *Eat This Book*, 105–6.
34. Green, quoted in Peterson, *Eat This Book*, 109.

not wasting any of it or hoarding any of it, but using it up in living. It is life formed by God's revealing word, God's word read and heard, meditated and prayed." It is a life rooted in the realization that

> the Word that was in the beginning is also the Word made flesh and continues to be the Word to which I say, *Fiat mihi*: "Let it be to *me* according to thy Word." The assumption underlying contemplation is that Word and Life are at root the same thing. Life originates in Word. Word makes Life. There is no word of God that God does not intend to be lived by us. All words are capable of being incarnated, because all words originate in the Word made flesh.[35]

The purpose of *lectio divina* is to live the text of Scripture. It is by living what we hear that we come to truly know and receive the Word. John Calvin once said that all right knowledge of God is born of obedience.[36] This is true. A few years ago, a friend challenged me to participate in a swimming race. It was to start at Rangitoto Island in the Hauraki Gulf and finish at St. Heliers beach on the Auckland waterfront—4.5 km. I did not have a swimming background. I was not a swimmer. So, I watched some videos online about swimming technique: reach, catch, pull to the waist, push up past the hip, swivel. I talked with experienced swimmers about how to breathe in open water, and which wet suit to acquire. But it was only when I actually got into the water and tried to swim that I really started to understand what they were all talking about. God's word cannot be understood from the beach, as it were. We must dive in and live the word that we hear if we are to fully taste and know the word of life.

Lectio divina is not a method or technique for just reading the text of Scripture; it is a way of living the text in Jesus's name. As Peterson says, "When we pray, 'Let it be done to me according to thy word,' we mean for it to take place in our flesh; a miraculous conception in the womb of our lives, 'Christ in me.'"[37] That is the ultimate goal of our engagement with Scripture: Christ in me.

Or Christ in *us*. Bible reading is not just something we do on our own and in private. The story of Scripture regularly pictures God's people assembling together in order to hear God's word read and explained—and to be formed together as a community of faith. On Mount Sinai,

---

35. Peterson, *Eat This Book*, 114.
36. Calvin, *Institutes* 1.6.2.
37. Peterson, *Eat This Book*, 115.

for example, Moses speaks and reads the words of God to the people gathered around the mountain (Exod 19–24). On the plains of Moab, he gives the law to the priests with the instruction to gather the people and read it to them, presumably explaining and applying it as they went along (Deut 31:9–13). On their return from exile, Ezra the priest brings the law before the assembly and reads from it, while his assistants make sure the people understand what is being read (Neh 8:1–8).

In the New Testament this pattern continues. We see, for example, Jesus entering the synagogue in Nazareth, reading from the scroll of Isaiah, and then explaining the word to the people gathered there. In Pisidian Antioch, we see Paul entering a synagogue and then, after the Law and the Prophets have been read, speaking a "word of exhortation for the people" (Acts 13:14–43). In turn, Paul instructs Timothy, "devote yourself to the public reading of Scripture, to preaching and to teaching" (1 Tim 4:13). This pattern of communal engagement with Scripture continues throughout church history, for "it is by means of the ministry of the Word that Christ is present in the congregation."[38] This practice of *lectio divina* provides an excellent framework for living in the word, not just when we are on our own, but when we are with others, whether that be around a dinner table, in a small group, at a leaders' meeting, or in a worship service.[39]

And live in the word we must, if we want to grow in Christ and bear fruit for him. It is, uniquely, in the words of Scripture that God draws near to us and speaks to us his powerful, creative, life-giving word. When we listen to the word of God, and live in the word of God, the Spirit of God renews us in the image of God. Yes, many of us struggle with reading the Bible. We know the Scriptures are important, but we read them and seem to hear nothing. Often, that it is because of how we read them. We are reading them in the wrong way. *Lectio divina* offers us an ancient yet fresh way of hearing the living Word speak through the written word. Together, these four elements of reading, meditating, praying, and living can transform our experience of God's word. *Read* the text out loud and slowly. *Reflect* on what captures your attention. Meditate on the text, enter the text, by engaging your imagination. Speak to yourself—preach to yourself—about what you are hearing. *Respond* to God by talking to him about what you have experienced. And make it your goal in all of this to

---

38. Adam, *Hearing God's Words*, 177.
39. Baab, *Power of Listening*, ch. 6.

live or *reside* in what you have heard. *Lectio divina* is not a technique for just reading the text of Scripture; it is a practice for embodying the text in Jesus's name.

I urge you to give yourself to this practice. Experiment with it. Persevere with it. And be saved from the I-land on which you are trapped. Four hundred years ago, Richard Baxter experienced the power of meditating on Scripture in this way and urged Christians to embrace this practice:

> Do it seriously and frequently. You will find that it will change you completely. It will elevate your soul, clear your understanding, and leave a pleasant savour in your heart. Your own experience will make you confess that one hour spent in heavenly meditation will more effectually revive you than many hours in bare, external duties. . . . Consider the matter, and resolve on the duty before you go any further. Let your family perceive, let your neighbours perceive, let your conscience perceive—yes, let God perceive—that you are one who will have your daily conversation in heaven. . . . I know it is your grief that your hearts are not nearer to him and that they do not love him with more feeling, passion, and delight. If ever you would have all this mended and enjoy your desires, try this life of meditation.[40]

Bibliography

Adam, Peter. *Hearing God's Words: Exploring Biblical Spirituality*. New Studies in Biblical Theology 16. Downers Grove, IL: IVP Academic, 2004.

Baab, Lynne M. *Joy Together: Spiritual Practices for Your Congregation*. Louisville: Westminster John Knox, 2012.

———. *The Power of Listening: Building Skills for Mission and Ministry*. Lanham, MD: Rowman & Littlefield, 2014.

Balthasar, Hans Urs von. *Seeing the Form*. Vol. 1 of *The Glory of the Lord: A Theological Aesthetics*, edited by Joseph Fessio and John Riches, translated by Erasmo Leiva-Merikakis. San Francisco: Ignatius, 1982.

Baxter, Richard. *The Saints' Everlasting Rest*. Abridged by Tim Cooper. Wheaton, IL: Crossway, 2022.

Boyd-MacMillan, Ron. *Explosive Preaching: Letters on Detonating the Gospel in the 21st Century*. Bletchley, UK: Paternoster, 2006.

Calvin, John. *Institutes of the Christian Religion*. Translated by Henry Beveridge. 3 vols. Edinburgh: Calvin Translation Society, 1845. https://ccel.org/ccel/calvin/institutes/institutes.iii.vii.html.

Craddock, Fred B. *As One Without Authority*. 3rd ed. Nashville: Abingdon, 1979.

Donoghue, Denis. *Ferocious Alphabets*. Boston: Little, Brown, 1976.

---

40. Baxter, *Saints' Everlasting Rest*, 159, 161.

Ellul, Jacques. *The Humiliation of the Word*. Translated by Joyce Main Hanks. Grand Rapids: Eerdmans, 1985.

Foster, Richard J., and James Bryan Smith, eds. *Devotional Classics: Selected Readings for Individuals and Groups*. New York: HarperCollins, 1993.

Guigo II. *The Ladder of Monks: A Letter on the Contemplative Life; and Twelve Meditations*. Translated by Edmund Colledge and James Walsh. Kalamazoo, MI: Cistercian, 1981.

Johnson, Darrell W. *The Glory of Preaching: Participating in God's Transformation of the World*. Downers Grove, IL: IVP Academic, 2009.

New, Geoff. *Imaginative Preaching: Praying the Scriptures So God Can Speak Through You*. Carlisle, UK: Langham, 2015.

———. *Live, Listen, Tell: The Art of Preaching*. Carlisle, UK: Langham, 2017.

New Zealand Bible Society. *New Zealanders and the Bible: 2017 Bible Engagement Survey*. https://adra.org.nz/wp-content/uploads/2021/06/Research_BookletBM17_v9final_webres.pdf.

Old, Hughes Oliphant. *The Biblical Period*. Vol. 1 of *The Reading and Preaching of the Scriptures in the Worship of the Christian Church*. Grand Rapids: Eerdmans, 1998.

Ortberg, John. *The Life You've Always Wanted: Spiritual Disciplines for Ordinary People*. Grand Rapids: Zondervan, 2015.

Quicke, Michael J. *360-Degree Preaching: Hearing, Speaking, and Living the Word*. Grand Rapids: Baker Academic, 2003.

Peterson, Eugene H. *Eat This Book: A Conversation in the Art of Spiritual Reading*. Grand Rapids: Eerdmans, 2006.

———. *Working the Angles: The Shape of Pastoral Integrity*. Grand Rapids: Eerdmans, 1987.

Ross, Michael F. *Preaching for Revitalization: How to Revitalize Your Church Through Your Pulpit*. Rev. ed. Fearn, UK: Christian Focus, 2006.

Wells, David F. *Above All Earthly Pow'rs: Christ in a Postmodern World*. Grand Rapids: Eerdmans, 2005.

Wiersbe, Warren W. *Preaching and Teaching with Imagination: The Quest for Biblical Ministry*. Grand Rapids: Baker, 1997.

3

Replacing Worldliness via Remembering the Word

TIM COLLINS

In our modern Western world where the Bible is readily available and accessible, the spiritual discipline of memorizing Scripture might seem like an outdated and old-fashioned practice. However, from the time that the Bible was written until now, followers of God have passionately engaged in this practice and seen the importance of it. Jesus himself modelled Scripture memorization to us as he was able to quote numerous Old Testament passages to the people he talked to. So why should we engage in this ancient practice today?

Much like cognitive behavioral therapy, where unhelpful ways of thinking get identified and replaced by more positive or life-enhancing ideas, learning Scripture by heart renews our mind and leads to transformation. So, is it possible to rewire our brain through Scripture memory? Neuroscience responds to this question positively. Neuroplasticity refers to the brain's ability to change, reorganize, or grow new neural networks in response to information or visuals that we feed our minds with. With the many online platforms that we engage in and the information influx that bombards us every day now, more than ever we need to not conform to the patterns of this world but to be transformed by the renewing of our mind so that we then are able to test and approve what God's will is—his good, pleasing and perfect will (Rom 12:2). Why not harness the power of neuroplasticity for transforming your thinking, emotions, and behavior through Scripture memory? Tim Collins shows us how to do that.

A Bit More like Jesus and a Bit Less like Mike

SOME YEARS BACK I was working as a marketing manager for Coca-Cola in New Zealand. When you work in marketing you constantly look at the ideas other businesses use for selling so you can find ways in which to sell your product in an innovative and unique way. At Coca-Cola we were no different. We were consistently trying to find ways to engage with the consumer in a fashion that was not stale or pedestrian.

Two examples stood out to me at that time. The first was McDonald's, who ran clever jingles showcasing their ingredients for the Big Mac. These got into my head and the heads of millions of others, I am sure. In fact, they were so effective that I memorized what was in a Big Mac. I can still list the ingredients of a Big Mac today. I do not eat them, but I know exactly what is in them.

The second industry stand out was the Gatorade ad with a catchphrase referencing Michael Jordan, who was a colossus at the time—big in stature both physically and in marketability. He had crossed over from being a basketball star to being an athlete; many people from both within and without the basketball audience wanted to be like him—cool, hip, and fashionable. Gatorade cleverly suggested that if you drank Gatorade, you would somehow transform into being more like him.

It has since occurred to me that those marketing campaigns employed by McDonald's and Gatorade were modern-day illustrations of an approach to learning, and that I should apply a similar repetitive practice to memorizing the Bible. If we can find a way to get the truth of Scripture into our minds that is not boring and tedious, we will thrive. We will develop a poise, joy, and a spiritual buoyancy in our souls. We might even displace the ingredients of a Big Mac in our minds with the ingredients of the Bible.

Paul writes about this displacement in Rom 12:2: "Do not conform to the pattern of this world, but be transformed by the renewing of your mind." The Greek word translated into "transformed" is the verb *metamorphousthe*.[1] In our everyday language we use the word *metamorphosis*. It means a change in the form or structure or character of something or someone.[2] Paul is encouraging the reader to replace the worldliness within each of us by deliberately renewing or changing what is otherwise in our minds.

One way that has helped me do this over the years is the process of remembering Scripture intentionally. This chapter explores practical ways of replacing worldliness through Scripture memory.

Memorizing the Bible

I tell my family that my old lawn mower is a daily example of a miracle in action. It is meant to take both petrol and oil. However, I have not put any oil in it since the day I bought it and yet it starts the first time, every time, and works beautifully. At first, I simply forgot to fill the oil tank. Now over the years I am too afraid to tinker with it. If it is not broken, then do not fix it!

The Christian walk is not like my lawn mower. It needs constant input from Scripture to achieve great output. It requires the discipline of continuous feeding to enable our Christian lives to be transformed and victorious. As we feed ourselves with Scripture, we are in effect sculpting ourselves into robust Christ-like individuals. We are cooperating with the Holy Spirit, the Master Sculptor who will "change our form" if we allow this change to take place.

Paul writes, "And we all, who with unveiled faces contemplate the Lord's glory, are being transformed into his image with ever-increasing glory, which comes from the Lord, who is the Spirit" (2 Cor 3:18). One of the most powerful opportunities to achieve this "ever-increasing glory" is to memorize Scripture. In essence the purpose of why we follow such a discipline is not so much to directly modify our behavior but to transform those internal drivers within from where our behavior comes from. It is in effect a circumcision of the heart.

---

1. Danker et al., *Greek-English Lexicon*, 639.
2. *Merriam-Webster*, "Metamorphosis."

I remember many years back reading an article by John Piper titled "Why Memorize Scripture." In the article, he painted the picture of the value of absorbing the bible into our soul through rote learning of Scripture. He quoted Chuck Swindoll as follows: "I know of no other single practice in the Christian life more rewarding, practically speaking, than memorizing Scripture. . . . No other single exercise pays greater spiritual dividends!"[3] Piper himself writes, "Bible memorization has the effect of making our gaze on Jesus steadier and clearer."[4] These authors, and others I have read over the years, declare that taking the time to replace the worldliness within us through remembering the word changes us from the inside out. In simple terms, we cannot live and understand what we do not know. When we lodge the living and inspired word of God into our inner being, then we are learning to cooperate with the Holy Spirit to live transformed and victorious Christian lives. We allow God's words to marinate our souls.

An Example in Action

I had the privilege of spending an afternoon in Oxford with Walter Hooper a few years ago. Hooper had been C. S. Lewis's personal assistant for two years before Lewis went to glory in 1963. When we met, Hooper regaled me with many stories and anecdotes about Lewis. He discussed why he believed Lewis has had such an impact in both Christian and secular circles with his fantasy and apologetic writings. At one stage I asked Hooper what he believed was the secret behind his obvious victorious Christian life? What enabled this Oxford and Cambridge academic to write some of the greatest literature of the last hundred years and have such a positive impact on the world for Christianity? His answer was simple and yet profound: "He just believed it." Hooper then said, "Lewis would spend time early each morning and at 5:00 p.m. each afternoon meditating and memorizing because he was convinced this was the primary source of spiritual growth."

Hooper added that there was no secret to what made Lewis the great man that he was, but the difficult part was having the discipline Lewis had to meditate on and memorize Scripture so regularly. He suggested most Christians agree on the benefit of this practice. Yet many Christians

---

3. Piper, "Why Memorize Scripture?," para. 3.
4. Piper, "Why Memorize Scripture?," para. 6.

struggle to master the process. Hooper is correct. We know we should take the time to let the word indwell us. But we often find all sorts of excuses to not allow that to happen. We ultimately need to be sold on the benefits so that we are prepared to pay the cost.

How I Got Sold on the Need to Memorize the Bible

There is an established selling technique that one learns in the business environment. It is called the four step SPIN cycle. *S* stands for Situation. What is the buyer's current situation? *P* represents Problem. What does my product offer that solves that buyer's particular problem? *I* points to Implication. What are the causes and effects of that problem for the potential buyer? And *N* equates to Need-Payoff. Why is my product worth the cost to the buyer? SPIN is aimed at meeting the buyer's need and ultimately to sell them something. It seeks to get them to accept that the price they pay is worth the benefit they will receive.

Up to a certain period in my life, I was not buying the need to memorize the Bible. And there was no one who took the time to show me, or to sell to me, the benefits of doing so. I could not see that I had a problem of little or no growth in my life and neither could I envisage the payoff of learning to memorize the Bible. My inner cost/benefit model was telling me the cost was too high. The payback on investment was lacking. But then God brought a couple into my life who showed me why I needed to change.

This is how the story unfolded. Early in our marriage, my wife Bronwyn and I met a retired couple from Seattle who had come to Auckland to work full time for the Navigators. They invited us to be part of their home group and during the two years we met with them they mentored us both. They modelled what it looked like in the flesh to live victorious Christian lives, and they taught us how to memorize Scripture. They even led us through the SPIN cycle without knowing it existed.

Bronwyn and I became aware that our situation meant that we were spending very little time with God and our problem that came from that was minimal growth in our Christian walk. The implication was frustration and a realization that other Christians seemed to have a deep relationship with Jesus, and we did not. But there was a solution. It did not cost in monetary terms, but it did cost in time and effort. Yet, the need-payoff was out of this world.

The couple sold us on a process of Scripture memory and the discipline to follow it through. The process went like this: Start with the topic. Then the verse reference. Then the verse itself. Then finish with the reference. Topic. Reference. Verse. Reference. Two verses a week from a set list. For example, the topic might be Christ the Center. The verses were 2 Cor 5:17 and Gal 2:20. Each morning I would keep going over and over these verses until they stuck.

At the end of each week the couple would test us. First, they would ask us to recite some verses we had learned previously; then we had to cite the current week's verses; in every instance it was: Topic, Reference, Verse, Reference—in that order. If we got it wrong, even slightly, we would repeat that verse. Their favorite mantra was "It is just as easy to get it right as to get it wrong. So, keep going until you do." Their other saying was "If you can remember your phone number you can remember a Bible verse." They would also have said that if you can remember a hamburger ingredient list like that for a Big Mac then you can remember a passage from the Bible.

After two years of following their process—week in and week out—we had learned decent chunks of Scripture. We had also learned the weekly discipline that was required, a little of the same discipline that made C. S. Lewis the man that he was. I did not want to be like Michael Jordan but I did want to be like Jesus and to do that required my setting aside time to let God's word dwell richly within me.

Our American friends returned to Seattle after two years and I found that, without direct accountability, I began to drop off the process they had taught me, and I began to forget those verses I had already learned. I needed to freshen things up to maintain the benefit without losing the discipline and it was then I set about constructing a different process.

What I developed looks something like this today: at the start of each week, I focus on one verse. I look to spend time memorizing that same verse each day for seven days. Then I start a new seven-day cycle with the next verse added to the previous verse(s). Because I memorize in groups of twelve verses, this process takes me twelve weeks. With those twelve verses, I choose six topics (with two verses in each one)—topics such as Christ the Center, Obedience, The Word, Prayer, Fellowship, and Witnessing. I put the starting letters into one "word" that I can remember as a prompt—in this case COTPFW.

I then repeat this process so that another three sets of twelve verses are added to my original set. For instance, ASCSMA, PSBSGD,

SSFPPH—each letter represents a topic, two references, and two verses. In total I end up with forty-eight verses per day after working on these four sets. Over time, by adding more sets, in one week that total can add up to five hundred verses.

I was seeing in action what Charles Duhigg, the author of *The Power of Habit: Why We Do What We Do and How to Change*, mentioned at a conference I attended. He said at one stage that there is nothing you cannot do if you get the habits right. I was able to retain so much Scripture in my mind because I had gotten the habit right. Changing my habits had changed the long-term trajectory of my Christian life.

I no longer practice memorizing at a set time each day. Rather, I remember verses remotely. I recall verses to myself at various times of the day and night looking for mental downtime when I am not required to be thinking of much else. For instance, I love to swim—sometimes up to three kilometers in a session. This can mean an hour or more in the sea. In the boring middle part, I will start to think of reciting memory verses. I will recite COTPFW while making sure no sharks are around me! I try to use the commonplace moments to incorporate the supernatural moments of the word.

I will recount this system at 2:00 a.m. in the morning while I am trying to get back to sleep. I will recap while sitting in a lecture, waiting at an airport, watching a cricket test match when the opposition are three hundred for one and scoring at a rate of 0.5 runs an over, and even while watching a boring movie. While visiting Myanmar, I once sat in an hour-long sermon, all in Burmese. Ten minutes in, out came PSBSGD. I have taken my daughter to her ice-skating lesson and watched her twirl over and over in the middle of the ice for extended periods. ASCSMA came to mind. There are countless further examples I could give of this practice.

For me, the unique aspect is not memorizing the Scripture but rather how and when I do it. I am not trying to learn new verses anymore but simply trying to keep the old ones in my head. I would estimate that at one stage I was repeating five hundred verses a week using this system. Twenty minutes a day over seven days a week is all the time it required.

What I Have Experienced Through This Practice

Paul writes, "Do not lie to each other, since you have taken off your old self with its practices and have put on the new self, which is being renewed in knowledge in the image of its Creator" (Col 3:9–10). Mature believers understand that we often do not feel that this "renewal" happens fast enough. But we also understand we are further along than we once were. Progress often feels slow, but we are still moving in the right direction. The old self is gradually being removed. New practices and attributes are developing, and our character is becoming more and more Christlike. The Bible calls this spiritual fruit.

Being reimaged to look like our Creator is reflected by greater humility in a person. It evidences God-given wisdom. It displays a peace that is supernatural. Over time my experience was that these fruits of the Holy Spirit had developed in me by the Spirit of God who again and again brought those now deeply ingrained verses to mind. Often these memorized verses come to me at the most unexpected times to convict me and renew me. Below are some helpful examples of how Scripture memory has impacted my life and transformed me.

Humility Through Business Success

I think of a particular time when I achieved some bona fide business success. I left Coca-Cola to start a coffee business. Along with my brother-in-law I built a significant Australasian organization. Some years later Coca-Cola approached us and indicated that they wished to purchase our business. After some tough negotiations we achieved an excellent price. On the day of finalizing the deal we were invited into the Coke boardroom for the signing and photos. There was something within me that day saying, "Tim, you have really made it. You have concluded a deal with one of the biggest multinationals in the world. What a star you are." Not a whole lot of humility existed in that moment. However, at the exact moment I was signing the documents a memory verse clearly came into my mind. As my pen touched that paper, I was hit by the following verse: "You may say to yourself, 'My power and the strength of my hands have produced this wealth for me.' But remember the Lord your God, for it is he who gives you the ability to produce wealth" (Deut 8:17–18). This came directly out of Deuteronomy. It was not as if I had even looked at that verse that morning. At that moment I was certainly not contemplating acknowledging God for his total hand in this success. But the Holy Spirit convicted me of my total lack of humility, and I realized that I would have achieved nothing without God's help and grace in this whole seven-year process.

Wisdom Through Conflict

Far less dramatic, but equally memorable, was a situation I found myself in with a family member who was not a believer. This person had decided that evening that she wanted to discuss the truth of the gospel in a confrontational and argumentative way. As the discussion unfolded, I could see that no matter what answer I gave her she was determined to push back. As I was about to articulate what was in my mind, some unkind blows to her arguments, Col 4:5–6 came to mind and made me pause: "Be wise in the way you act toward outsiders; make the most of every opportunity. Let your conversation be always full of grace, seasoned with salt, so that you may know how to answer everyone." Again, this was a memory verse I had been trying to put into practice. At that moment I was totally convicted of my lack of grace. The verse hit me, and it felt as if an explosion had gone off. I instantly changed my tone of voice, words, and attitude. The conversation became far less intense and inflammatory. I think that was a divine-wisdom encounter at that moment.

Some would say that these two examples are just coincidences. All I know is that over time these situations kept happening as I learned to hide God's word in my heart. They play a role in my personal transformation. As I continue to replace worldliness with remembering Scripture my mind is filled with what I need. God's word within renovates my soul. The result is a deep subterranean river of joy that flows within me no matter what I am facing externally. It produces *shalom* in my life—an inward sense of completeness and wholeness.

Conclusion

The big idea of this chapter is that when we take the time to memorize the Bible, it will reproduce in us this wholeness, harmony, and tranquility that we once had but lost through the Fall. There are no shortcuts to the process. What does work, however, is first, to start this new practice by setting aside the same twenty-minute time slot each day in the same location with the same journal.

In the very ordinary moments of our everyday life, we have many chances throughout the day to practice putting and keeping verses in our mind and heart by remembering and reciting them—all in many individually shaped, creative, and novel ways. We can keep this spiritual practice fresh and vibrant just by doing the same discipline differently each time. Henri Nouwen once wrote the following words about this ordinary life:

> This is what life is about. It is being sent on a trip by a loving God, who is waiting at home for our return and is eager to watch the slides we took and hear about the friends we made. When we travel with the eyes and ears of the God who sent us, we will see wonderful sights, hear wonderful sounds, meet wonderful people . . . and be happy to return home.[5]

There is no better way to travel with the "eyes and ears of God" than to be familiar with God's words and to be creative in finding spaces in our lives where we intentionally feed ourselves from Scripture. We can grasp the downtime, enjoy the dull, and recognize the humdrum as an opportunity to recite what we have learned by heart. The cost of this practice is high. It takes discipline, time, and effort. But the payback is out of this world.

Bibliography

Danker, Frederick W., et al. *Greek-English Lexicon of the New Testament and Other Early Christian Literature*. 3rd ed. Chicago: Chicago University Press, 2000.

Duhigg, Charles. *The Power of Habit: Why We Do What We Do and How to Change*. New York: Random House, 2013.

Merriam-Webster Dictionary. "Metamorphosis." Updated Apr. 26, 2025. https://www.merriam-webster.com/dictionary/metamorphosis#dictionary-entry-1.

Nouwen, Henri J. M. *Bread for the Journey: A Daybook of Wisdom and Faith*. San Francisco: HarperSanFrancisco, 2006.

Piper, John. "Why Memorize Scripture?" Desiring God, Sept. 5, 2006. https://www.desiringgod.org/articles/why-memorize-scripture.

---

5. Nouwen, *Bread for the Journey*, 45.

4

Reading the Bible Missionally

GEORGE M. WIELAND

Throughout church history the regular practice of reading Scripture has been a cornerstone of the Christian faith. Reading God's word informs and encourages all other spiritual disciplines. The Bible is not just a record of what God has done throughout the ages, but it is an ongoing story of which this world and we humans are part. As we read God's word, we learn what God has done, is currently doing, and what his intentions and plans are for this world. It invites us to find our place and purpose within this story in order to live meaningfully in this world as participants in the mission of God.

As we read the Bible, we discover that mission is a central theme. The very identity of the church is closely connected with God's purposes and calling. Widening and deepening our understanding on missional hermeneutics can be part of how we engage with God's word. In this chapter, George Wieland shares how his own background informed the way he approaches his spiritual practices and invites us to read Scripture missionally and to use mission as a key interpretive lens.

From "What Did It Mean?" to "What Does It Do?"

FOR AS LONG AS I can remember the Bible has been a constant companion in my life. Before I could read for myself, my mother would read to me daily from a large and colorful children's story Bible. As I grew, I continued the practice of daily Bible reading, guided by Scripture Union notes. When I made a faith commitment in my early teens, I was given a reading plan that would take me through the entire Bible in three years. There were no explanatory notes, just a prescribed portion for each day with a set of questions to think about. I bought a notebook and got started, answering every question so diligently that it actually took me seven years to complete the plan. Then I started again just in case I had missed anything the first time through!

Some years later at theological college I acquired the tools of careful exegesis, trying to uncover the "original meaning" of the text before relating that meaning as closely as possible to contemporary life. And then as a pastor, I preached and taught through biblical books. Naturally, when I had the opportunity to undertake further study, I chose a biblical topic, and my research took me even deeper into the linguistic, cultural, and historical world in which the New Testament letters that I was focusing on had been written. As a lecturer in biblical studies, I tried to pass on that concern for understanding what biblical texts might have meant to their original readers and, as a subsequent step, taught my students how to apply that meaning to our different contexts today.

Worthwhile and important as I believe that to be, I did begin to wonder if there was more to be learned and experienced about how the Bible speaks and does its work in people's lives. Although I valued the insights gained through knowledge of the biblical languages, historical and geographical background, literary forms, etc., it did not seem plausible that God's communication through the Bible could only be accessible to trained scholars. There were innumerable examples of all sorts of people being challenged, encouraged, directed, and drawn into deeper relationship with Jesus through reading or hearing the Bible without following accepted rules of interpretation.

I was also noticing that I was hearing the Bible differently in different contexts. Passages that were so familiar that I could recite them by heart resonated with fresh significance when I read them in unfamiliar places or new circumstances. They were not only yielding unexpected insights but also producing changed attitudes and action. Rather than resisting such contextual influences as impediments to discovering the real meaning of a biblical text, I began to embrace them as part of the environment within which the voice of Scripture may be heard, in ways that could be transformative for both the hearers and their contexts. A course I developed on Intercultural Bible Reading gave an opportunity to explore how readers' cultural and social contexts were at play as they heard and responded to the Bible.

All this has served to expand the range of questions that I ask when I approach a passage of Scripture. I still want to know, "What did this passage mean when it was first written and heard or read?" but I am now also asking, "What does this passage do in those who read or hear it today?" I understand that to be a missional question. If God is at work in the world with saving purpose (the *missio Dei*) and the Bible is an instrument of that activity, then to ask, "What is the effect of the Bible on its readers and hearers in their diverse cultures and contexts?" will help us discover more about God and comprehend more fully God's purpose for the world. A missional Bible reading attempts to be open to such learning and to being shaped and resourced by it for participation in realizing what God desires for us and for the world.

Aspects of a Missional Reading of the Bible

It is my privilege to curate a missional formation group as part of an intercultural practice program at Carey Baptist College, Auckland, in Aotearoa New Zealand. This has been the context in which I and successive small and culturally diverse groups of students have practiced a missional reading of the Bible. By engaging in this together, several aspects of what a missional reading of the Bible involves have emerged. I gather those aspects here (recognizing that there may be others yet to be added), not to serve as a method or process, but to identify some of the attitudes, intentions, and awarenesses that we try to bring to our hearing of Scripture. This reading has a missional focus. It approaches the Bible as a revelation of God's missional character and purpose. We read this passage to know the God of mission and to understand what God desires and is working toward for the world and its people.

We interpret the various parts of the Bible within a missional framework. We discern in the Bible, as a whole, the outlines of a mission narrative. Beginning with the missional act of God's creation, the story moves toward the full realization of the kingdom of God, the rule of God declared in the gospel to be exercised in and over all things through the agency of God's anointed King, the Lord Jesus Christ. We ask how each part of the Bible relates to the unfolding of that story, and what it contributes to it.

We are conscious of the missional locatedness both of the biblical documents and of ourselves as readers. We recognize that each of the writings that comprise our Bible came into being in a particular geographical, historical, and social environment, in the contexts of real relationships and situations. We want to understand how the biblical document spoke within that mission context, and to hear it within the realities of our own mission contexts.

Our reading is motivated by a missional intentionality. We are not only students of God's mission, but participants in it. We look to the Bible to reveal the mission of God to us in order to shape and resource us to play our part in that mission as it continues today. We find ourselves in the Bible's story of God's mission and experience it with the empathy and immediacy of co-participants, sharing joys, fears, challenges, and wonder, rather than looking on from a distance as disinterested observers.

We are aware that the Bible is given not to individual people or autonomous groups but to a missional community, the people of God across space and time. Accordingly, we read as partners with others in the mission of God. Our missional formation group values its diversity. As part of our practice, we read the selected passage in at least two of the languages represented in the group and are enriched and often surprised when different languages lend distinctive flavors and connotations to what we are reading. We are curious about different cultures and assumptions within which what is read is intuitively understood. We share divergent experiences of life and faith that stretch our horizons. Beyond the group itself we try where possible to be attentive to the insights and challenges heard in the Bible by people in very different environments and the witness of God's people through history. In this great missional community, global and local, contemporaneous and across time, we strive to hear more truly and interpret more faithfully the Bible's message to God's missional people.

We read in an attitude of missional receptivity. More than a record of the mission of God, the Bible is itself an agent of that mission. As we read it, we are ourselves objects of God's mission toward us. We read the Bible, therefore, with an eager openness to being engaged by what we read. We offer our minds to be renewed, our hearts to be cleansed, and our lives to be oriented toward God's character, purpose, and kingdom.

In all of this we recognize the role of the Holy Spirit both in the production of the writings that comprise the Bible and in their effect on those, including us, who read them. And we anticipate that a missional reading of the Bible will bring us into fuller knowledge and more faithful following of Jesus who is the center and goal of God's mission.

An Example: Missional Reading, Missional Resonances

I have always loved the book of Acts. I have read it, preached it, and taught it. But since I came to live in the hyper-diverse city of Auckland, I have read it differently. Adopting a missional approach, asking how the story of the mission of God that unfolds in Acts resources me and others for participation in God's continuing mission in our context here, opens us to correspondences between the Acts story and our own. In particular, reading with missional intentionality here in Auckland, in this "city of migrants," we notice the presence of so many people in Acts who are on the move. Our eyes and hearts thus are opened to the significance of migration and migrants in God's mission, both then and now. Here are some examples.

Diaspora people (Acts 2): In Jerusalem on the day of Pentecost there were people "from every nation under heaven" (v. 5). In some ways they regarded Jerusalem as their home, but they struggled to fully belong. These people had been born and brought up in other parts of the world, were most at ease in the languages of their places of birth and did not have the social and family networks that gave identity and security to the local born residents. Through the miracle of Pentecost, they heard the wonders of God in their native tongue or the language of their heart and were embraced into the new community of those who shared life and faith in the risen Jesus. Diaspora people make up almost half of Auckland's population. They too struggle to find acceptance and belonging. Whether they arrived here with a Christian faith or find it in Auckland, a missional reception of the Acts story impels us to welcome people from elsewhere into Jesus communities of shared joy, diversity in culture and language, and mutual care.

A spiritual seeker (Acts 8:26–39): A foreign dignitary had turned up in Jerusalem which probably happened a lot in the world of international relations, but this man's purposes were different as he had come specifically to worship. As a wealthy person, he had been able to purchase a valuable scroll, part of the Jewish Scriptures, and he was reading it intently on the long, slow journey home. At God's prompting, Philip joined him on the road, answered his questions, pointed him to Jesus, and at the man's request baptized him there and then. A missional reading of this passage opens us to the possibility that travelers and visitors to our city unknown to us may also be on a spiritual quest. We are encouraged here to be open to surprising promptings of the Spirit that invite us to engage with people who might seem to be just passing through and to develop an awareness that their journey could be significant in God's purpose for them and, through them, for other people and places.

An international student (Acts 8–9): A young man called Saul left home to study in another country where he came across dedicated followers of Jesus. His first reaction to them and their strange beliefs was extremely negative. He opposed them vigorously and violently. This was his mission and pursuit until he met Jesus for himself, and his life was transformed. He then became an amazingly effective witness, teacher, and leader. Auckland hosts many thousands of international students. A missional reading of Saul's story stirs us to ask who are those whom God has brought here so that they can encounter followers of Jesus like me and get to know him for themselves? What can I do to meet them?

Refugees (Acts 11:19–26; 13:1–3): As we read Acts with attentiveness to the story of God's mission and the participants in it, it seems significant that the people who carried the gospel to the influential city of Antioch were refugees. They had been driven out of Jerusalem by persecution and made their way to Antioch with few resources with which to make a new home for themselves. But what they did carry with them was a faith strengthened by what they had endured and a deep commitment to Jesus for whom they had been prepared to lose so much. It was from these refugees' witness that the first truly intercultural church was birthed from which the gospel was sent out to the world. All refugees who arrive in New Zealand spend their first few weeks in the Refugee Reception Center in Auckland, and many remain there for longer periods of time. Our missional reading challenges our limited perception of refugees as people in need of help, hospitality, and welcome. That is certainly part of their reality, but we are also led to ask, particularly when we recognize that many come with a Christian faith, what their witness and vitality will bring to the life and mission of the church here and how we can make room for their contributions and gifts.

A bicultural young person (Acts 16:1–5): In this chapter, it seems that a girl from a diaspora Jewish family had got involved with a local boy who was not of the same culture and religion. This caused tensions in that migrant community, and the child born of the relationship was not fully accepted by them. When both mother and son became believers in Jesus, they found themselves part of a new, welcoming community where young Timothy's qualities and gifts were recognized. Furthermore, the bicultural young man now had a new motivation to work at rebuilding the relationship with his mother's people so that he could take the good news to them. In the formation of an authentic, diverse Christian community, bicultural people who can relate across barriers of cultural differences have a significant role to play. Many young people growing up in Auckland are unsure of their cultures, who they truly are, or where they belong. We learn from Timothy's story that they don't have to choose one over another part of their cultural identity. God has a purpose in it all, and it is the church's responsibility to affirm and value their background and all aspects of their being.

A foreign business owner (Acts 16:13–15, 40): A woman moved to another continent to look after the sales end of the family export business, and it was there where she started meeting with some other women to pray. When Paul and Silas turned up at their group and introduced Jesus to them, Lydia became a believer. Immediately, she opened her home not only to the missionaries but also to other local people who were interested in the gospel and became believers. Soon her home had turned into the gathering place for the first church in that city, that was used in significant ways in missions throughout their region and beyond. Business brings many people to Auckland, but that is not the totality of their lives. Who are the "Lydias" among them who are on journeys of faith and whose hearts God is touching so that they respond to the message about Jesus? What part might their skills and resources play in God's mission here and elsewhere? And how can I support them on their faith journey and mission?

Many other examples could be cited, but these might serve to illustrate some ways in which God's continuing mission in and through us can be experienced as we read the Bible not only as observers from another time and place but as participants in the continuing story of God, the community of Jesus, and the world.

Practicing Missional Bible Reading

Any reading of the Bible that is undertaken with an attitude of engagement in God's purpose for the world and for us could be considered missional. If you want to enrich your devotional times with an intentionally missional approach to your reading you might find the following questions and instructions helpful. Select a unit of manageable length—it could be a chapter, a few verses—preferably a reasonably short but coherent unit. As a way of exploring the chosen text's content and its effect in terms of God's mission, choose some of the following questions and ponder them as you bring them to your selected verses. Of course, you do not have to be limited to these questions, they are just a starting point. If you are unable to answer the question you started with, move to another one. These questions are meant to open windows into the text, so begin with one you can see through!

- Reading to know the God of mission
    - In what ways do we meet God in this passage?
    - What do we discover about God here?
    - How does God challenge, teach, encourage, and/or call us?
    - What do we want to ask God as we read this text?
- Approaching the Bible as the story of God's mission
    - What stage in the overarching story of God's mission does this part of the Bible belong to?
    - What does it add to that story?
    - How might it connect to other parts of the story?
- Understanding the Bible as a product of God's mission
    - In what ways has this part of the Bible come into being as a result of God's mission?
    - What aspect or stage of God's mission caused it to be written?

- How was this historical record/worship/letter/etc. intended to serve the purposes of God's mission when it was written and first received?
- Entering into the Bible as participants in God's mission
  - What may be learned from this part of the Bible about the goals, character, and scope of God's mission, what sorts of people can participate in it, and what does such participation involve?
  - Is there any specific instruction, encouragement, or wisdom to be derived from this part of the Bible relevant to my/our participation in mission?
- Reading together with partners in God's mission
  - With whom am I sharing this encounter with the Bible? What do they see, hear, and feel in the text from their various cultures, languages, histories, and situations?
  - Who are the partners not around the table now whose perspectives and insights we want to receive? How will we do that?
- Reading in the context of God's mission
  - What is my/our location right now, as we read the Bible?
  - How does the passage we are reading resonate in this particular context of God's mission?
  - What does the God of mission prompt us to see, pray, and do in this location?
- Welcoming the Bible as an act of God's mission
  - How does this part of the Bible affect God's mission toward me/us?
  - How does it speak to, inspire, disturb, or challenge me/us?
  - What might God be wanting to do in me/us that aligns with the purposes of God's mission?

Having sat with Scripture and (where possible) with others, take time to pause and gather your impressions and reflections. Acknowledge the presence of God and the activity of God's Spirit with you and those you have been reading with, in the place where you are and the places into which you will go, and in the passage of Scripture that you have read.

Consciously adopt attitudes of missional readiness through practicing a stance of:

- attentiveness to God, to each other, to places and people;
- availability to God and to others as God prompts; and
- adaptability to hold our assumptions about God's mission and our part in it lightly, and a willingness to see, think, and behave differently as God shows the way.

Part 2

Transformed Through Returning to the Wild Earth and the Beauty of Creation

5

An Unexpected Journey
Hiking as a Spiritual Practice

SANTHOSH GEORGE

There is a great amount of research about the physical benefits of hiking. Hitting the trails improves muscle strength, boosts your mood, enhances respiratory fitness, improves your sleep, and reduces your risk of heart disease. During a hike you immerse yourself in nature, jump over rocks, navigate your way across rivers and around trees, and climb over uneven surfaces. All these activities provide a wonderful workout and fitness training for your body. However, have you ever considered that hiking can also be a valuable spiritual practice with spiritual and emotional benefits?

Multiday hiking can be compared to a pilgrimage where you leave the comfort of your life and the trappings of civilization. As you pack your backpack in preparation for the hike you practice simplicity by reducing your belongings to the mere essentials. You then move from what is familiar into unknown territory in search for new insights or a special meeting with God. There are three movements—a withdrawing from noise to silence, from work to rest, and from loneliness to solitude. In this chapter, Santhosh shares how his discovery of hiking as a spiritual practice has strengthened his faith and led him to a place of reverence and adoration. He leaves the city to meet with his Creator in the beauty of nature and in everything he encounters. Let's join him on his hikes and learn from his insights and discoveries.

Beyond the Discomfort

THE ROUTE AHEAD SLOPED relentlessly upward. The forest around us cast a canopy of shadows in the fading light of dusk. All conversation had died a while back—we were utterly exhausted. The silence was punctuated by the squelching of our boots on wet mud. My fifteen-kilogram backpack dug into my shoulders, my legs felt like lead, and I began to feel a rising sense of panic—where was the hut?

My friends and I were on a hike up Mount Pirongia, near Hamilton, New Zealand. The plan was to spend the night at the hut near the summit before heading back down the next day. This was my first ever multiday hike, and this grueling grind was not what I had expected. Later we discovered that we had failed to read the fine print—the track we were on was classed as advanced! Nearly ten hours into the hike, the mud path gave way to a wooden boardwalk. Suddenly, we rounded a corner and there was the hut! A wave of relief and joy washed over me. We made it! As I stumbled into the hut, I remember thinking, "That's it. Never again! I'm done with hiking. Give me a holiday by the beach any day."

Ten years and countless hikes later, I now regularly escape with my friends into the pristine national parks of New Zealand on hikes that last for five or six days. It turns out Mount Pirongia was not an ending, but a beginning. We have discovered that beyond the many hardships and discomforts of hiking there is an incomparable refreshment and renewal of body, mind, and spirit, all within a relatively short time. In this chapter, I would like to explore what it is about this recreation that makes it such a transformational experience, especially when approached as a spiritual practice. But first, let me give you a glimpse into what is involved.

Multiday hiking involves heading into the wilderness and leaving behind the comforts and trappings of civilization—there are no roads, no supermarkets, and most unsettlingly for some, no cell phone coverage. Packing the right gear and provisions is mission-critical—food, water bottles, spare clothes, wet weather gear, cooking equipment, crockery, a first aid kit, toiletries, and so on. Forgetting an item can have catastrophic consequences, as a friend of mine who forgot to pack toilet paper soon discovered (we helped him out). A typical day involves four to seven hours of actual hiking. This is usually along well-marked tracks but can involve clambering over rocks and tree roots as well as crossing streams and rivers. You will spend the night in a tent or, here in New Zealand, at one of the many huts managed by the Department of Conservation (DOC). A typical DOC hut is spartan. The sleeping area comprises foam mattresses arranged side by side, usually over two levels, bunk-bed style. A benchtop, sink, dining table, trestle seating, and a wood-burning fireplace occupy the rest of the open-plan space. The toilets, which are basic long drops, are mercifully situated several meters away from the hut. There is no electricity or hot water, no clean sheets, or showers. The Hilton this is not.

If you are still reading, let us deconstruct the elements that make hiking so nourishing for the soul.

Withdrawing

> But Jesus often withdrew to lonely places and prayed.
>
> —LUKE 5:16

Life is busy. As the pastor of a local Baptist church in East Auckland, I have discovered that the demands of ministry can be a bottomless pit. Do not get me wrong—I love my work. I love making a difference in people's lives and feeling useful and needed. But there are times when I get so busy that I miss out on the very thing I am trying to help others experience—namely, quality time with God. In his book *The Ruthless Elimination of Hurry*, John Mark Comer warns that we can become "too busy to live emotionally healthy and spiritually rich and vibrant lives."[1]

Yet busyness is not unique to our age. By all accounts, Jesus and his disciples had hectic schedules. Everywhere Jesus went, he was pursued by large crowds eager for his teaching (Mark 2:2) and healing (Matt 15:30). At one point, we read that "so many people were coming and going that [Jesus and his disciples] did not even have a chance to eat" (Mark 6:31). So how did Jesus manage to fit in uninterrupted quality time with his heavenly Father? By *withdrawing* to quiet and "lonely places." Much like the ebb and flow of the tides, the rhythm of ministry that Jesus modelled was one of pressing in and withdrawing. Jesus was quite the

---

1. Comer, *Ruthless Elimination of Hurry*, 21.

outdoorsman, regularly withdrawing to spend the night on the Mount of Olives (Luke 21:37) or escaping to the Sea of Galilee (Matt 14:13).

Hiking is a radical form of withdrawing, especially for a city slicker like me. The world I leave behind and the world I step into are totally different; it feels like stepping through that magical wardrobe into Narnia. I have noticed three movements—a withdrawing from noise to silence, from work to rest, and from loneliness to solitude. Let us look at each of these in turn.

From Noise to Silence

The world we live in is saturated with noise, both literally and figuratively. The noise of traffic, smartphone notifications, emails, advertising billboards, YouTube clickbait, and so on all clamor for our attention and so often drown out the still, small voice of God (1 Kgs 19:12 KJV). In *The Screwtape Letters*, C. S. Lewis pictures the demons working to "make the whole universe a noise in the end" while shouting down the "melodies and silences of heaven."[2]

But what better way to escape the noise of busy, modern living than to withdraw into the silence of the wilderness? Even the "noise" of nature—the friendly greeting of a curious fantail, the thunderous roar of a waterfall, the soothing tones of a gentle forest stream—all seem to encourage an inner "silence of the soul" that heightens one's awareness of God's gentle whisper, and enable what Brother Lawrence calls "a wordless and secret conversation between the soul and God."[3] Saint Augustine simply described it as "entering into joy."[4]

From Work to Rest

Hiking also provides the perfect transition from work to rest. Work can so easily pursue us into our places of rest—our always-connected smartphones mean that a single phone call, text message, or email can instantly pull our consciousness back into the office. A hike provides the perfect excuse to turn that device off, have a screen detox, and fully disconnect from the siren song of work—after all, you are out of cell phone coverage

---

2. Lewis, *Screwtape Letters*, 114.
3. Brother Lawrence, quoted in Foster, *Streams of Living Water*, 52.
4. Augustine, quoted in Comer, *Ruthless Elimination of Hurry*, 131.

anyway. I can release my unfinished tasks to "lie in their places where I left them, asleep like cattle."[5] Away from the trenches of life, I can process my feelings, collect my thoughts, and "allow the mud to settle in the mud puddle of my mind."[6]

Being completely disconnected and uncontactable is a little unsettling at first. What if you miss some major news event? I once emerged from a hike to the news that Russia had invaded Crimea. Or what if someone urgently needs you? In moments like this, I am reminded of the words of Father Cavanaugh in the movie *Rudy*: "Son, in years of religious studies . . . I've come up with only two hard, incontrovertible facts: there is a God . . . and I'm not Him."[7] Being uncontactable is a way of letting God be God, and reminding myself that the world can carry on quite happily without me.

Hiking also provides rest and refreshment for the body. You ask, "What is so refreshing about lugging a fifteen-kilogram backpack for four to seven hours over five to six days?" Well, for someone who spends so much of his waking life sitting—in traffic or hunched over a laptop or lounging in front of a Netflix show—a few days of strenuous walking is the perfect counterweight to an otherwise sedentary lifestyle. Breathing in the oxygen-rich air of lichen-covered forests,[8] drinking from alpine streams, and winding down for bed in natural darkness unsullied by excessive artificial light all contribute to a profound sense of physical well-being and help the body reset to natural rhythms. I also notice a boost in fitness—my Fitbit invariably records a drop in resting heart rate of three to four beats per minute.

From Loneliness to Solitude

The final form of withdrawing involves a transition from loneliness to solitude. One of the barriers to the spiritual life is the primal fear of being alone. This is not a misplaced fear. Many of us experienced the pernicious effects of prolonged isolation during the COVID-19 pandemic, and for good reasons. Psychobiologists have proven that long-lasting loneliness not only makes you sick but can also kill you—emotional isolation is on

- 5. Slee, *Sabbath*, 27.
- 6. McKay and McKay, "Podcast #822: Developing the Warrior Within."
- 7. Quoted in Smith, "There Is a God," para. 1.
- 8. Incidentally, lichen only thrives in pollution-free, oxygen-rich environments.

par with smoking as a risk factor for mortality.[9] Solitary confinement as a means of enforced loneliness is used as the ultimate form of mental torture in many oppressive regimes.[10] Frieda Fromm-Reichmann, a pioneering therapist on loneliness, has proposed that loneliness lies at the heart of nearly all mental illness.[11]

And so, we understandably try to avoid feelings of loneliness like the plague. We dial up the background noise of our lives—the always-on TV or radio; the over-busy schedules that expunge periods of emptiness; the superficial interactions with others that create what Thomas Merton called a "vapid togetherness."[12]

But what if, by intentionally withdrawing to quiet and "lonely places" and opening our hearts to God in a leap of faith, we encounter Presence, not absence? What if, as Henri Nouwen puts it, we find "a threshold instead of a dead end, a new creation instead of a grave, a meeting place instead of an abyss?"[13] That is when loneliness can become solitude. John Mark Comer writes, "Loneliness is inner emptiness. Solitude is inner fulfilment."[14]

The gift of solitude is what the desert fathers and mothers of early Christianity pursued as they withdrew by themselves into the desert. Father Anthony, the most well-known "abba," lived by himself in an old, abandoned Roman fort for some twenty years. These Christian hermits found in the desert's profound exterior silence "an unnerving, interior silence for which one is usually ill-prepared. Yet the fruit of this silence is a vulnerability absolutely essential to the spiritual life."[15]

I love the camaraderie and the sense of shared adventure that comes from hiking with friends. But I also appreciate the many opportunities for solitude that withdrawing into the wilderness presents, opportunities that may be harder to come by in an urban environment. Listen to Henri Nouwen: "It is probably difficult, if not impossible, to move from loneliness to solitude without any form of withdrawal from a distracting world, and therefore it is understandable that those who

---

9. Shulevitz, "Lethality of Loneliness," 25.
10. Sturt and Sturt, *Created for Intimacy*, 8.
11. Shulevitz, "Lethality of Loneliness," 25.
12. Merton, *Contemplation*, 44.
13. Nouwen, *Reaching Out*, 13–14.
14. Comer, *Ruthless Elimination of Hurry*, 134.
15. Lane, *Solace of Fierce Landscapes*, 222.

seriously try to develop their spiritual life are attracted to places and situations where they can be alone."[16]

I have also discovered that on the far side of a satisfying experience of solitude is a renewed capacity for connection with others. Nouwen writes:

> Without the solitude of heart, our relationships with others easily become needy and greedy, sticky and clinging, dependent and sentimental, exploitative and parasitic, because without the solitude of heart, we cannot experience others as different from ourselves but only as people who can be used for the fulfilment of our own, often hidden, needs.[17]

The periods of solitude that Jesus enjoyed undoubtedly fueled his seemingly boundless capacity for connection and service to others (Matt 14:13–14).

The Beauty of Gardens

> I think that I shall never see a poem lovely as a tree.
>
> —JOYCE KILMER

Lee Kuan Yew, the man responsible for transforming Singapore into a garden city, famously observed that "a concrete jungle destroys the human spirit."[18] From the Hanging Gardens of Babylon built in the sixth century BC to modern-day Central Park in New York to simple backyard flower patches, the gardens we create in our urban environments are a testament to our primaeval longing to escape into nature. A multiday hike provides a fuller escape, putting you in an environment where, for an extended period, nature is all there is, as far as the eye can see.

I recently came across an article in the *National Geographic* magazine that referenced multiple studies on the therapeutic effects of nature. For instance, being in nature encourages the brain's prefrontal cortex to dial down and rest. According to attention restoration theory, "Spending time in nature relieves the stress and mental fatigue caused by the 'directed attention' that work and city life require."[19] Nature can boost

---

16. Nouwen, *Reaching Out*, 16.
17. Nouwen, *Reaching Out*, 22.
18. Lee Kuan Yew, quoted in Lee, "Speech by SMS Desmond Lee," para. 23.
19. Williams, "This Is Your Brain on Nature," 56.

creativity by up to 50 percent and reduce the incidence of fifteen diseases including depression, anxiety, heart disease, diabetes, asthma, and migraines.[20] Even a short walk in the woods (which in Japan is known as forest bathing) can reduce the stress hormone cortisol by 16 percent and lower blood pressure by 2 percent.[21] If nature could be bottled, it would truly be a miracle drug!

Awe and Wonder

> Not all who [wonder or] wander are lost.
>
> —J. R. R. TOLKIEN

From our elevated perch on the Cascades Saddle in Mount Aspiring National Park, we looked out over the majestic Matukituki Valley. The snow-capped peak of Mount Aspiring loomed beyond, and behind us lay the Dart glacier. Silently, almost reverentially, we drank in this achingly beautiful scene. And then my friend spoke: "Santhosh, would it be appropriate to say a prayer?" I was taken aback because this friend is not religious. Yet, could there have been a more appropriate response to such awe-inspiring beauty? The feelings of awe that the grand vistas of nature evoke can draw us into a posture of worship. "The world is charged with the grandeur of God," wrote Gerard Manley Hopkins, echoing the words of David—"The heavens declare the glory of God" (Ps 19:1).[22]

Awe can help us feel "briefly, deliciously, insignificant."[23] It can pull us out of our self-absorption and self-referential state and restore in us a proper sense of our place in the world. When Job became preoccupied with his suffering, God's response was to point to the wonders of creation to heal Job's perspective. It was God's way of saying to Job, "There are more things in heaven and earth, Horatio, than are dreamt of in your philosophy."[24]

The profound therapeutic effects of awe have only been properly studied in the last twenty years. Awe can increase feelings of compassion, generosity, and humility, and even help us feel less impatient. It can

---

20. Williams, "This Is Your Brain on Nature," 57.
21. Williams, "This Is Your Brain on Nature," 58.
22. Hopkins, "God's Grandeur," line 1.
23. Morgan, "Oh Wow!," para. 1.
24. Shakespeare, *Hamlet* 1.5.187–88.

reduce rumination associated with depression as well as decrease chronic inflammation associated with heart disease, cancer, diabetes, arthritis, and bowel disease.[25] Einstein waxed lyrical about this "wonder emotion," writing, "The most beautiful emotion we can experience is the mysterious. It is the power of all true art and science. He to whom this emotion is a stranger, who can no longer wonder and stand rapt in awe, is as good as dead."[26]

Awe can also shatter our preconceptions about God. The language and meaning we draw on to describe God can often be shaped and constrained by our own limited life experiences. "When we give a thing a name," as Gregory of Nyssa pointed out, "we imagine we have got hold of it. . . . Perhaps we should do better not to flatter ourselves too soon that we can name God."[27] Yet experiences of awe can help us transcend these limitations. The majesty of creation can inspire us to see the Creator with new eyes, casting what John Cassian described as "an imperfect yet astonished gaze at God's ungraspable nature."[28]

Simplicity

> Civilization is the limitless multiplication of unnecessary necessities.
>
> —MARK TWAIN

Before a hike, I sometimes catch myself looking at my eighty-five-litre Osprey backpack in amazement. Almost everything I'll need to live on for the next several days will fit into this one backpack. So why do I have so much stuff filling up my home?

Possessions can consume our attention. They need to be shopped for, stored, maintained, repaired, and eventually replaced. They can exhaust and dissipate our attention away from the things of God.[29] Thus, to live the spiritual life is to "live freely and lightly,"[30] keeping in mind the words of Jesus: "Life does not consist in an abundance of possessions" (Luke 12:15). This involves practicing the spiritual discipline of

25. Morgan, "Oh Wow!," para. 5.
26. Einstein, quoted in Shiota et al., "Nature of Awe," 944.
27. Gregory, quoted in Lane, *Solace of Fierce Landscapes*, 62.
28. Cassian, quoted in Lane, *Solace of Fierce Landscapes*, 12.
29. Merton, *Contemplation in a World of Action*, 101.
30. Comer, *Ruthless Elimination of Hurry*, 10.

simplicity—the spiritual equivalent of Marie Kondo-ing our lives.[31] At the heart of this discipline is the realization that, ultimately, God alone suffices.[32] The careful packing that goes into a multiday hike, with the ruthless elimination of anything superfluous or excessively burdensome, is a continual reminder to pack for the larger pilgrimage of life with the same spirit of simplicity.

The Strenuous Life

> Over-sentimentality, over-softness, in fact washiness and mushiness are the great dangers of this age and of this people. Unless we keep the barbarian virtues, gaining the civilized ones will be of little avail.
>
> —Theodore Roosevelt

Some degree of hardship, discomfort, and inconvenience are part and parcel of multiday hiking, whether it is fighting off sand flies, washing dishes in ice-cold water, or trying to sleep in a hut full of snorers. On top of that, there is the risk of sprained ankles, broken bones, and hypothermia. Yet these elements of hardship and danger have a fortifying effect on the soul. As that panicky overnighter hiking trip up Mount Pirongia taught me, no matter how challenging the path gets, if you will just keep putting one foot in front of the other, you will eventually make it to the hut—that proverbial place of safety and rest. Hikers will tell you that the resilience, grit, and hardiness that hiking fosters usually overflows into other facets of life. The spiritual life certainly demands these qualities—this is why the apostle Paul likens it to running a race (1 Cor 9:24–27).

Belden Lane, a fellow hiker, has beautifully captured this interplay between the rigors of wilderness hiking and its fortifying effects on the spiritual life. He writes:

> Exposure to the harsh realities and fierce beauties of a world not aimed at my comfort has a way of cutting through the self-absorption of my life. The uncontrolled mystery of nature puts the ego in check and invites the soul back (in more than one way) to the ground of its being. It elicits the soul's deepest desire, enforces a rigorous discipline, and demands a life marked by

---

31. Marie Kondo is a Japanese author and TV presenter widely known for her teachings on organization and minimalism.

32. Merton, *Contemplation in a World of Action*, 24.

activism and resistance. It reminds me, in short, that spiritual practice—far from being anything ethereal—is a highly tactile, embodied, and visceral affair.[33]

Beginning the Journey

As I trudged up Mount Pirongia all those years ago, I could never have imagined that multiday hiking would one day become such a life-giving spiritual practice. One that enables a withdrawing from noise to silence, from work to rest and from loneliness to solitude. One that connects me with nature and inspires feelings of awe and wonder. One that encourages simplicity and fortifies the soul for the spiritual life by persevering through physical hardship and discomfort.

Getting into multiday hiking does require a basic level of fitness. It is best to start with some day hikes, and then move on to an overnighter before going away for longer periods. A few essentials are a good pair of hiking boots, a sleeping bag, a comfortable backpack, and effective wet and cold weather gear. Odor-inhibiting merino clothing is also a must if you want to avoid dark looks from fellow hikers. Nip around to your nearest outdoor adventure store for further advice on gear.

While the many rewards of multiday hiking accrue to all, there are unique benefits to those who intentionally approach it as a spiritual practice rather than just a recreational pursuit. In one sense, a multiday hike is simply a vessel that can hold any number of spiritual practices in a distraction-free environment conducive to those practices. I have engaged in spiritual practices such as contemplative prayer, *lectio divina*, gratitude, and journaling. Solo hiking offers unique opportunities for silence and solitude, although I prefer simply detaching from my group from time to time. Someone I know even incorporated fasting into their hike. I recommend packing a notebook to journal any thoughts and prayers, and either packing a small Bible or accessing one on a Kindle. But above all, bring along your sense of adventure. Look beyond the discomfort to the delights ahead. And prepare to meet God in new and unexpected ways.

---

33. Lane, *Backpacking with the Saints*, 4.

Bibliography

Comer, John Mark. *The Ruthless Elimination of Hurry: How to Stay Emotionally Healthy and Spiritually Alive in the Chaos of the Modern World*. Colorado Springs: WaterBrook, 2019.

Foster, Richard J. *Streams of Living Water: Celebrating the Great Traditions of Christian Faith*. San Francisco: HarperCollins, 1998.

Hopkins, Gerard Manley. "God's Grandeur." Poetry Foundation. https://www.poetryfoundation.org/poems/44395/gods-grandeur.

Kilmer, Joyce. "Trees." Poetry Foundation. https://www.poetryfoundation.org/poetrymagazine/poems/12744/trees.

Lane, Belden C. *Backpacking with the Saints: Wilderness Hiking as Spiritual Practice*. Oxford: Oxford University Press, 2015.

———. *The Solace of Fierce Landscapes: Exploring Desert and Mountain Spirituality*. Oxford: Oxford University Press, 1998.

Lee, Desmond. "Speech by SMS Desmond Lee at the Launch of the Therapeutic Garden at HortPark." Singapore Ministry of National Development, May 14, 2016. https://www.mnd.gov.sg/newsroom/speeches/view/speech-by-sms-desmond-lee-at-the-launch-of-the-therapeutic-garden-at-hortpark.

Lewis, C. S. *The Screwtape Letters*. London: Centenary, 1945.

McKay, Brett, and Kate McKay. "Podcast #822: Developing the Warrior Within." *Art of Manliness*, Aug. 1, 2022. https://www.artofmanliness.com/career-wealth/leadership/podcast-822-developing-the-warrior-within/.

Merton, Thomas. *Contemplation in a World of Action*. 2nd ed. Gethsemani Studies in Psychological and Religious Anthropology 1. Notre Dame: University of Notre Dame Press, 1998.

Morgan, Eleanor. "Oh Wow! How Getting More Awe Can Improve Your Life—And Even Make You a Nicer Person." *Guardian*, Sept. 23, 2022. https://www.theguardian.com/lifeandstyle/2022/sep/23/how-getting-more-awe-can-improve-your-life-and-even-make-you-a-nicer-person.

Nouwen, Henri J. M. *Reaching Out: A Special Edition of the Spiritual Classic Including Beyond the Mirror*. London: Fount, 1998.

Shakespeare, William. *Hamlet*. Edited by Barbara Mowat et al. Folger Shakespeare Library. https://www.folger.edu/explore/shakespeares-works/hamlet/read/1/5/#line-1.5.187.

Shiota, Michelle N., et al. "The Nature of Awe: Elicitors, Appraisals, and Effects on Self-Concept." *Cognition and Emotion* 21 (2007) 944–63. https://doi.org/10.1080/02699930600923668.

Shulevitz, Judith. "The Lethality of Loneliness." *New Republic* 244 (2013) 22–29. https://newrepublic.com/article/113176/science-loneliness-how-isolation-can-kill-you.

Slee, Nicola. *Sabbath: The Hidden Heartbeat of Our Lives*. London: Darton, Longman & Todd, 2019.

Smith, Randall. "There Is a God; I Am Not Him." Catholic Thing, Sept. 1, 2018. https://www.thecatholicthing.org/2018/09/01/there-is-a-god-i-am-not-him/.

Sturt, John, and Agnes Sturt. *Created for Intimacy: Discovering Intimacy with Yourself, Others and God*. Guildford, UK: Eagle, 1996.

Williams, Florence. "This Is Your Brain on Nature." *National Geographic* 229 (2016) 54–67.

6

Fostering a Contemplative Gaze Toward Creation

Katrina Tulip

Nature reveals the divine. For those who are open and perceptive to its messages, everything in creation bears God's fingerprint or footprint. Spending quality time in nature or going for contemplative walks can open our hearts and minds toward our Creator and lead to sacred encounters that are often accompanied with new insights and feelings of awe.

In this chapter, Katrina shares her own experiences of spending time and wandering in nature throughout her life and shares how her contemplative nature-gazing practice developed and took shape. Oftentimes she received solace and inspiration through her adventures in the cathedral of the outdoors. As you read her story you will be invited to pause and relate these ideas to your own life. You will also be encouraged through many practical guidelines to foster your own contemplative gaze toward creation. Katrina interweaves insights from the desert fathers, mystics, and saints, as well as theologians and creation spirituality advocates into the tapestry of her personal story.

"Pink Beach," the signpost read. Drawn in by the name and my love of exploring, I continued my walk beyond the lookout and came to a pretty cove nestled below the cliffs on the far side of Shakespear Regional Park in Auckland, New Zealand. Sparked by the excitement of discovery, I descended the wooden steps and jumped from rock to rock until my feet touched the pink-toned sand, where I paused and gazed around, breathing in the beauty. I noticed a black-backed gull sitting on her nest under the cliffs, and a pair of oystercatchers with a lone dotterel feeding at the water's edge. No other people—delicious solitude! I sat on the sand and listened for the hundredth time to the soft, haunting voice of Enya singing "So I Could Find My Way" and redirected the lyrics toward the Nurturer and Sustainer of my life.

When the song ended, I remained silent and still, soaking in the beauty of my surroundings. The sun was shining, the mood mellow, and the milky-smooth surface of the sea sparkled like diamonds, dazzling my eyes. A gentle breeze caressed my skin. Small waves were gliding in and breaking softly on the shore with soothing regularity. As they approached, one after the other, I felt the vastness of divine love—wider, longer, higher, and deeper than the ocean—flowing toward me and all else that had been made (Eph 3:14–19; Ps 145:9). I felt connected to both the Creator and creation. The invitation here could not have been clearer: "Open your heart and receive from my infinitely generous flow of love and goodness." Overwhelmed with gratitude, my heart responded and dissolved, and I sobbed uninhibitedly.

The rich, mystical[1] experience described above seemed like a culmination of many smaller encounters with the divine in nature over recent months. Graced gifts have come my way—undeserved, unforced, and unexpected. They have nourished, strengthened, enlivened, sustained, encouraged, inspired, and healed me. Reflecting on these experiences, I see how the spiritual practice of fostering a contemplative gaze toward creation[2]—a way of truly seeing and deeply listening with the eyes and ears of the heart (Eph 1:18) to each and all living and nonliving beings[3]—

---

1. Mystical as in experiencing divine presence, as well as having a sense of oneness with creation.

2. Creation, Mother Earth, Mother Nature, nature, the natural environment—each name has its own nuance and I use them all at different times. You, dear reader, will have your own preferred name. Feel free to substitute it. I extend the same invitation regarding your favored name/s for God.

3. I deliberately choose the word "beings" here, as opposed to "things" to honor the sacredness of creation, and to highlight the need for those of us in the West to

enhances my openness and receptivity to the loving, indwelling presence of God. For God is not *out there* but is in all, through all, and with all.[4] Elizabeth Barrett Browning expresses this beautifully in her oft-quoted lines: "Earth's crammed with heaven, and every common bush afire with God, but only [she] who sees takes off [her] shoes."[5]

The contemplative practice of being in creation is transforming me as it deepens my trust in the goodness of God, renews me daily, and helps me journey toward wholeness. On top of that, it strengthens my desire to respect and care for creation and inspires me to exhort others to do likewise.

Invitation to Pause and Reflect

- Have you had any mystical experiences within nature? If so, recall what happened in detail.
- How has this changed your relationship with the divine and with nature?
- Express gratitude for any insights given. Record your experiences in a journal and/or share them with a trusted friend to help savor the experience.

How Do I Engage with God's Creation as a Spiritual Practice?

My early morning routine begins with centering prayer, which is a method of contemplative prayer where the pray-er rests silently in the presence of God.[6] When practiced once or twice daily for about twenty minutes, it opens the deeper parts of one's being to God and helps to sustain contemplative awareness throughout the day. Jesuit theologian Walter Burghardt described contemplation as taking a "long loving look

---

avoid objectifying creation, because this mindset can lead to possessive, utilitarian, and consumerist behavior, which is damaging to our planet.

4. Rohr, "Everything Is Connected," para. 4.
5. Browning, "Aurora Leigh: Book 7."
6. Boyer, "Guide to Centering Prayer."

at the real."[7] In other words, having an open, nonjudgmental, soft, compassionate gaze toward oneself, others, the Creator, and creation.

After praying, I usually head out for a walk or bike ride. Sometimes I have an inner sense beforehand to go to a specific location—perhaps along a familiar trail toward a local reserve. If time allows, I may go further afield to a beach, forest, mountain, lake, or river. I am solitary on these outings so I can be attentive to my surroundings. As I wander along, I consciously use my senses, noting what I see, hear, smell, or touch. I pause when something catches my attention.

I may stop and receive the gift of a spectacular sunrise reflected on the sea. Such moments of transient beauty remind me to savor good things but not cling to them. I might pick up a walnut from under a mature tree in the park and receive an insight about my future growth potential as a spiritual director given the right conditions and time. I am invited to kneel in the dewy grass to look more closely at a dainty mushroom sheltering a tinier one and consider how any caring action—however small—counts for something. I am stirred to chase a tumbleweed rolling along the beach in a fresh breeze and feel the joy of spontaneous playfulness. Open clam shells inclined toward the morning sun speak to me as they symbolize cupped hands resting and receiving from God. They remind me to follow suit during my gradual recovery from post-COVID fatigue. I am captivated by faithful parent terns feeding hungry, dependent chicks. They speak of and symbolize the nourishment provided by daily engagement in contemplative prayer. Monarch butterflies sipping nectar from open flowers, rapidly growing caterpillars and darkening chrysalises provide me with a feast of metaphors for the spiritual journey.

If I have noticed something small and appealing—a koru-shaped shell, skeleton leaf, opening seedpod, soft feather, or smooth stone—I pick it up and feel its shape and texture. Sometimes I bring it home and add it to my personal altar. The altar I created serves as a visual prayer focus. It contains meaningful items such as a candle, a holding cross, photos, pictures, and names of people I am praying for, as well as these treasures from nature.

When a noticing—or a "nature *divina*," as I sometimes call it—lingers in my mind, I spend time pondering its message. I do this by dialoguing with God and recording my thoughts and feelings in a journal. Occasionally the noticing has a disturbing aspect to it, touching into an

---

7. Burghardt, "Contemplation."

inner wound or vulnerability, and I need to attend to what is surfacing. One of those experiences was when I saw an adult tern viciously peck a lone chick in a neighboring nest.[8] Themes may emerge over time. All these observations and movements are rich fodder for discussion with my spiritual director.

I delight in sharing my "nature noticing" with others. As an extension of my morning practice, I regularly upload photos accompanied by written reflections onto social media. They are easily adapted and become individual messages of encouragement for friends in need. They also make wonderful cards for all occasions.

Invitation to Pause and Reflect

- How would you describe your gaze toward yourself, other people, God, and the natural environment? Would you agree that the way we gaze toward one of these realities influences how we gaze toward the others?

- Where do you sense an invitation to foster intentionally a more open, softer, compassionate, less judgmental gaze? You might want to share this with God and invite the Holy Spirit to give you fresh eyes.

How Did This Spiritual Practice Emerge?

There are several contributing factors that have led to the emergence of my contemplative gaze toward creation. I have had an affinity with Mother Nature from childhood. During those formative years she was a source of comfort and a place I could escape. My school friends and I spent hours exploring the beach, pine forest, mountain, and harbor. This love of the outdoors continued into adulthood and was nurtured by activities such as running, hiking, cycling, kayaking, and travelling.

In my mid-twenties, I was introduced to contemplative spirituality by a spiritual formation lecturer, Sheila Pritchard, at the Bible College of New Zealand. This opened new ways of seeing and intimate ways of being with the mystery that is God. I began attending multiday silent prayer retreats where I discovered the riches offered by those salient *s*-words:

---

8. Interactive Drawing Therapy (IDT) is a very useful tool for processing anything that disturbs our equilibrium.

solitude, silence, stillness, and space—that were all savored by the Source. When I practiced these disciplines, I noticed that I became more attuned to God's presence. On contemplative walks on retreats, I was amazed at how spiritual insights from nature just leaped out at me!

My forties felt like a dark valley where God seemed silent and attending church felt like a chore. Thankfully, I received solace through many adventures in the cathedral of the outdoors. In the spiritual reawakening that followed a decade later, I was graced with numinous experiences of being wrapped in God's love. I began to understand how this love is pivotal to life, and how the experience of it brings profound inner transformation and naturally flows into life-giving action.

During 2019, I received a long-awaited divine "green light" to apply for the Spiritual Directors' Formation Programme (SDFP) run by Spiritual Growth Ministries in New Zealand, which teaches the art of spiritual direction based on a contemplative, incarnational model.[9] I learned how God uses any aspect of our lives to connect with us, which is why it is so important to take time to pause and pay attention to whatever is happening in our lives and attracting our attention. I became familiar with the catchphrase "Notice what you notice," and endeavored to make this a habit.

An introduction to Christian mystics of old during the SDFP deepened my awareness of the connection between divine love and the cosmos. I was drawn to the extraordinarily gifted, Spirit-filled mystic St. Hildegard of Bingen (1098–1179), and seized the chance to get a taste of her music, art, poetry, science, and theology through an online course with Matthew Fox.[10] Hildegard spoke of love abounding in all things, and of everything in the universe being interconnected and interdependent. She exulted in how the whole cosmos is a symphony of joy and jubilation. Hildegard explained that all of creation is holy and warned humans not to use their power to rupture that holiness by committing unjust acts and lacking compassionate action. If we let ourselves fall in love with creation deeper and deeper, we will naturally respond to its endangerment with passion. For Hildegard, being virtuous meant doing good works, which she understood as acting justly toward all of creation.[11] I resonate with

---

9. Spiritual director Sue Pickering defines spiritual direction as taking place "when one person (the director) prayerfully supports and encourages another person (the directee) to attend and to respond to God." Pickering, *Spiritual Direction*, 3. For a more detailed explanation of this model, see Pickering, *Spiritual Direction*, 26–27.

10. Fox, *Answer the Call*.

11. Fox, *Answer the Call*.

these teachings and am inspired by Hildegard's courage in speaking out and acting upon her God-given convictions.

During the SDFP, a version of St. Francis of Assisi's "Canticle of the Creatures," adapted by singer-songwriter Simon de Voil, became a favorite song of mine. Written toward the end of his life, the theology underpinning the lyrics of this song reflected St. Francis's understanding of nature as a sacramental expression of God's generous love and goodness. It also explained how God's love binds all things together in a family of relationships.[12] Just over one hundred years later, theologian and mystic Julian of Norwich—who, like us, lived through a pandemic—described how all things in the universe are held together in love, and how our task is to love all that God loves.[13] These insights confirmed my growing sense of the centrality of love and of love being the best motivation for effective action.

Creation spirituality advocate Matthew Fox reminded me that Gen 1 begins with cosmology and is a celebration of the intrinsic goodness of the universe, which he terms "original blessing." To Fox's mind, the relatively modern emphasis on fall and redemption has caused us to lose sight of this important beginning. Fox adds: "The eco-crises of our time are witnesses to the failures of religion and spirituality to contextualise our understanding of the sacredness of creation."[14]

The fact that we are part of "the web of creation" was also covered under the topic of Māori spirituality.[15] During a SDFP workshop, I learned about whanaungatanga, which, in its broadest sense, refers to the interconnectedness of all living and nonliving things. The cosmos is a complex whānau (extended family) in which everything belongs, and we humans are the kaitiaki (guardians), involved in caring for, and protecting it all.[16] Twentieth-century quantum physics supports this ancient worldview by demonstrating that matter and energy, at its most fundamental level, are about relationship—things only exist in relation to other things: "The world is, at its most primal level, an undivided whole."[17]

Two months earlier, I had attended a six-day prayer retreat with the inviting theme "Your Place at the Table: Enjoying the Hospitality of the Trinity," based on Andrei Rublev's famous *Trinity* icon. From this retreat,

12. See Delio, *Franciscan View of Creation*.
13. Francis, "Spiritual Direction and Justice."
14. Fox, *Essential Writings*, ch. 1.
15. A description used by St. Hildegard. Fox, *Answer the Call*.
16. Francis, "Spiritual Direction and Justice."
17. Fox, *Essential Writings*, ch. 3.

as well as from a recent reading of Richard Rohr's *The Divine Dance*, I gained a deeper understanding of the continual harmonious relational flow between the Triune Godhead and us. We are all invited to be part of this circle dance of love and communion to become conduits for this life-giving, compassionate flow within our beautiful and broken world.[18]

The COVID-19 pandemic contributed to the development of my contemplative gaze. Social distancing restrictions resulted in me spending more time outdoors where I was nourished by nature. On Easter 2020, which occurred during a significant period of lockdown, I initiated a treasure hunt with my home group from church where everyone had to go outdoors to search for symbols of the cross on Good Friday and for resurrection metaphors on Easter Sunday. This was followed by an online sharing of our findings, which turned out to be a remarkably rich and satisfying exercise. It showed me how nature is replete with "metaphors, symbols and illustrations that we can identify with, learn from and be encouraged by."[19]

The pandemic coincided with the SDFP, and, as is often the case when undertaking Christian ministry formation, I was invited by God to go through the unpleasant-but-necessary-for-your-growth process of facing and processing baggage lurking within my "shadow."[20] Thankfully, I was graced with many consolations during this harrowing time, of which many came through Mother Nature. American nature poet Mary Oliver describes my experience so eloquently in her poem "Loneliness" when she speaks of these Mother Earth comforts like flowing water and blooming flowers.[21]

Invitation to Pause and Reflect

- Ponder your life journey so far. What has informed and influenced your relationship and response to nature? What particular aspects can you thank God for? What is emerging for you right now to process further that you might need God's help for?

---

18. Rohr with Morrell, *Divine Dance*, 26–31.
19. Foster, "Hannah Anderson—God Revealed in Nature."
20. Carl Jung's famous concept of the hidden aspects of the personality, or psyche, that the conscious mind doesn't want to admit to.
21. Oliver, "Loneliness," 51.

- What could you do to enhance and deepen your connection with God and nature?
- Prayerfully consider the following options to draw closer to God: Attending a silent prayer retreat; talking with a spiritual director; practicing solitude, silence, and/or stillness; making it your habit to "notice what you notice"; exploring centering prayer; learning about a Christian mystic; listening to nature-themed music; reading Mary Oliver's poetry; looking for Mother Earth comforts within nature.

Gazing, Noticing, and Responding

Here are some memorable nature *divina* encounters selected from the plethora filling my kete (woven flax basket) of knowledge. One morning I felt prompted to go to Otanewainuku Forest Reserve. I was in deep need of solace and trusted that it would be found within this rich, pulsing-with-life community. While I hugged a huge rimu tree and felt her strength and stability, I reflected on how she has outlived several pandemics during her lifetime. I felt reassured. Further along the trail, a moss-covered, low-lying bough invited me to sit and rest awhile. Moving along, I noticed an alcove between the extended flanks of a tall kahikitea which beckoned me to lean in and savor being sheltered. At regular intervals along the track, solitary North Island robins gifted me with their friendly interaction. Feeling uplifted, I spied a thin, curved branch looping across the trail. It coaxed me to swing on it, and so I did—in a rather ungainly fashion! These gentle, life-giving encounters soothed my anguish sufficiently and resourced me with courage to share my feelings and struggles with trusted others.

The precise timing of a meaningful encounter with nature can be very powerful and encouraging. There have been occasions in my life when, within moments of having poured out my heart to God over some issue, I received an unexpected response from nature. The sudden noticing of a small, but heavily laden lemon tree, for example, spoke to me of my own potential fruitfulness and generativity as a fledgling spiritual director. Turning a corner and seeing a double rainbow filling the sky just as the words of Jer 29:11 dropped into my mind filled me with hope for a difficult situation. Another time, a white dove swooping in and landing on the walking track in front of me indicated to me that I had been heard. I received this sign as a promise of future restoration and peace.

Watching fur seals in the South Island last summer provided insights around themes of rest, recreation, and enjoying life's simple pleasures. Two seal pups play fighting invited me to embrace fun-filled spontaneity. An adult male soaking leisurely in a rock-pool spa inspired me to fully savor the joys of the present moment. A mother seal blissfully engaged in a lengthy back scratch against a rock reminded me of the need to pamper my sometimes-neglected physical body. These experiences have caused me to indulge more frequently in relaxing soaks at the local hot pools, which is such a contrast to years of engaging in high-intensity exercise!

As well as personal messages, nature encounters can be metaphors for national and international current events. When strolling along the beach at Pilot Bay recently, I noticed two different species of starfish lying upside down on the sand. One was tiny, dainty, and blue, and the other big, spiky, and orange. Both were out of their natural element and suffering. The starfish reminded me of the effect the COVID restrictions had on us all. As I returned the starfish to the sea, I thought about how we all need to help each other get back on our feet.

Another morning on my walk along a beach in Tauranga, I saw hundreds of kelp seaweed plants lying on the sand, having been ripped away from their undersea rock homes in the recent storm. I gazed with concern at their exposed roots and was prompted to pray for the millions of Ukrainian refugees who have been uprooted from their homes during the current Russian invasion. Then I noticed single pipi shells hosting clusters of tiny barnacles and was moved to give thanks for the residents of neighboring countries of Ukraine, who have opened their hearts and homes to these refugees.

Invitation to Pause and Reflect

- What kinds of places in nature soothe and comfort you? How about setting an intention to visit one of those spots whenever you are in need of solace?

- Have you had encounters within nature that were remarkably well-timed alongside other events happening in your life? How does that influence your understanding of the connection between the Creator, creation, and you?

- How has nature inspired you to pray for other people and situations?

Transformational Potential

The habitual practice of contemplatively gazing toward creation is and has been transforming me in several ways. The caring mother-heart of God, expressed by nurturing and sustaining Mother Earth, is supporting my journey toward healing and wholeness. Again and again, I am getting resourced through nature in very specific ways. For example, recently I have discovered an aspect of God I never knew existed—namely God's incredible softness! Like most spiritual encounters, this new experience is hard to describe, but I noticed something akin to a very gentle, soft, tender, delicate sense of divine presence. I had first observed it in the language, tone, and manner of someone I met during the SDFP, and it birthed a longing within me for that same kind of softness in my life. A few months later, out of the blue, I was twice graced with a sense of being enfolded in a beautiful, exquisite, divine softness—the like of which I had never felt before! For several months afterward, my eyes were continually drawn to softness and gentleness within nature: feathers lying on the ground; mother birds sheltering their young; a trail of soft bulrush seed heads; long grass rippling in the wind; the caress of a gentle breeze; and delicate, pink-toned skies heralding dawn and dusk caught my attention. This growing awareness of the soft gaze of the universe is now helping me to shift from a self-protective, defensive stance to a much softer, more open, and healthily vulnerable way of being.

One night during the Hildegard course, I woke up thinking of her description of how earth is the mother of all, because she contains all the seeds, and is in so many ways fertile and fruitful.[22] I pictured earth as our mother who is giving herself so generously and freely to us all, and then thought how we humans have been greedily taking what we have wanted, while ignoring her needs. I lay there, sensing Mother Earth shuddering and groaning, desperately trying to maintain her equilibrium but not quite managing to. This unusual and somewhat mystical experience left me feeling that we, her human offspring, need to respond quickly to save her. Creation care is now a matter of great urgency.

My growing awareness of the interconnectedness of all things has led me to understand that every act of love, no matter how small, is important and counts. Sheila Pritchard writes about this in her blog: "An apparently small thing can have a significant and lasting impact. That is exactly what quantum science tells us. We influence the world around us

22. Fox, *Answer the Call.*

by every action and attitude."[23] I often pick up rubbish on my walks—not from a sense of duty, but as an expression of my love for Mother Earth. As I do this, I pray earnestly for a multiplication of eco-warriors around the globe, people of all ages, religions, cultures, and political persuasions. May they all be united in voice and action on Mother Earth's behalf.

I am increasingly motivated to learn about environmental sustainability and am trying to adjust my lifestyle accordingly—though it can be a challenge to change old habits! I trust that the sharing of my "nature noticing" on social media will have ripple effects for good. I hope, among other things, that they will help foster an awareness of nature as "a communion of subjects" to be loved and respected, rather than "a collection of objects" to be utilized and possessed.[24]

Memorable encounters with native birds on my walks inspire me to learn more about their species. If in my research I discover that they are endangered or in decline, I may feel stirred to join an organization that is actively supporting their preservation. This was the case for the kea. Engaging with these curious, sociable, and intelligent parrots on hiking trips to Mt. Arthur and Mt. Cook National Parks endeared them to me. It was a shock to discover later just how vulnerable kea are, and a relief to find I could contribute to their preservation through the Kea Conservation Trust.

I wonder how else my God-given creative energies might be harnessed to help guide others into a compassionate and intimate reconnection with nature? Pastor and eco-spiritual director Victoria Loorz states that the very real and concrete changes our world desperately needs but desperately resists will not happen without this deep reconnection.[25] I have learned about the emerging wild church and forest church movements overseas.[26] I am intrigued by these diverse eco-faith communities who meet outdoors and are committed to inner and outer transformation, and am alert to what might emerge within Aotearoa New Zealand.

Invitation to Pause and Reflect

- How have you felt the soft gaze of the universe?

23. Pritchard, "Emerging from Emergency," para. 7.
24. Berry, quoted in Loorz, *Church of the Wild*, ch. 1.
25. Loorz, *Church of the Wild*, ch. 1.
26. Loorz, *Church of the Wild*, ch. 1; Williams, *Forest Church*.

- What is your response to the statement "Every act of love counts, no matter how small"?
- Think of a time when you have experienced pain over the suffering of Mother Earth. How does this stimulate your desire to give back to her?
- How environmentally sustainable is your lifestyle? What changes could you make to make it more so?
- Which endangered species do you especially care about? What one thing could you do to enhance their protection?

Contemplative Nature Gazing: Practical Guidelines

Having shared aspects of my personal journey of fostering a contemplative gaze toward nature and how this practice has transformed me, I hope that you, dear reader, have been inspired to explore this practice for yourself. Here are some guidelines to get you started. Read this how-to section slowly and prayerfully. Are there one or two activities that you feel drawn to exploring further? Record your plan in a journal and/or share it with a trusted friend—then put it into practice. Wonder awaits you!

Nurture a desire for God to speak to you through nature. Pray for an increased openness and receptivity to perceiving God in nature. Decluttering one's interior space by attending to personal issues as they surface will increase this capacity. If you feel drawn to silence, explore contemplative ways of praying. A daily practice of centering prayer can help to remove accumulated emotional and psychological baggage from the body in a gentle, gradual way. This will free up interior space and increase your receptivity to perceive God in nature and in other ways.

Wander in the outdoors. The optimum frequency and duration of these walks will vary from person to person. A twenty-minute contemplative walk twice a week is a good place to start.[27] If you have mobility constraints, be inventive. Sit in a garden, listen to the birds, or gaze at a flower. You could also buy swan plants and watch the Monarch butterfly

---

27. Recently I heard an interview with Julia Cameron, author of *The Artists Way: A Spiritual Path to Higher Creativity*. She recommends walking twice a week for twenty minutes to enhance creativity and spirituality. Watkinsbooks, "Julia Cameron Interview."

life cycle; drive somewhere scenic, park up, and gaze at the view; or watch a nature program and pause it when something strikes you.

Solitude is desirable. Walking companions, whether people or pets, or listening to music while you are outdoors can be a distraction from being fully attentive to your surroundings. Be intentional about being fully present to the moment and situation that unfolds before you. Walking contemplatively with others is possible if the participants agree to the purpose of the walk, maintain silence, and give each other physical space. Richard Rohr has facilitated many group walking meditations on retreats and provides useful guidelines on this.[28]

Let go of any agenda you may have for the walk. This practice is not about covering a specific distance at a particular speed in a certain amount of time. "The journey is the total destination," states Rohr.[29] Try to be unhurried: amble or saunter.[30] This is a contemplative practice. A slow, gentle approach will allow you to listen deeply and notice what calls for your attention.

Be flexible about your route and let the walk unfold. Sometimes I have an inner nudge to head to a certain location, and other times I have no idea where I will end up! Be ready to stop and pause at any point if something catches your attention. Expect the unexpected!

Look with the eyes of your heart. Try to engage with the world around you through a soft, compassionate, nonjudgmental gaze, welcoming and receiving all that comes your way. Use all of your senses and try not to analyze or label everything with your mind.

Begin with a sense of wonder. These nature noticings "are usually small and humble moments of awe."[31] Rohr expands on this: "When you allow yourself to be led into awe and wonder, when you find yourself in an *aha* moment and you savor it *consciously* (remember that joy and happiness take a minimum of fifteen conscious seconds to imprint on your neurons), then you have a genuinely new experience—as opposed to it being merely a passing diversion or momentary distraction."[32]

---

28. Rohr with Morrell, *Divine Dance*, 201–2.

29. Rohr with Morrell, *Divine Dance*, 202.

30. Naturalist and conservationist John Muir once said, "Now these mountains are our Holy Land, and we ought to saunter through them reverently, not 'hike' through them." Quoted in Palmer, "Parable of Sauntering," para. 4.

31. Loorz, *Church of the Wild*, ch. 5.

32. Rohr with Morrell, *Divine Dance*, 124.

Have a posture of reverence. This will make room for relationship, which in turn makes room for the presence of the holy. According to Celtic poet and philosopher, John O'Donohue, "What you encounter, recognize or discover depends to a large degree on the quality of your approach. . . . When we approach with reverence, great things decide to approach us."[33]

Be childlike in your approach. That is, open to adventure, wide-eyed, curious, exploratory, spontaneous, playful and responsive. Saunter "freely and lightly" (Matt 11:30 MSG). Retain a sense of humor—what you notice may be quirky and surprising, or even confronting and challenging.

Be fully present in the moment of noticing. It can be tempting to whip out the mobile phone camera in an effort to capture the moment. However, doing so may distract us from being wholly present to the total experience. As Burghardt advises, try not to possess the object of your delight but instead receive it as a gift. Having said that, there are times when a photographic record is helpful as it provides *visio divina* images for future reflection.[34] Christine Valters Paintner similarly suggests that we view such photography as *receiving* rather than *taking* images, "because contemplative practice is receptive practice."[35]

Reflect on your nature noticing afterward. Draw a picture of the image that spoke to you, or apply the *visio divina* process to a photo of it. Dialogue with God, journal, and share your experiences with trusted friends or with a spiritual director.[36] This follow-up will help to clarify and deepen the effect. Occasionally the meaning of our nature noticing may remain unclear, even though we intuitively sense that it is significant somehow . . . and so we simply choose to rest in the wonder and mystery of who and what we have encountered.

Read The Green Bible. In this particular Bible, Scripture passages on nature- and creation-care themes are highlighted in green, and several helpful articles from a variety of contributors are included at the front.

Make friends with remarkable men and women of old. There are godly men and women or sages such as Jesus, the desert fathers and mothers, and medieval mystics such as St. Hildegard of Bingen, St. Francis, and

---

33. O'Donohue, quoted in Loorz, *Church of the Wild*, ch. 4.

34. *Visio divina* means "sacred seeing," and is essentially applying the steps of *lectio divina* to a visual image. Burghardt, "Contemplation."

35. Paintner, *Eyes of the Heart*, ch. 2.

36. Individual profiles of spiritual directors within the Christian tradition in New Zealand can be found at https://acsd.org.nz.

Julian of Norwich who practiced contemplation as they looked long and lovingly at the real. We can use them as our mentors and learn from them.

Read Māori whakataukī (proverbs). Māori have a very close connection to the land; many of their proverbs encourage respect and care for earth, sea, and sky, and all life contained therein.[37] Reading Paul Hawker's gripping account of his forty-day spiritual journey in the Tararua Ranges might further enhance your understanding of this practice.[38]

Learn about eco-spirituality. This is a goal that could entail learning from contemporary nature mystics, poets, and theologians such as Teilhard de Chardin, Thomas Berry, Mary Oliver, Wendell Berry, Sister Ilia Delio, Matthew Fox, Victoria Loorz, Stephen Chase, and father-son duo Douglas and Jonathan Moo. Pope Francis's encyclical *Laudato si'* is also well worth reading.[39]

Expect to be changed. Practicing a contemplative gaze toward creation will inevitably alter us. May each of us be open and willing to embrace any ongoing transformations initiated by God in this way.

A Final Word

A year or so has passed since first drafting this chapter. I have been reflecting on my journey since then. It is gratifying to see how this practice has become firmly established in my life. The fact that God is everywhere has become a precious and meaningful reality in my daily experience. It is like a wellspring that I can always draw from. Within this posture of receptivity to divine presence, a vast storehouse of specific nature noticings has accumulated. They can be called to mind at any time, and thus continue to be a source of blessing.

Further, in my work as a spiritual director, I seek to help others be attentive to the presence, action, and invitations of the Other in their daily lives. Sometimes these are experienced within nature. My job is to encourage the person to pause, clarify, and explore what happened, to get in touch with their feelings about it, and to share their response with God. It is a joy to see how this process can help to deepen the person's connection with the amazing revelation of God that is all around them.

---

37. See Elder, *Aroha*.

38. Hawker, *Soul Survivor*.

39. Helpful websites include: arocha.org.nz and blessedearth.org. Facebook pages include: Christian Environmentalists NZ; and New Creation New Zealand.

In light of what you have read in this chapter, what do you sense is God's invitation to you?

Bibliography

Boyer, Lindsay. "Guide to Centering Prayer." Spirituality for Questioning Minds. https://www.lindsayboyer.com/centering-prayer.

Browning, Elizabeth Barrett. "Aurora Leigh: Book 7." American Literature. https://americanliterature.com/author/elizabeth-barrett-browning/poem/aurora-leigh-book-7.

Burghardt, Walter J. "Contemplation: A Long Loving Look at the Real." In *An Ignatian Spirituality Reader*, edited by George W. Traub, 89–98. Chicago: Loyola, 2008.

Cameron, Julia. *The Artist's Way: A Spiritual Path to Higher Creativity*. New York: Tarcher, 2002.

Delio, Ilia. *A Franciscan View of Creation: Learning to Live in a Sacramental World*. Franciscan Heritage 2. St. Bonaventure, NY: Franciscan Institute Publications, 2003.

Elder, Hinemoa. *Aroha: Māori Wisdom for a Contented Life Lived in Harmony with Our Planet*. Auckland, NZ: Penguin Random House, 2020.

Enya. "So I Could Find My Way." Track 2 on *Dark Sky Island*, lyrics by Roma Ryan, produced by Nicky Ryan. Killiney, Ireland: Warner Bros. Records, 2015.

Foster, Nathan. "Hannah Anderson—God Revealed in Nature." *Life with God: A Renovaré Podcast*, episode 220. https://renovare.org/podcasts/lifewithgod/hannah-anderson-god-revealed-in-nature.

Fox, Matthew. *Answer the Call for an Uncommon Life Through the Mystical Teachings of St. Hildegard*. 7-module video training, Shift Network, June–July 2021. https://theshiftnetwork.com/course/01MFox05_21.

———. *Essential Writings on Creation Spirituality*. Edited by Charles Burack. Modern Spiritual Masters. Maryknoll: Orbis, 2022. Kindle.

Francis, Fran. "Spiritual Direction and Justice." Workshop, Spiritual Directors Formation Programme, Auckland, NZ, June 11, 2021.

Francis, Pope. *Laudato si'*. https://www.vatican.va/content/francesco/en/encyclicals/documents/papa-francesco_20150524_enciclica-laudato-si.html.

Maudlin, Michael G., et al., eds. *The Green Bible, NRSV*. New York: HarperCollins, 2008.

Hawker, Paul. *Soul Survivor: A Spiritual Quest Through 40 Days in the Wilderness*. Oxford: Lion, 2001.

Loorz, Victoria. *Church of the Wild: How Nature Invites Us into the Sacred*. Minneapolis: Broadleaf, 2021. Kindle.

Oliver, Mary. "Loneliness." In *Blue Horses*, 51. London: Corsair, 2018.

Paintner, Christine Valters. *Eyes of the Heart: Photography as a Christian Contemplative Practice*. Notre Dame: Sorin, 2013. Kindle.

Palmer, Albert W. "A Parable of Sauntering." Sierra Club. https://vault.sierraclub.org/john_muir_exhibit/life/palmer_sauntering.aspx.

Pickering, Sue. *Spiritual Direction: A Practical Introduction*. London: Canterbury, 2008.

Pritchard, Sheila. "Emerging from Emergency: Callings, Sacred Activism and Quantum Leadership." Concentric Circles, Feb. 21, 2022. https://sheilapritchard.blogspot.com/2022/02/emerging-from-emergency-callings-sacred.html.

Rohr, Richard. "Everything Is Connected." Center for Action and Contemplation, Jan. 19, 2022. https://cac.org/daily-meditations/everything-is-connected-2022-01-19/.

Rohr, Richard, with Mike Morrell. *The Divine Dance: The Trinity and Your Transformation*. New Kensington, PA: Whitaker House, 2016.

Voil, Simon de. "Canticle of the Creatures." YouTube, July 20, 2019. https://www.youtube.com/watch?v=VskkeyYEvbo&t=6s.

Watkinsbooks. "Julia Cameron Interview on *The Artist's Way* and *The Listening Path*." YouTube, Feb. 26, 2021. https://www.youtube.com/watch?v=vJ7BDa2S9pU.

Williams, Cate. *Forest Church: Earthed Perspectives on the Gospel*. Cambridge: Grove, 2019.

7

Contemplative Gardening
A Spiritual Practice that Prevents and Heals Burnout

Angelika Halstead

In search for a place to heal we often feel drawn to the natural world. Spending time outside in creation can be deeply restorative and life-giving, especially in a season of burnout or a time when we feel wounded in body, mind, or spirit. For some people, it is a walk along a beautiful beach, the lushness of a forest, or the spaciousness experienced from a mountain top. For others it is the garden around their home that presents a place of healing and solace to them.

In this chapter, Angelika describes her experience of burnout and shares how gardening as her new spiritual practice healed her. Spending time in her garden every morning helped her to evaluate her life and welcome a new season. Gardening introduced her into a new way of living that was built on some important guidelines which are explained further in this chapter. These precepts are practicing presentness; enfolding our personal story into God's grander narrative; counting our blessings and practicing gratefulness; reclaiming our innocence and goodness; surrendering to God's timing, plan, and will; and planting seeds of hope and of a good tomorrow. As you read this chapter may you also find a way to connect with God in nature and feel the magic of living a more creative, empowered, balanced, and soul-filled life.

> Come forth into the light of things, let Nature be your teacher.
> —William Wordsworth

> To forget how to dig the earth and to tend the soil is to forget ourselves.
> —Mahatma Gandhi

> In many cases, gardens and nature are more powerful than any medication.
> —Oliver Sacks

I wish I had known earlier in my life what I now know about the phenomenon of burnout. I would have recognized its signs and developed strategies to prevent it. I might have also understood that people like me, who are highly sensitive, caring, and giving, often do not know their limitations and are naturally susceptible to both burnout and compassion fatigue.

I learned these lessons the hard way and through my own experience discovered that the emotional, physical, social, and spiritual exhaustion that comes with burnout is very hard to bounce back from. In my career as a counselor and spiritual director I have known symptoms of compassion fatigue. There have been times when my desire, ability, and energy to feel and care for my clients declined and my positivity, soulfulness, staying power, and healing resources reached a state of depletion. However, last year was the first time that I experienced burnout.

This was when I turned to gardening as a spiritual practice and allowed nature to become my teacher. As I dug the earth and tended the soil, I learned not only to forget myself but also to find my way back home to God and to my deeper self. Connecting with God in my garden became the medicine that restored my body, soul, and spirit.

Understanding Burnout and Compassion Fatigue

My healing journey also included learning all that I could on the nature of burnout and compassion fatigue. While there are many similarities between these conditions there are also very clear distinctions. The term *burnout* was first used in Graham Greene's 1960 novel *A Burnt-Out Case*, which tells the story of a spiritually tormented, disillusioned architect who suffered an attack of indifference which resulted in him not finding any meaning in art or pleasure in life. Thereafter, in 1974 the German-American psychologist Herbert Freudenberger introduced the term *burnout* to the clinical world. Freudenberger himself experienced severe burnout when he worked up to sixteen hours a day, first in his own practice and then in a community-based clinic offering free medical care to people who had been rejected by the more dominant culture. Freudenberger's self-diagnosis and personal experience of burnout informed his writing on this topic.[1] More empirical studies on burnout were then led by Christina Maslach, a social psychologist who developed the field's principal diagnostic tool, the Maslach Burnout Inventory.

Ayala Pines and Elliot Aronson define burnout as "a state of physical, emotional and mental exhaustion, that typically occurs as a result of working with people over long periods of time in situations that are emotionally demanding."[2] The gradual and cumulative synthesis of emotional exhaustion, depersonalization, and a reduction of personal accomplishment results in symptoms such as self-doubt, failure, loss of motivation, isolation, and cynicism.[3] On a physical level it can include exhaustion, fatigue, frequent headaches, gastrointestinal disorders, sleeplessness, and shortness of breath. There are also emotional and behavioral signs that present themselves as frustration, anger, suspicious attitudes, feelings of omnipotence or overconfidence, excessive use of tranquilizers and barbiturates, anxiety, and depression. People whose personalities are naturally predisposed to suffer from burnout are primarily "the dedicated and the committed."[4] Burnout can develop due to high workload, high emotional load, low autonomy, and challenging work relationships.[5]

1. Fontes, "Herbert J. Freudenberger."
2. Pines and Aronson, "Combatting Burnout," 263.
3. Johnson et al., "Experience of Work-Related Stress," 180.
4. Freudenberger, "Staff Burn-Out," 161.
5. Johnson et al., "Experience of Work-related Stress across Occupations," 179.

Compassion fatigue, on the other side, has been defined as reducing "our capacity or our interest in bearing the suffering of others."[6] There is a quicker onset of symptoms than burnout, and its behavioral response is directly related to exposure of traumatic material or events.[7] Compassion fatigue is most common in the helping professions. It results in a reduced capacity to care for others,[8] feelings of overwhelm, a variety of physical and emotional stress symptoms, and a lack of professional confidence. While burnout often requires a complete break from work, and sometimes a long time to heal from, compassion fatigue can usually be recovered from relatively quickly and can be treated through the implementation of self-care strategies.

In my case, burnout was caused by adding a new and challenging job as an online lecturer to my already busy private practice. On top of this, my husband and I did some major house renovations, were greatly impacted by the COVID-19 pandemic with its lockdowns, sense of uncertainty, and ever-changing policies which also prevented us from going on our yearly holiday. Although I noticed health problems in early January caused by the stress I was under, I continued to push myself to the limit and consequently saw my symptoms getting worse and worse throughout the year.

The symptomatology of burnout can be complex and, in my case, progressed through a series of five stages which clearly reflected the commonly used simplification of Freudenberger's original twelve-stage model.[9]

Stage 1: Honeymoon Phase

When I started my new lecturing job, there was a lot of excitement and stimulation as I was introduced to interesting people and new topics to teach. Consequently, I experienced high job satisfaction, commitment, energy, optimism, and creativity. This was accompanied by an acceptance of many new responsibilities and a desire to prove myself.

---

6. Figley, "Compassion Fatigue," 1434.
7. Figley, "Compassion Fatigue," 1436.
8. Figley, "Compassion Fatigue," 1434.
9. Hert, "Burnout in Healthcare Workers," 173–75.

Stage 2: Onset of Stress

A few months into my new job I noticed stress symptoms that affected me physically, mentally, and emotionally. I started to lose focus, reduced my social interaction, avoided making decisions, and experienced certain levels of anxiety, fatigue, and forgetfulness. At times I also observed unusual heart rhythms.

Stage 3: Chronic Stress Phase

To manage my private practice and the demands of my new job, I worked long hours and used both my Saturdays and Sundays to catch up on various tasks. The stress I experienced had become more persistent and affected my work. Feelings of apathy and resentment arose. I felt tired and listless in the morning, experienced nausea throughout the day, and had to stop my activities frequently to lie down and rest. I also noticed that I withdrew socially from family and friends, my thinking was not as sharp and clear as usual, and feelings of overwhelm, pressure, and being out of control became more frequent.

Stage 4: Burnout Phase

Unfortunately, I did not have the wisdom to reduce my workload or take a break, but rather carried on burning the candle at both ends. This, over time, resulted in me reaching the end of my tether and no longer functioning well. My stomach and bowel problems became chronic, I felt nauseous all the time, and spent a lot of my time in bed, resting. Emotionally, I constantly vacillated, felt empty inside and unsure of myself, and noticed a pessimistic outlook on work and life. My devotional times in the morning was grounding me but everything else in my world seemed totally out of balance.

Stage 5: Habitual Burnout Phase[10]

As the year progressed my burnout symptoms became part of my everyday life, my autonomous nervous system felt very dysregulated, and I

---

10. The five stages of burnout are further explained in Hert, "Burnout in Healthcare Workers."

experienced chronic mental and physical fatigue, constant sadness, and high levels of anxiety. It was then that I resigned from my lecturing job and went on a sabbatical. I started a new chapter and discovered gardening as a holistic spiritual practice and as an activity that can help to revert burnout.

Motivated by Irish theologian and philosopher John Scotus Eriugena, who believed that Christ can be understood through two forms of revelation, namely Scripture and nature, I moved away from my desk to the outside world.[11] Nature, and more specifically gardening, became not only my new spiritual routine but also my medicine and cure.

The Therapeutic Effect of Gardening

In recent years the therapeutic effects and benefits of gardening to mental and spiritual health have been widely acknowledged. There are many ways in which mind and garden interact; essentially, caring for a garden is a nurturing and restorative activity that fosters the healthy growth of the mind, and in a profound way connects you to God and his creation.[12] The famous neurologist Oliver Sacks believed in the calming and organizing effects of gardens on our brains and nervous system. He regularly took his patients to the New York Botanical Gardens and observed not only spiritual and emotional but also physical and neurological changes.[13]

The idea that gardening and time in nature can help us to thrive and recover from mental illness started to become prominent in Europe in the eighteenth century and is by now well confirmed. A large-scale survey—conducted by the UK charity Mind—of people taking part in various green activities and gardening showed that 94 percent of participants found it beneficial for their mental health.[14]

The Alnarp campus of the Swedish University of Agricultural Sciences developed a specific healing garden for people suffering from burnout diseases. This garden invites its visitors to experience nature through their senses as well as through gardening activities. The designers of these gardens considered colors and forms to offer both harmony and contrast and create a welcoming, safe, and secure space with a serene feeling of beauty. All participants spent four hours per day both working

---

11. Carabine, *John Scottus Eriugena*.
12. Stuart-Smith, *Well-Gardened Mind*, 14–15.
13. Sacks, *Everything in Its Place*, 245.
14. Bragg et al., *Ecominds Effects on Mental Wellbeing*, 36.

and enjoying the various areas of the healing gardens.[15] Similarly, the impact of burnout on nurses taking daily work breaks in a hospital garden rather than spending their lunch break indoors was measured and showed a significant reduction.[16] These findings also reflect my personal experience and the reasons why I engaged in gardening as a therapeutic tool and spiritual practice.

Gardening as an Invitation to Heal and Grow

> Everybody needs beauty as well as bread, places to play in and pray in, where nature may heal and give strength to body and soul.
>
> —John Muir

Motivated by Muir's words, I created a flower garden at the entrance to our home and a large vegetable garden in an enclosed area behind our house. A very gifted landscape designer assisted me in choosing a combination of plants that flower in different seasons, complement the color of our home, and for visual appeal grow to various heights. I also received help from a woman who specializes in establishing organic vegetables gardens. In both situations I learned that the quality of the soil is the most important aspect of successful gardening. It is the health of the soil that is responsible for the color of the flowers, the size of the potatoes, the tastiness of the tomatoes, and the sturdiness of the bean vines. As gardeners we are always in partnership with our soil. Similarly, to nurture our spiritual growth we need to first explore the soil of our experience and create conditions we can grow and thrive in. Adding fertilizer without first knowing and improving the soil of our hearts can lead to shallow-rooted spirituality, and mindless activism. Understanding what has depleted the soil of our inner garden and reworking the conditions of our life to bring nourishment to our soul is the first step on this healing-from-burnout journey.

Burnout as a God-Sent Intervention

For me, the physical symptoms of burnout that I experienced came from adrenal overload and a totally dysregulated autonomous nervous system.

---

15. Stigsdotter and Grahn, "Experiencing a Garden."
16. Cordoza et al., "Impact of Nurses."

Feeling so unwell caused me to stop burning my candle at both ends and felt like a divine intervention and invitation to rest. Thomas Merton's words served as an admonition: "To allow oneself to be carried away by a multitude of conflicting concerns, to surrender to too many demands, to commit oneself to too many projects, to want to help everyone in everything is to succumb to succumb to the violence of our times."[17] When I read these words, I suddenly knew that I had succumbed to the rush and pressure of life and allowed it to destroy my health, inner peace, and the root of inner wisdom and the fruitfulness of my work.

Reaching stage five of burnout, with all its physical and emotional symptoms, was a wake-up call. I felt that God invited me to conclude what I was doing, restructure my life, and make some significant changes to combat the violence of our time. Paying more attention to my physical needs and listening to my body was part of this invitation. Rather than treating my body as a servant I slowly learned to attune to its voice and relate to this part of my being as a beloved friend. Similarly, when working in a garden there is no negotiation with the march of the seasons or the natural growth force.[18] You cannot speed the process up, you just have to step back and let nature unfold, work with the dynamics at play, and submit to the natural rhythm of garden time. As everything in a garden happens in slow time, gardening helped me to calm down and live at a different pace. Recovery from severe burnout takes patience and time. It is necessarily slow.

Gardening and healing from burnout require the same posture and attitude as most formative spiritual practices. We need a lot of patience, attentiveness, diligence, perseverance, and self-control. Similar to all spiritual disciplines, gardening cultivates within us mindfulness, creativity, curiosity, and surrender. It draws us closer to God and opens our eyes to the sacred. In my recovery from burnout, the deepening of my spiritual journey and my growing interest in gardening paralleled each other. I found that what is true for my garden is also true for my body, soul, and spirit.

---

17. Merton, *Conjectures of a Guilty Bystander*, 82.
18. Stuart-Smith, *Well-Gardened Mind*, 237.

Contemplative Gardening—My Morning Ritual

> Father, teach me presentness, as prayer.
>
> —STRAHAN COLEMAN[19]

1. Practicing Presentness

As I step out of our home and enter our garden, it transforms into both a sacred cathedral and a therapeutic tool. I consciously leave all my day-to-day activities, worries, and cares behind and become fully present to what is right in front of me. I ground myself in the Here and Now and become mindful of how the trees filter out potentially distracting and intrusive noises from the outside world and the plants clean the air as they convert water, carbon dioxide, and minerals into life-giving oxygen and energy-rich organic compounds. My garden soothes and stimulates all five senses. I attend to the beauty around me, experience God, or as John O'Donohue calls him, "The Beautiful," and gain a sense of completion, sureness, and homecoming.[20] The combination of openness and enclosure within my garden generates strong feelings of safety and peace. It becomes a space without fear, a place where I am free. Gradually the need to be hyper-vigilant or on the defensive disappears and a sense of confidence and trust emerges.

2. Enfolding My Story in God's Grander Narrative

Every morning as I walk into my garden, I remind myself that the sun, soil, plants, my body, soul, and spirit, and everything else is interconnected. My personal story, with all its ups and downs, is embedded in a cultural and contemporary discourse or the story of my group, community, church, nationality, gender, ethnicity, and experience. These stories again are part of a greater narrative. As I step out into nature, I ponder these thoughts and consciously place my story and our story into the hands of God. I become aware of the bigger, cosmic story, the principles that are always true, the greater pattern that is not bound on cultural or temporary understanding and confines, and I worship the Source of life and Creator of all. I become mindful that all started in a beautiful garden

---

19. Coleman, *Beholding*, 33.
20. O'Donohue, *Beauty*.

called Eden, a garden which Adam was asked to take care of (Gen 2:15). My story will one day end in another garden—namely, in paradise—a place where God will wipe every tear from my eyes. There will be no more death or mourning or crying or pain, for the old order of things has passed away (Rev 21:4). Anchoring the journey of my life in this bigger story and grounding myself in biblical truths helps me feel at peace knowing that I am held and guided by a force that is greater than me.

3. Counting My Blessings—Being Grateful

A prayer of thanksgiving flows out of these considerations, and I experience what Garofalo wrote: "Gratitude is a core value engendered and amplified by gardening and gardens. One cannot help but appreciate the beauty and bounty of our unique Earth."[21] I am grateful for the green color around me with its restorative and healing functions, which the physician Esther Sternberg calls "the default mode for our brains," the color that strikes my eye in such a way as to require no adjustment and thus automatically takes me to a lower level of arousal.[22] I am grateful for the "intimate relation of the mind upon the nervous system" and that my garden "employs the mind without fatigue and yet exercises it; tranquilizes it and yet enlivens it; and thus, through the influence of the mind over the body, gives the effect of refreshing rest and reinvigoration to the whole system."[23] I breathe deeply and greet this day and my beautiful garden with a smile. As my daily practice I then pick some leaves of the four medicinal herbs I planted, eat them, and give thanks to God for providing me with all I need to improve and maintain my health, heal, and get better. Thank you, God, for allowing me to be in this world of wonder.

4. Reclaiming My Innocence and Goodness

My attention then goes to the weeds in my garden. No matter how intentional I am about my vegetable beds or flower gardens, nature always finds a way of growing something that I have not planted or sown, and these unwelcome visitors compete with my plants for the same space, soil, and nutrients. Weeding is a daily and consistent discipline and as I

---

21. Garofalo, "Gardening to Lift One's Spirit," under Gratitude.
22. Sternberg, quoted in Stuart-Smith, *Well-Gardened Mind*, 73.
23. Olmsted, quoted in Stuart-Smith, *Well-Gardened Mind*, 91.

remove these troublesome plants, I am aware that they need to be pulled out with their roots if I don't want them to come back the next day.

As I weed these fertile and delightful spots in my garden, I examine the garden of my heart and utter the following prayer: "Search me, God, and know my heart; test me and know my anxious thoughts. See if there is any offensive way in me, and lead me in the way everlasting" (Ps 139:23–24). I listen to what the Holy Spirit brings to my consciousness and not only become aware of judgments I have made, unkind words I have spoken, negative thoughts I have focused on, but also other sins of omission and commission I have committed, and destructive habits and attitudes that are not yet transformed. As thoughts and memories arise, I release them to God and replace them with loving, positive, and productive ideas. Confessing my wrongdoings and asking for forgiveness are part of this process. Sigmund Freud referred to this exercise as sublimation, or converting unwanted, disturbing, anxious, and destructive thoughts, impulses, or desires into something more constructive.[24] We thus create a way of being that is in alignment with how God intended it.

Ripping up weeds is one expression "of care in which destructiveness can be put to use in the service of growth. In discharging quantities of aggression and working off anxieties, tilling the earth works on the inner landscape as well as the outer; quintessentially, it is a transformative action."[25] Burnout has taught me that how I manage negative thoughts, feelings, and experiences greatly influences my healing and well-being. It is a way of regaining my innocence and making peace with God, myself, and others.

5. Surrendering to God's Timing, Plan, and Will

So many garden activities are done kneeling, in the position of prayer and surrender. I kneel to weed, to plant, to dig the soil, and to harvest. On my knees I let go of the cares of the day, my worries, and concerns. I entrust these into the loving hands of God and transform them into a prayer. I let go of my need for certainty and to predict the future, my need for power and control, my preconceived ideas of how things should turn out, and my need for fast solutions and outcomes. I let go of all that has caused my burnout, doing too much in too short of a time, and instead say a

---

24. Freud, summarized in Cornell, "15 Sublimation Examples."
25. Stuart-Smith, *Well-Gardened Mind*, 42.

wholehearted yes to life as it comes to me with all its pain, surprises, joys, and wonders. Gardening has a lot to do with acceptance, patience, and surrender and an appreciation for the natural order of all things with its perfect timing and seasons. No fertilizer can make a flower bloom before its time. There is no point in pushing against the stream or gardening against the rhythms and processes of nature. Like gardening, surrendering to God's ways and work within us allows us to enter the natural cycles of life. I therefore step back and let my life and nature unfold—slowly—one petal at a time.

6. Planting Seeds of Hope and a Good Tomorrow

All the flowers of all the tomorrows are in the seeds of today.

—YEN

Planting seeds, seedlings, or bulbs and caring for them is a very frequent activity in my contemplative gardening ritual. Seeds are symbols of hope. With each seed, I plant a narrative of future possibility. While not all the seeds I sow germinate, I am still left with a sense of security that comes from knowing that there are seeds in the soil of my garden. The fruits, vegetables, and flowers that come from seeds symbolize a form of goodness that is real and worth believing in as they are not out of reach.

Early Celtic Christians saw planting a seed as a worshipful action and connected the life, death, and resurrection of Christ to the planting of seeds that in time burst into life from their earthy tomb. Three days before sowing, Celtic farmers sprinkle the seeds with water in the name of the Father, Son, and Holy Spirit. Planting in the Celtic tradition was always symbolic of the planting of Christ's resurrection life within us and all of creation.

As I plant seeds in my garden, I become mindful that every thought I entertain and every word I speak is a seed that effects my emotions, my body, and my future. I consciously move away from stress-producing overthinking patterns, which are part of burnout, to more productive, positive, future-oriented thoughts and focus on ideas that embrace life with all its complexity, mystery, and magic. Pursuing healing and health is not a passive process, our mind and emotions need to be gardened too.

Cultivating a caring and compassionate attitude toward myself and knowing what nourishes both my soul and my spirit are part of the constant tending and reworking of my inner garden that is required for me to flourish. Cynicism and pessimism, despair of the hopelessness, and doomsday-thinking dominate these challenging times we live in, and little attention is paid to what is right in the world. Optimism is a choice, as is building our lives on God's word and promises and on how he views us. Celebrating life's beauty, goodness, and truth—the joy and wonder of being alive on this amazing planet—can all nourish and feed us.

When I finish planting new seeds, I become aware that "seeds have tomorrow ready-built into them. They set off the pleasure of planning and new possibilities."[26] This thought invites me into a time of prayer where I ask God to inspire me with one specific word seed that will feed my soul throughout the day and will serve as a source of guidance, hope, and motivation.

I am grateful for the many lessons burnout and gardening have taught me. In a season of burnout recovery, I reevaluated my life, reduced my stress levels, and learned to live in greater harmony with God, myself, and nature. A new awareness that God is the very soil or ground of my being then emerged. I have learned some of the mysteries of the garden and how its external characteristics model the heart itself. Removing weeds, slugs, bugs, and anything that endangers the growth of my plants goes hand in hand with cultivating good soil and ideal growing conditions. Similarly, removing all obstacles to the deepening of my relationship with God and actively cultivating a burning love for God belong together. As I detach or let go of unhelpful attitudes and motives, thoughts that stall my pursuit of God, and emotional ties that complicate my inner journey, I remove aspects of my false self and gain a clearer understanding of my truest self. It is this true self in the soil of interior freedom that connects deeply with God, the source of all spiritual nourishment and growth. Gardening as a spiritual practice taught me to intentionally let go of all that kept me from the single-minded pursuit of God. It invited me to unclutter my mind and heart and develop a mindful, grounded sensitivity, and keen attention to my inner world. My spiritual growth and greater direct experience of the divine presence was nourished by the abundant simplicity of my true self. This simplicity in balance and harmony with my community, and the created world around me, led to the restoration of my health and body.[27]

Gardening has become one of my most cherished spiritual practices. It has been the vehicle to shift my life from languishing to flourishing. I

---

26. Stuart-Smith, *Well-Gardened Mind*, 23.
27. Swan, *Forgotten Desert Mothers*, 21–25.

encourage you, the reader, to engage in this beautiful practice and on a daily level:

- Practice presentness.
- Enfold your story into God's grander narrative.
- Count your blessings and be grateful.
- Reclaim your innocence and goodness.
- Surrender to God's timing, plan, and will.
- Plant seeds of hope and of a good tomorrow.

My prayer for you is that your garden becomes both your sanctuary and your playground, a place that helps you to slow down to listen for the sound of the genuine within.[28] In a time where we are glued to our screens and live largely separated from the natural world, may you find the vitality that derives from gardening. May it also be a space where you ground yourself in the divine mystery of the present moment. As you engage in gardening as a spiritual practice may you move away from all the things that distract you in life, and as you embrace simplicity, may you find peace and clarity. I pray that this practice helps you anchor yourself in a radical trust in God's love and that your garden becomes a space for spiritual awakening, healing, and discernment. As you observe nature's reliable and trustworthy rhythms and patterns, may you feel safe and adjust positively to change. I pray that this spiritual practice encourages you to yield more to your Maker, and to flow with the movement of life rather than against it—trusting that all will be well. I pray that your garden is like a book that is filled with simple wisdom about how to live well. And in your garden may you connect more deeply with the Creator of all that is true, good, and beautiful.

Bibliography

Bragg, Rachel, et al. *Ecominds Effects on Mental Wellbeing: An Evaluation for Mind.* London: Mind, 2013. https://www.mind.org.uk/media/4418/ecominds-effects-on-mental-wellbeing-evaluation-report.pdf.

Carabine, Deirdre. *John Scottus Eriugena.* Great Medieval Thinkers. Oxford: Oxford University Press, 2000.

Coleman, Strahan. *Beholding: Deepening our Experience in God.* Colorado Springs: Cook, 2023.

---

28. Adapted from Thurman, "Sound of the Genuine."

Cordoza, Makayla, et al. "Impact of Nurses Taking Daily Work Breaks in a Hospital Garden on Burnout." *American Journal of Critical Care* 27 (2018) 508–12. https://doi.org/10.4037/ajcc2018131.

Cornell, Dave. "15 Sublimation Examples (In Psychology)." Helpful Professor, May 28, 2024. https://helpfulprofessor.com/sublimation-examples-psychology/.

Figley, Charles R. "Compassion Fatigue: Psychotherapists' Chronic Lack of Self Care." *Journal of Clinical Psychology* 58 (2002) 1433–41. https://doi.org/10.1002/jclp.10090.

Fontes, Flávio Fernandes. "Herbert J. Freudenberger and the Making of Burnout as a Psychopathological Syndrome." *Memorandum* 37 (2020). https://doi.org/10.35699/1676-1669.2020.19144.

Freudenberger, Herbert J. "Staff Burn-Out." *Journal of Social Issues* 30 (1974) 159–65. https://doi.org/10.1111/j.1540-4560.1974.tb00706.x.

Garofalo, Michael P. "Gardening to Lift One's Spirit." Green Way Research, February 2001. https://www.gardendigest.com/garsp.htm.

Greene, Graham. *A Burnt-Out Case*. London: Vintage, 2004.

Hert, Stefan de. "Burnout in Healthcare Workers: Prevalence, Impact and Preventative Strategies." *Local and Regional Anesthesia* 13 (2020) 171–83. https://doi.org/10.2147/LRA.S240564.

Johnson, Sheena, et al. "The Experience of Work-Related Stress Across Occupations." *Journal of Managerial Psychology* 20 (2005) 178–87. https://doi.org/10.1108/02683940510579803.

Merton, Thomas. *Conjectures of a Guilty Bystander*. New York: Image, 2014.

O'Donohue, John. *Beauty: The Invisible Embrace*. New York: Harper Perennial, 2004.

Pines, Ayala, and Elliot Aronson. "Combatting Burnout." *Children and Youth Services Review* 5 (1983) 263–75. https://doi.org/10.1016/0190-7409(83)90031-2.

Rossi, Alberto, et al. "Burnout, Compassion Fatigue, and Compassion Satisfaction Among Staff in Community-Based Mental Health Services." *Psychiatry Research* 200 (2012) 933–38. https://doi.org/10.1016/j.psychres.2012.07.029.

Sacks, Oliver. *Everything in Its Place: First Loves and Last Tales*. New York: Vintage, 2019.

Stigsdotter, Ulrika A., and Patrik Grahn. "Experiencing a Garden: A Healing Garden for People Suffering from Burnout Diseases." *Journal of Therapeutic Horticulture* 15 (2003) 39–48. https://www.researchgate.net/publication/234071989_Experiencing_a_Garden_A_Healing_Garden_for_People_Suffering_from_Burnout_Diseases.

Stuart-Smith, Sue. *The Well-Gardened Mind: Rediscovering Nature in the Modern World*. London: HarperCollins, 2020.

Swan, Laura. *The Forgotten Desert Mothers: Sayings, Lives, and Stories of Early Christian Women*. Mahwah, NJ: Paulist, 2001.

Thurman, Howard. "Sound of the Genuine." Awakin. https://www.awakin.org/v2/read/view.php?tid=2648&op=audio.

Part 3

Transformed Through Principles
and Radical Ways of Being

8

Counting Down Our Days

Philip Halstead

Keeping eternity in mind is important. Visitors to Sydney, Australia, might come across a piece of copperplate script graffiti between the town hall and St. Andrew's Cathedral spelling the word "Eternity." This is not the only eternity graffito tag that Arthur Stace, a former alcoholic and criminal, recorded after his conversion and encounter with God. Captivated by John 5:24 that says, "Whoever hears my word and believes him who sent me has eternal life and will not be judged but has crossed over from death to life," Stace rose every morning before daylight and chalked that one-word sermon on footpaths across the city for over thirty-five years. It is estimated he etched his iconic message half a million times and became known and celebrated as Mr. Eternity.[1]

In this chapter, Phil encourages us to become more heavenly minded and focus on eternity. We are pilgrims here on earth. We are homeward bound and on our way to another world. The spiritual practice that Phil introduces you to in this chapter will help you to live more consciously in the here and now while considering your eternal future. Understanding that this present life is temporary invites us to invest in what is important. It will add

1. Patowary, "Story Behind Sydney's 'Eternity' Graffiti," para. 3.

> *more meaning to your earthly life and profoundly affect your daily decisions. Looking at life through the lens of eternity will infuse you with joy and a sense of purpose that can, as in Phil's situation, sustain you in your daily life even as you face great challenges and difficult situations.*

> How did it get so late so soon? It's night before it's afternoon.
> December is here before it's June. My
> goodness how the time has flewn.
> How did it get so late so soon?
>
> —Dr. Seuss

It All Comes to Pass

Following in the footsteps of numerous sages, Dr. Seuss, in his inimitable style, reminds us that time waits for no one—not you, not me. Time marches on relentlessly and oftentimes ruthlessly. It accelerates as we age. Where children's summers last forever, older people merely need to blink or sneeze and another year has passed![2] Whether we acknowledge it or not, the daily obituary columns confirm this and remind us that our days are numbered, and our lives are finite. And if these realities aren't sobering enough, the author of Hebrews declares that after we die each one of us will face God's judgment (Heb 9:27).

But all is not lost. There is a wonderful invitation in this equation—namely, the spiritual practice of counting down our days and/or numbering our days aright. As we reflect daily on the impermanence of our lives, we get inspired to seek God in the here and now, trivialize the trivial,[3] and live our todays in a much more meaningful way. Great temporal and eternal benefits will flow from this ritual.

Having said that, I do recognize that the practice of counting down our days is not everyone's cup of tea. When I told a friend, who is an experienced therapist, that I was planning to write about the wisdom of thinking regularly about the brevity and fragility of life, she said with considerable vexation, "That's an awful topic, a toxic idea. It's especially dangerous for individuals who are grappling with mental health issues,

---

2. Goldingay, *Psalms 90–150*, 35.
3. Adapted from Yalom, *Staring at the Sun*, 34.

disappointment, and suicidal ideation." I see her point and agree. So, if you sense that pondering the transient nature of your life to connect more closely with God will not benefit you, feel welcomed to skip this chapter and focus on other spiritual practices depicted in this book. All of them are designed to nurture your union with God.

The Genesis of the Practice

My custom of counting down my days began shortly after I was diagnosed with Parkinson's disease. I was sitting on my favorite couch at home considering what the possible implications of the disease may mean for myself, my loved ones, and our future. I was also thinking about the death of a friend who had died inside of three years of his Parkinson's diagnosis, because the disease had stolen his ability to swallow. The sobering realization was that he was of a similar age to me.

As I mulled over these grim facts, I wondered how many more days I might have left. Moses's words in Ps 90:10 came to mind: "Our days may come to seventy years, or eighty, if our strength endures."[4] This prompted me to do some calculations. There are 365 days in a year (excluding leap years), and I am a few months shy of my fifty-fifth birthday. I crunched the numbers and wrote in my prayer journal that there were 9,184 days to go to my eightieth birthday. The following day I wrote 9,183 beside the date of that day's journal entry and the day after that 9,182. As you would expect, I realized with my condition that there was no guarantee that I would make it through to the end of another nine-thousand-plus days, but this did not deter me from engaging with this new practice.

While the mechanics of counting down the days to my eightieth birthday and entering them into my prayer journal may be unique, the idea of contemplating the brevity of life is not. Moses prayed, "Teach us to number our days, that we may gain a heart of wisdom" (Ps 90:12). David implored God to show him his life's end. He prayed, "Let me know how fleeting my life is. You have made my days a mere handbreadth; the span

---

4. I realize that the specifics of this verse do not match reality. For instance, the average life expectancy for someone in New Zealand in 1870 was slightly over thirty-four years and in 2020 it was just over eighty-two years. See O'Neill, "Life expectancy." Further, Goldingay argues that, in the Old Testament, seventy years refers to long periods of trouble, not one's lifespan; see Goldingay, *Psalms 90–150*, 30. Nonetheless, everyone concedes that human life on earth is finite and for this reason I have remained with my initial literal interpretation of Ps 90:10.

of my years is as nothing before you" (Ps 39:4–5). Solomon stated, "It is better to go to a house of mourning than to go to a house of feasting, for death is the destiny of every [person]; the living should take this to heart" (Eccl 7:2).

When spiritual giants of this stature accentuate the same message—and there are many other luminaries who do likewise—it is imperative that we pay attention to what they are saying. It is also noteworthy that our own experience confirms the transitory nature of life. Who has not identified an upcoming milestone—such as a significant birthday, the passing of an aged loved one, or a rite of passage—at some distant point in their future only to witness the event come and go?[5] And who has not tasted the velocity of life when they have attended a funeral, an Ash Wednesday church service, or the birth of a grandchild?

By now, I have been entering the ever-decreasing number of days to my eightieth birthday into my prayer journal for over two thousand days. When I commenced this exercise, it never crossed my mind that it would become a daily spiritual practice in my life, let alone a transformative one. I thought I was merely contemplating my mortality. Nonetheless, as I have continued with this simple routine, I have realized that it is replete with benefits.

Benefits of Counting Down Our Days

The first gain that I noticed via the spiritual practice of numbering my days was a deeper connection with God. The route to this joyous reality was surprising. As I began the practice, a handful of pressing yet unsolicited questions emerged within me. Examples include, "Am I on the right track?" and "Am I investing the remaining time that I have into relationships and tasks that truly matter?" As I reflected on these questions, I decided to change the time of day that I read the Bible and prayed. For the previous twenty-five years I had swum three times per week in a squad that began at 6:00 a.m. An upshot of these thrice-weekly early morning fitness appointments was that I would have my devotional time after I had finished work on those days. However, the problem with this approach was that I was tired and often dozed off as I read the Bible and prayed. Counting down my days helped me to reevaluate my priorities and begin *every* morning with Bible reading and prayer (and of course a

---

5. Adapted from Yalom, *Staring at the Sun*, 36–37.

good cup of coffee). The jubilant result of this new rhythm is that I have experienced a more intimate relationship with God since I changed the order of my day.

Moses also had change in mind when he beseeched God—the Timeless One, and the Creator of time—to teach Israel to number their days, so that they might gain hearts of wisdom (Ps 90:12). Moses believed that changes of this nature could assist Israel to repent of their sins, revere God more, and from this healthier position experience more of God's blessings (Ps 90:13–17).[6]

This has been my exact experience. Some months into the practice of counting down my days I felt compelled to repent of the uncountable hours I had wasted on selfish and sinful diversions. I sought forgiveness for not developing and using the talents I had been entrusted with and experienced remorse about not prioritizing God and others. New clarity and freshness of vision emerged from this seedbed of regret and repentance.

I realize that some of you may be too time-pressed or overwhelmed to contemplate the kind of choices and commitments that I am mentioning here. When children are young, when cows are in calf, when health is compromised, when exams are just around the corner, it is difficult to create quality time for prayer, God's word, and soul-searching reflection. Nonetheless, I am hopeful that you may be able to find a few minutes in your schedules to think and pray about the direction of your lives and make a helpful change or two. The adjustments do not need to be large. I have heard it said that if you fly from London to New York and you are one degree off course you will end up in South America! While I cannot vouch for the geographical veracity of this claim, the message is clear: Incremental changes to our trajectories over time can make a continent of difference.

Goldingay argues that David was aware of the shortness of his life when he asked God to help him fathom that life was like a handbreadth (Ps 39:4–5), which was the smallest recognized measuring unit of that epoch. What David was really asking God for here was "the willingness to live with the facts, for the grace to acknowledge and accept the nature of human life," and the wisdom to orient his life accordingly.[7]

We know that it is one thing to appreciate a principle like counting down our days and quite another to put it into practice. It is far easier

---

6. Adapted from Goldingay, *Psalms 90–150*, 36.
7. Goldingay, *Psalms 90–150*, 557.

to say "one day" than it is to say "Day One." I feel convicted here. Thirty years ago, I was encouraged to memorize one Bible verse per week and at the time I was convinced that this was an excellent idea. Well, I started a few months ago, and I am averaging about half a verse per week! Still, if we do not begin now, when will we start? Solomon puts it this way: "Whoever watches the wind will not plant; whoever looks to the clouds will not reap" (Eccl 11:4). Another way of putting this is that perfect conditions seldom occur; now is the time to act.

Some classic counselling truisms reflect these points. One is, "If you always do what you have always done, you will always get what you have always got." Another is, "What can you do now in your life so that one year or five years from now, you will not look back and have similar dismay about the new regrets you've accumulated? In other words, can you find a way to live without continuing to accumulate regrets?"[8]

Insights like these motivate me because I do not want to generate new regrets. Do you? Might today be the day that you make the apology and/or commence that forgiveness process that you have been toying with for years? Is there a better moment than now to surprise your spouse and complete the task you promised you would finish last year? Could this be the afternoon to start a Scripture-memory program? Might you trial reading the Bible and praying first thing in the morning for a month? Could this be the moment you start counting down your days and living more consciously and mindfully of your life's impermanence? You get the idea.

The poet John Greenleaf Whittier writes, "For of all sad words of tongue or pen, the saddest are these: 'it might have been!'"[9] How profound is that! I once worked with a man who detested his monotonous job and frequently beat himself up for not moving on. It is hard to imagine what that did to his soul. Johann Hari identifies disconnection from meaningful work as one of nine major causes of depression and anxiety.[10] My former colleague would not dispute this as he struggled with depression. I do not mean to belittle him for his indecision as I have been stuck myself. I realize that persistence is often admirable and that there are many

---

8. Yalom, *Staring at the Sun*, 101.

9. Whittier, quoted in Yalom, *Staring at the Sun*, 144.

10. The other eight major causes of depression and anxiety in Hari's view are disconnection from: other people, meaningful values, childhood trauma, status and respect, the natural world, a hopeful or secure future, and the role of genes and brain changes. See Hari, *Lost Connections*, 61–155.

factors that contribute to inertia. However, this man freely acknowledged that several doors of opportunity had opened for him and that he simply was unable to walk through them. While I appreciate that the practice of counting one's days is not the panacea to all of life's ills, I think it could have assisted my former colleague. Meditating on the concept everyday may have given him the impetus to step beyond "it might have been" and find his true vocation.

Contemplating the brevity of my life has made it easier for me to make wiser decisions. I used to say yes to many requests that I wanted to say no to and found myself attending these events begrudgingly. Now, however, I find it less painful to say no to certain social and speaking invitations. Reciprocally, I am more able to enjoy the possibilities that open for me via saying no, such as spending time with family and friends, reading good books, and resting.

Another positive outcome of counting down my days is that my relationship with time has improved. I have become more appreciative of the gift of today and each moment. Smelling the roses, jesting, lingering with those I love, working hard, and serving God wholeheartedly are now what I try to do. Those closest to me have noticed this and said that I am a *little more* accommodating of impromptu ideas and surprises these days.

The Irish filmmaker Simon Fitzmaurice confirms how comprehending the finitude of life can change one's perspective. He was diagnosed with motor neuron disease in his thirties and died at forty-three. In one of the haunting lines in his book, *It's Not Yet Dark*, he describes how he longed to tell his beautiful six-, four-, and three-year-old children to "wake up, learn something. It's all there for the taking."[11] I can relate to this call to embrace life more fully.

Considering the rapid passing of my days has fueled my desire to pass on my learning to our daughter and to the students who attend my classes while I am still able to do so. In the case of our daughter, I started to joke with her that I was going to write her a *Life Lessons Learned Lecture* (LLLL) that would contain seven principles and could be read inside of seven minutes. She in turn told some of her friends and before I knew it several of them were teasing me about the idea. We had a lot of fun. Expectations grew, the banter built, and the pressure was on. I ended up giving a printed and framed version of the LLLL to our daughter a few months later as a surprise Christmas present just before she commenced

---

11. Fitzmaurice, *It's Not Yet Dark*, 105.

her university studies. I reprise the lecture here with her permission. The principles mirror much of my learning from counting down my days.

1. *Put God first*: God loves you! Obey and follow God; fear God; know that God's rules/laws are always given with your/others' best interests in mind. To obey God is to live with and not against the grain of life—thus, we need to do things God's way. We need to use our schedules to become the people we were created to be (e.g., always allocate time each day to read the Bible and pray), as opposed to filling up our daily planners with appointments. We are not our own—we have been purchased for a price!

2. *Live your one and only (earthly) life really well*: Enjoy! Celebrate! Seek progress not perfection. If something is worth doing, it's worth doing badly until you become good at it. Sow toward heaven. Every day everyone is getting closer to the other side of life. Rehearse the consequences (i.e., think about what will happen if you do or don't do what you are considering) before you make big decisions.

3. *Bad and good rubs off*: Choose your closest friends very wisely and prayerfully. Think about the effect they have on you. If they lead you toward God, righteous living, serving, and life, that's great—their good has rubbed off. If they lead you away from God and toward the world and rubbish, their bad has rubbed off. The people you hang out with *will* have an influence on you. Wisdom is needed. Of course, you will relate with, enjoy, help, and receive from all kinds of friends, but make sure your key friends are people who rub off good on you. And remember, "friendship is a verb."[12] Demonstrate friendship to your key friends. To be a good friend involves initiating and sowing. Rejoice with those who rejoice; mourn with those who mourn (Rom 12:15).

4. *Feeling your feelings*: Your feelings are important. You need to listen to them. But you must not let them rule your life. Don't follow your feelings if they go against God's laws; don't "follow your heart" if doing so goes against the Bible. Feelings come and go—you can ride them out. Sometimes you need to overcome feelings and simply do your study, do your chores, do the right thing, bless the person, go

---

12. With Baab, I know that the word *friendship* is a noun. Baab's point is we need to *do* in our friendships. We need to be proactive in our friendships if we want them to be fulfilling. See Baab, *Friending*, 96.

for the swim; other times, you may need to rest. Heed your feelings but don't let them rule you. Practice delayed gratification. I've heard it said that it's a case of fact, faith, feeling: find the biblical fact, put your faith in the fact, your feelings will catch up.

5. *Education baby*: Get a good education while you can. It will pay off. This involves the university studies you are about to embark on, but also things like reading for, say, twenty minutes each day for the rest of your life. Play the long game; lasting success generally takes effort over time.

6. *Money Honey*: Make money your friend. If possible, earn more than you need. Never spend more than you earn. Always give a percentage away and save a percentage. Don't borrow money on things that depreciate. An 8 percent return on your money is a very good return; if someone promises you a far better return it's probably a scam. Never gamble on your house. Start a superannuation fund through your employer from the get-go; it's a great way to save money painlessly. Contentment is better than envy.

7. *Body matters*: Respect your body. Look after it. Treat it very well. Avoid extremes (e.g., getting sunburnt) and dangerous sports/situations. Exercise regularly, eat sensibly, drink lots of water, get enough sleep. Eat for strength, not drunkenness (Eccl 10:17). Your body is God's temple. Enjoy and respect it. (I love you!)

Some Concluding Thoughts

No doubt by now you sense that I experience the positive impact of counting down my days. The practice has worked wonders for me. It has helped me to strengthen my connection with God. It has enabled me to be more present in my key relationships. It has motivated me to trivialize many of life's less important features, give precedence to that which matters the most, and get my house in order.[13] The practice has also positively impacted my work as a lecturer, pastoral caregiver, and pastoral counselor. Stated differently, counting down my days has assisted me to live more consciously and intentionally. It has aided me to love God, my neighbor, and myself more (Mark 12:29–31). Without doubt, the practice

13. Billy Graham argues that getting our houses "in order is one of the most important things parents can do for their children." See Graham, *Nearing Home*, 69.

has transformed my life and made it richer, more meaningful, and much more enjoyable.

Still, the proof is in the pudding. Why not trial the practice for yourself? You do not need to ponder the brevity of your life for lengthy periods of time to reap heartening benefits. The exercise takes me no more than thirty seconds per day. I simply write the number of days to my eightieth birthday into my journal each day, observe how the days are racing by, and pray that God would help me to make the most of *this* day. You might choose an alternative approach that is tailor-made to your circumstances. You may count down the days to a major birthday or event. Or you could arrange to meet with an accountability partner to discuss the big questions of life and out of each conversation nominate a concrete action to implement before you next meet. Whatever method you choose, the key is that it is doable and not too onerous. I know that blessings would come your way if you were to count down your days.

Bibliography

Baab, Lynne M. *Friending: Real Relationships in a Virtual World*. Downers Grove, IL: IVP, 2011.

Fitzmaurice, Simon. *It's Not Yet Dark*. Dublin: Hachette, 2014.

Goldingay, John. *Psalms 90–150*. Vol. 3 of *Psalms*. Baker Commentary on the Old Testament Wisdom and Psalms. Grand Rapids: Baker Academic, 2008.

Graham, Billy. *Nearing Home: Life, Faith, and Finishing Well*. Nashville: Thomas Nelson, 2011.

Hari, Johann. *Lost Connections: Uncovering the Real Causes of Depression—And the Unexpected Solutions*. New York: Bloomsbury, 2018.

O'Neill, Aaron. "Life Expectancy (from Birth) in New Zealand, from 1870 to 2020." Statista, Aug. 9, 2024. https://www.statista.com/statistics/1041182/life-expectancy-new-zealand-all-time/.

Patoway, Kaushik. "The Story Behind Sydney's 'Eternity' Graffiti." Amusing Planet, Jul. 20, 2018. https://www.amusingplanet.com/2018/07/the-story-behind-sydneys-eternity.html.

Yalom, Irvin D. *Staring at the Sun: Overcoming the Terror of Death*. San Francisco: Jossey-Bass, 2008.

9

The Joy of Having Less

JAIMEE VAN GEMERDEN

"We spend so much time on the hunt, but nothing ever quite does it for us," says Dan Harris in the film Minimalism: A Documentary About the Important Things.[1] *Many of us in the Western culture spend a lot of time hunting for satisfaction, enjoyment, and happiness by consuming material things, but nothing ever seems to fulfil our deepest desires and needs. To achieve the "American dream" we have chosen the high-consumption lifestyle and sacrificed a sense of balance, moderation, solitude, and inner peace. Although there is nothing wrong with consumption itself, a lot of our behavior has become automatic, habitual, and compulsive. So, what is the answer to this dilemma? How do we find true happiness and awaken from this dream? How can we learn to consume what we need in a measured, intentional, and decisive way?*

In this chapter, Jaimee expands on those ideas and introduces you to practices of simplicity and asceticism within a range of Christian spiritualities. These practices are based on the teachings of Jesus and lead to a transformation of our desires and a new level of engagement with the divine. Jaimee also draws from ancient teachings of asceticism and especially from Clare of Assisi's

1. D'Avella, *Minimalism*.

> contributions, which show how the narrowing of choices ultimately leads to the fullness of life as it generates a greater level of freedom. Experiencing this freedom then improves well-being and creates spiritual space. Ascetic practices will also lead to an aesthetic life as these practices offer us an invitation to order, coherence, and unity, to purify the lens of our heart and help our souls to become alive to beauty.

An Excess of Things

IN THE PROCESS OF recently moving house, I found myself sitting on the floor of my bedroom sifting through two drawers that had been barely accessible for three years. My difficulty in accessing these drawers had led them to be repositories of "things that seem important and don't belong elsewhere" with little logical connection between the items (as I could never remember the sorts of things that had previously been placed there). Arrayed around me was a collection of out-of-warranty device receipts, photos, DVDs, heirloom prayer books, expired and unneeded medicine, miscellaneous technology accessories, and little cardboard boxes that I thought might one day come in handy. More than half of these items quickly found their way to the rubbish bin.

I generally consider myself to be a person who does not have an excess of things. All my worldly possessions fit into a small bedroom, and I all too regularly sort through and reorganize my space to limit my retention of unnecessary objects. However, as I sorted through these two drawers, I realized the extent to which the consumption and collection of strange items was endemic in my life, as much as it is in the lives of many others in the Western world. I hemmed and hawed over which expired first aid supplies should be kept, and I could not bear to throw out the DVDs even though I have no device capable of playing them. For some reason, there is a security in things that makes them difficult to dispense with. The question must be asked why having less is so challenging for some of us, and whether there is value in reducing the extent of our belongings.

In recent years, minimalism has become something of a buzzword. I think of the popularity of Marie Kondo, whose *Tidying Up* streaming series was Netflix's number-one nonfiction release in 2019. The book which launched Kondo to fame, *The Life-Changing Magic of Tidying Up*, has sold more than thirteen million copies in forty-four different languages.[2] Her KonMari method sparked a revolution and changed the way people looked at things: suddenly we were asking whether our possessions "sparked joy" and, if they did not, we were thanking them and moving them on. The popularity of Kondo's work capitalizes on the fact that it feels like an unnatural practice. The modern, consumerist world teaches us how to get more things, not how to purge or have less. Yet, intrinsic to, and part of the draw of, Kondo's method is the belief that having less is a good thing—that a change needs to be made for the well-being of those who have too much.

The art and belief in the value of having less is by no means a new practice, although it has been reframed and remarketed for the consumer age. Within a range of Christian spiritualities, practices of simplicity and asceticism have been central to following in the way of Jesus. These practices draw on the teaching of Christ as a basis and, further than just obedience, they also help to shape and form the life of believers. The traditional practice of asceticism is as much about the reshaping of desire as it is about having less. When we shift our desire and create space in our lives, there is an opportunity for a new level of engagement with God.

The Reordering of Desire

The practice of asceticism, or religious self-denial, in Christianity has been part of following Jesus since the very beginning. New Testament scholar Susan R. Garrett suggests that the focus of Luke's Gospel on spiritual healing draws on Greco-Roman connections between the task of a doctor and the practice of *askesis*.[3] Throughout this Gospel there is an emphasis on moral discipline and the mastering of desire, as well as numerous encouragements to give up one's earthly possessions (e.g., Luke 9:23; 12:13–34; 14:25–33). At the heart of these passages, Garrett argues, is Jesus's teaching to find freedom by living "a life characterized by *denial of self*."[4] This connection likely draws on common principles from the Greek world. As Garrett shows, for Greek philosophers such as the Stoics "failure to break the grip of desire for possessions, family, and even

---

2. Greenstreet, "Marie Kondo."

3. *Askesis* can be understood as a practice of self-discipline, especially for religious purposes. Garrett, "Beloved Physician," 71.

4. Garrett, "Beloved Physician," 86.

life itself leads inevitably to a kind of enslavement and unhappiness."[5] In the ancient world, through the New Testament, and all the way to the minimalist movements of today, lines are drawn between freedom and well-being, and the discipline of having less.

In many diverse ways the practice of self-denial became a key part of Christian monasticism. From monastic traditions that isolate themselves to refocus their attention to God, to forms of chastity and fasting that seek to temper and control desire, asceticism can manifest in a wide variety of practices. One notable community that outworked their belief in the importance of self-denial sprouted up in the early thirteenth century in the Italian town of Assisi. Clare of Assisi, a follower of Francis, held strongly to a commitment to a life of poverty, even in the face of church and political structures that were put in place to protect the vulnerability of women who lived in this way.[6] In addition to the creation of the religious order of the Poor Clares, following the Rule of St. Clare, Clare's legacy includes the affirmation of what she called the "privilege of poverty."[7] Throughout her life Clare fought vehemently for the privilege for her and her nuns to own nothing as she believed that it was integral for them to "be dedicated to God alone."[8] Correspondence between Clare and Pope Gregory IX shows Clare's passion and her fervent belief that "the left hand of the Heavenly Spouse would support their physical needs."[9]

For Clare, to live in the privilege of poverty was a matter of following the gospel. It was a process that supported her belief that dedicating oneself to God was closely connected with renouncing the distractions and cares of worldly life. Clare's Rule, which was approved in 1252 just before her death, encourages the Poor Sisters to "serve the Lord in highest poverty so that, in freedom of soul, you may be the Lord's servants."[10] The Sisters did own land sufficient for the proper enclosure of the monastery, but this was not to be used for any purpose other than the care of

---

5. Garrett, "Beloved Physician," 87.

6. See Joan Mueller's excellent book on the life of Clare and the formation of her religious order, *The Privilege of Poverty*.

7. It is worth noting here that there is an important distinction to be made between the privilege to choose poverty as part of an ascetic practice, and the state of enforced poverty that is experienced far too widely in the modern world.

8. Mueller, *Privilege of Poverty*, 39.

9. Mueller, *Privilege of Poverty*, 39.

10. Clare of Assisi, "Rule of Saint Clare," 128.

the Sisters.[11] Clare strongly affirmed this choosing of poverty as both a practice of obedience and a way of gaining freedom from the worries of the world, or "freedom of soul." This concept of freedom resonates well with Laura Hartman's definition of asceticism. She writes that "saying no to one's desires is saying yes to something better."[12] In Clare's language, "something better" means the freedom of soul that can be found in the privilege of poverty.

However, at the forefront of ancient practices of asceticism is not really having less things. The reduction of possessions is an outworking of the spiritual discipline, but the driving force behind it is the reorientation of desire. Theologian Sarah Coakley helpfully sums up this process: "When the ascetic life works, and works well, it unifies, intensifies and ultimately purifies desire in the crucible of divine love, paradoxically imparting true freedom precisely by the narrowing of choices."[13] A "narrowing of choices" is a simple way to explain the practice of asceticism. In a range of different areas of life, to live ascetically is to live with less in order to train and reorient desire. This is also captured in Maria Antonaccio's consideration of traditional literature concerning asceticism. She shows how "asceticism is interpreted not only as a renunciatory practice aimed at mortification of the flesh and restriction of bodily pleasures,"[14] but also that it can be seen as the "acquisition of a skill, the practice of an art or *techne*, the education of desire in the constructive aim of living well."[15] These reflections show the ultimate focus and value of asceticism: having less is not an end in itself, it can also be a waypoint for the process of reorienting desire and inhabiting freedom in relationship with God.

Part of this outcome for ascetic practice is the idea of the fullness of life. What Luke's Gospel offers is an image of consumption that is radically different to that of our modern world. Jesus teaches a model of simplicity tied to his call to discipleship. An example of this is found in his response to a question concerning an inheritance. Before the story of a rich fool, Jesus says: "Take care! Be on your guard against all kinds of greed, for one's life does not consist in the abundance of possessions" (Luke 12:15 NRSV). Jesus reinforces his point through a parable in which the rich man stores up enough so that he can rest in his investment. Instead, Jesus

11. Clare of Assisi, "Rule of Saint Clare," 134.
12. Hartman, *Christian Consumer*, 49–50.
13. Coakley, *New Asceticism*, 6.
14. Antonaccio, "Asceticism," 80.
15. Antonaccio, "Asceticism," 80.

encourages his listeners to focus their desire toward God, to "be rich toward God" (Luke 12:21 NRSV). Jesus's first statement is worth pausing on. Caught up in his warning is the statement that hoarding possessions is not the substance of living. In her reflections on Lukan asceticism, Garrett highlights how "cultural models of asceticism . . . seek to replace a more conventional way of looking at and relating to the self, others, and the world with a new vision of what we might call 'the flourishing self.'"[16] Life, understood as the ideal mode of human living, is characterized by Jesus as more than simply the pursuit of possessions. An ascetic vision of simplicity can draw on this characterization and offer a practical way to pursue the type of life that Jesus encourages.

Consumption in the Modern World

As a spiritual practice, asceticism has a unique value in the modern world. By the end of the twentieth century a stark change had taken place in terms of how people exist in society: in Sallie McFague's language, "We have become consumers—not citizens, or children of God, or lovers of the world, but *consumers*."[17] Part of the impetus behind this shift to a consumer identity is that, particularly in the Western world although increasingly globally, to consume is the inherent mode of participation in society. There is a sense where, in Michelle Gonzalez's words, "I shop therefore I am"; my existence in this world is to be defined by my consumption.[18]

The problem of consumerism in the modern world is well-documented and plays into the popularity of phenomena like *Hoarders*[19] or Marie Kondo's *Tidying Up*. Fashion is often highlighted as one of the worst industries for over-consumption, particularly in connection with fast fashion. Fast fashion is the system of production that emphasizes low-cost weekly cycles of trends and significant overproduction, and leads to over-purchasing through a cheap, throw-away culture.[20] Shoppers are purchasing more, but not necessarily wearing or using all that they buy; it is estimated that most consumers wear less than 50 percent of

16. Garrett, "Beloved Physician," 72.
17. McFague, *Life Abundant*, 96.
18. Gonzalez, *Shopping*, 23.
19. *Hoarders* is an American reality TV show on the A&E network. It has run since 2009 and features the struggles of those living with a compulsive hoarding disorder.
20. Bardey et al., "Finding Yourself in Your Wardrobe," 114.

their wardrobe.[21] This form of consumption not only encourages greater purchasing, but also shifts the way that goods are viewed. As Gonzalez notes, "Material goods are transient and disposable, they have little authentic value for us."[22] This was not always the way, but the social condition of being a consumer is such that objects are *consumed* rather than valued for the need that they meet.[23]

In her discussion of consumerism, Hartman offers the image of *askesis* as "consumptive self-denial for the sake of holiness."[24] Just as asceticism is more about the redirection of desire than the simple act of having less, consumerism is about the act of consuming, and the follow-on implications this has for human wants, more than it is about the things that we consume. Mindy Makant describes how "the joy of desiring becomes a never-ending cycle as the very act of acquisition fuels rather than satisfies the desire."[25] What we purchase and fill our life with, and how we go about this consumption, is an outpouring of where we direct our desire. What asceticism offers, as a spiritual practice, is a way to redirect our desire. It is a form of "consumptive self-denial" that is ultimately a denial of our consumer self.

Creating Spiritual Space

The value of the practice of asceticism in the modern world remains the same as it was for Clare of Assisi, although it may carry even more import given the ubiquity of consumerism. The privilege of poverty as the art of having less generates a greater level of freedom which improves well-being and creates spiritual space. In a study published in 2020, psychologists Kasey Lloyd and William Pennington illustrate the connections between a low consumption lifestyle and numerous well-being benefits—namely, autonomy, competence, mental space, awareness, and positive emotions.[26] Of particular interest are their findings concerning

21. Bardey et al., "Finding Yourself in Your Wardrobe," 114.
22. Gonzalez, *Shopping*, 17.
23. It is also worth noting the ethical and environmental problems of consumption that are, thankfully, becoming more central concerns for consumers. Gonzalez explores this idea and argues that "through our consumerism we participate in global slavery, whether we admit it or not." Gonzalez, *Shopping*, 11.
24. Hartman, *Christian Consumer*, 31.
25. Makant, "Pursuit of Happiness," 293.
26. Lloyd and Pennington, "Towards a Theory," 125.

mental space. Rather than a cluttered home that generated mental clutter, a life with less things was identified by participants as a life with more mental clarity.[27] As a friend of mine once described it, "messy room, messy brain." This description of mental spaces as an outcome of low consumption is an interesting connection with ancient beliefs concerning the practice of asceticism, which Clare of Assisi argued opened the door for the freedom of soul. This freedom describes the mental space that helps to focus elsewhere, the clarity and presence for the reordering of desire.

The belief that having less supports well-being is intrinsic to contemporary minimalist movements. Popular duo The Minimalists argue that "minimalism is a tool to rid yourself of life's excess in favor of focusing on what's important—so you can find happiness, fulfilment, and freedom."[28] In the Christian tradition, this can be reframed as a way of reordering desire to find freedom in the pursuit of God, rather than the pursuit of things. Minimalism is then not simply a lifestyle where there is a limited number of allowable possessions. It does not mean that you cannot have a full bookshelf, or a few extra things in the closet. Instead, it is the process of considering the value of our things, of asking where our desire is being ordered, and of offering a challenge to our consumeristic way of being. Just like the ancient discipline of asceticism, a minimalist lifestyle asks where our focus is being directed. This practice releases us from needless pursuits and redirects our attention to desire freedom and well-being—a flourishing life following Jesus's model.

An Ascetic Life

When I consider Clare of Assisi's story, I am struck by her commitment to a way of obedience to Christ that seems remarkably foreign to a modern Christian in the West. The idea of barely having enough to get by is scary but, even more than that, I am challenged through her teaching to reorder my desire. Where is my focus? Why do I need these new things? So instead of shifting my focus to God, I look over my (metaphorical) neighbor's fence. The social media narrative that is all too easy to buy into is one of comparative consumption: they look like they are succeeding, and they have things I do not have; therefore, I need those things.

27. Lloyd and Pennington, "Towards a Theory," 127.
28. Minimalists, "What Is Minimalism," para. 3.

Instead, how can I embody the challenge laid out by Jesus in Luke's Gospel as he declares that "one's life does not consist in the abundance of possessions" (12:15 NRSV). In comparison to those obedient to Clare's Rule, I have an excess of things—far more than I need to survive. But rather than requiring strict adherence to a life of intentional poverty, there are modern practices of minimalism which can help us achieve similar goals to traditional ascetic practices. The goal in this spiritual practice is the reorientation of desire, not simply the task of having less things.

As a first practical step, I encourage you to do a critical audit of your possessions. This involves taking time with each item to consider not only its place in your life, but also the reason why you would like to keep it. Begin with one group of items—books, clothes, etc. To make this a manageable task take one book/piece of clothing and ask the following questions: Is this something I use regularly, or is it something that offers me security? Would I be uncomfortable handing it on to someone else? While this audit might help to reduce some of your possessions, it will more importantly show you your attitude to the things that you own. Does your response to your belongings show a freedom of soul or does it reveal a reliance on an abundance of possessions? Let this audit be the first step on your journey to reorienting your desire by identifying your response to the challenge of having less.

Bibliography

Antonaccio, Maria. "Asceticism and the Ethics of Consumption." *Journal of the Society of Christian Ethics* 26 (2006) 79–96. https://doi.org/10.5840/jsce200626122.

Bardey, Aurore, et al. "Finding Yourself in Your Wardrobe: An Exploratory Study of Lived Experiences with a Capsule Wardrobe." *International Journal of Market Research* 64 (2022) 113–31. https://doi.org/10.1177/1470785321993743.

Clare of Assisi. "The Rule of Saint Clare." In *In Her Words: Women's Writings in the History of Christian Thought*, edited by Amy Oden, 127–39. Nashville: Abingdon, 1994.

Coakley, Sarah. *The New Asceticism: Sexuality, Gender and the Quest for God*. London: Bloomsbury, 2015.

D'Avella, Matt, dir. *Minimalism: A Documentary About the Important Things*. Missoula, MT: Netflix, 2015.

Garrett, Susan R. "Beloved Physician of the Soul? Luke as Advocate for Ascetic Practice." In *Asceticism and the New Testament*, edited by Leif E. Vaage and Vincent L. Wimbush, 71–95. New York: Routledge, 1999.

Gonzalez, Michelle A. *Shopping*. Minneapolis: Fortress, 2010.

Greenstreet, Rosanna. "Marie Kondo: 'My Greatest Achievement? Organising the World.'" *Guardian*, Jan. 8, 2022. https://www.theguardian.com/lifeandstyle/2022/jan/08/marie-kondo-owe-my-parents-items-i-threw-out.

Hartman, Laura M. *The Christian Consumer: Living Faithfully in a Fragile World*. Oxford: Oxford University Press, 2011.

Kondo, Marie. *The Life-Changing Magic of Tidying Up: The Japanese Art of Decluttering and Organizing*. New York: Ten Speed, 2014.

Lloyd, Kasey, and William Pennington. "Towards a Theory of Minimalism and Wellbeing." *International Journal of Applied Positive Psychology* 5 (2020) 121–36. https://doi.org/10.1007/s41042-020-00030-y.

Makant, Mindy G. "The Pursuit of Happiness: The Virtue of Consumption and the Consumption of Virtue." *Dialog: A Journal of Theology* 49 (2010) 291–99. https://doi.org/10.1111/j.1540-6385.2010.00555.x.

McFague, Sallie. *Life Abundant: Rethinking Theology and Economy for a Planet in Peril*. Minneapolis: Fortress, 2001.

The Minimalists. "What is Minimalism." https://www.theminimalists.com/minimalism/.

Mueller, Joan. *The Privilege of Poverty: Clare of Assisi, Agnes of Prague, and the Struggle for a Franciscan Rule for Women*. University Park: Penn State University Press, 2006.

Part 4

Transformed Through Love
and Living in Community

10

Catching Up with a Brother
The Intimacy of Fellowship

Simon Moetara

Friendships enrich our lives and promote our well-being. They bestow us with purpose and meaning and offer us a platform to evolve as human beings. In the presence of a true friend the superficial aspects and half-truths of social acquaintance fall away, and we feel safe to share our hearts. As John O'Donohue writes, "One of the deepest longings of the human soul is the longing to be seen."[1] The author of this chapter found that true friends are like mirrors that reflect our soul and make room for us to be seen and understood as we are—without the usual masks or pretensions. When we are fully seen, loved, and understood, we come home to ourself, and we grow. This homecoming also brings us closer to God and to all that is real and eternal.

We often think of spiritual practices in individualistic terms; however, as we meet with a friend in honest, intimate fellowship, Christ is in our midst. In this chapter, Simon shares his experiences of regularly meeting with his Christian brothers and invites us to find the encouragement and building-up, presence and comfort, challenge and confession that this spiritual practice provides.

---

1. O'Donohue, *Anam Cara*, 49.

> In this wise does one, whom God has placed in common life
> with other Christians, learn what it means to have brothers.
>
> —Dietrich Bonhoeffer[2]

> Ka whakahoa tātou tētahi ki tētahi
>
> —1 John 1:7

I recently went through a very difficult time. I was feeling pretty low and quite anxious about the future. I chatted with my wife, and she encouraged me to press into God. Interestingly, in that moment, "pressing in" meant quite different things to each of us. For my precious wife this usually means retreating to a solitary place, playing some worship music, and seeking God in prayer. However, for me it inspired a completely different approach. I realized that I needed to "get out" of my aloneness and catch up with a Christian brother. For I find it is often in the embrace and intimacy of tētahi ki tētahi (one to another) fellowship that I feel God's presence and hear God's voice.

Reflections on Fellowship

It is easy to think of spiritual practices in individualistic terms. For my own devotional life, I employ several practices. I spend time in prayer. I read the Bible. I write and reflect as I journal. Such disciplines are important and can indeed be beneficial; but they are also often performed alone. However, there is also a communal dimension to spiritual practices, with fellowship being a key for Christian living.

John Wesley preached that "Christianity is essentially a social religion; and . . . to turn it into a solitary one is to destroy it."[3] Mathis speaks broadly of three means of God's grace: his voice (the word), his ear (prayer), and his people (fellowship).[4] Peter urges Christians everywhere to "love the family of believers" (1 Pet 2:17 NLT). For Peter, the church "is family, brothers and sisters, and therefore has a call upon the Christian's

---

2. Bonhoeffer, *Life Together*, 25.
3. Wesley, "Sermon 24," para. 5.
4. Mathis, *Habits of Grace*, 37.

love in a way others do not."⁵ Peter alone uses the word *adelophotēta* to describe Christians, translated as "brotherhood" in many translations. It is a word that describes family ties established by covenant relationships, the basis of Christian fellowship.⁶ In the Māori Bible this phrase is translated "Arohaina nga teina, nga tuakana," employing the terms for older and younger siblings, reinforcing a deeply familial and relational connection as part of our Christian reality.

Dallas Willard declares that the Christian life "is one that requires some regular and profound conjunction with others who share it," and when such a connection is lacking it "is greatly diminished."⁷ We were never meant to live as self-reliant, autonomous beings. We were not designed to journey through this world on our own. "In order to grow," writes Siang Yang Tan and Douglas Gregg, "we need other people who will give us affirmation, encouragement, care, unconditional love, and forgiveness."⁸ We all need people who know us and love us, people with whom we can share our struggles and triumphs, who will support us and challenge us, and who will partner with us in our service and witness to the world. Fellowship is being with other Christians in ways that help us to grow in our faith and, therefore, closer to Jesus. In fellowship we "become agents of the Holy Spirit in one another's growth and transformation."⁹ For example, Dietrich Bonhoeffer speaks of our roles as communicators of God's truths to one another:

> God has willed that we should seek and find His living Word in the witness of a brother. . . . Therefore, the Christian needs another Christian who speaks God's Word to him. He needs him again and again when he becomes uncertain and discouraged, for by himself he cannot help himself without belying the truth. He needs his brother man as a bearer and proclaimer of the divine word of salvation. He needs his brother solely because of Jesus Christ. The Christ in his own heart is weaker than the Christ in the word of his brother; his own heart is uncertain, his brother's is sure.¹⁰

---

5. Davids, *First Epistle of Peter*, 103.
6. Hillyer, *1 and 2 Peter, Jude*, 82.
7. Willard, *Spirit of the Disciplines*, 186–87.
8. Tan and Gregg, *Disciplines of the Holy Spirit*, 161.
9. Tan and Gregg, *Disciplines of the Holy Spirit*, 159.

10. Furthermore, Bonhoeffer writes, "And that also clarifies the goal of all Christian community: they meet one another as bringers of the message of salvation." Bonhoeffer, *Life Together*, 23.

Jesus has anointed us with his Spirit, and we are set apart in service to each another. As C. S. Lewis says of God, "Above all, He works on us through each other. Men are mirrors, or 'carriers' of Christ to other men."[11]

This encouragement can occur in fellowship in larger gatherings such as church services, prayer meetings, or Bible study groups. However, the fellowship that I wish to reflect on further here is somewhat smaller in scope, a more personal connection between intimates. In my mind, it is "catching up with a brother." It is often in such times and connections that I meet with Jesus, hear his voice, and feel his love and presence.

God and the Intimacy of Face-to-Face Encounter

Rabbi Jonathan Sacks notes a beautiful detail in the construction of the sanctuary in Exodus. Above the ark of the covenant were two figures, cherubim, "their faces one to another" (Exod 25:20 ESV). The Israelites had been commanded not to make anything that might be worshiped as an idol, and the sanctuary was constructed after the incident of the golden calf. Why, then, were these angelic forms present in the Holy of Holies?

God spoke to Moses from between the two cherubim (Exod 25:22). According to Sacks, the message was so important for God that it outweighed any danger of misunderstanding: "God speaks where two persons turn their face to one another in love, embrace, generosity and care." Sacks concludes, "When we open our 'I' to another's 'Thou'—that is where God lives. We discover God's image in ourselves by discerning it in another."[12] Sacks believes that societies are only human, and humanizing, when communities are built on face-to-face encounters—covenantal relationships. *Hesed* (the Hebrew word for loyal, steadfast love), Sack contends, is "a relationship of face-to-face."[13]

This has been my experience. As I meet with my brother in honest, intimate fellowship, Christ is in our midst. It is in that sacred space that I feel close to God. As I am heard in loving nonjudgment, I find my thinking corrected and my emotions settled as I experience a divine perspective in the presence of my brother. When I meet face-to-face with my brother in love and acceptance, I find that God speaks.

---

11. Lewis, *Beyond Personality*, 37.
12. Sacks, *To Heal a Fractured World*, 54.
13. Sacks, *To Heal a Fractured World*, 54.

Kanohi ki te kanohi (face-to-face) is an essential Māori cultural value for flourishing relationships. The social meaning of the phrase emphasizes physical presence and even a sense of commitment to whānau (extended family) or a kaupapa (purpose).[14] In our post-pandemic digital age, it is a great reminder that there is no substitute for actual, in-person presence.

This desire to be real before God is reflected in my sharing the "real me"—my weaknesses, my temptations, and my struggles—with a brother. True fellowship begins when we can bring ourselves authentically and openly to the conversation, free to take off any masks and pretense and be honest with one another. Tan and Gregg explain further:

> When we are willing to be open with others about our personal problems and needs—risking shock or rejection—and when we are willing for others to be equally open with us, we find ourselves together at the foot of the cross, the place of God's healing and grace.[15]

The Benefits of Catching Up

I have found such catching up to be valuable in my faith journey, especially in the following areas: for encouragement and being built up, experiencing God's presence and comfort, and as a safe place to be challenged and to confess my struggles.

1. Encouragement and Building Up

Encouragement is a key part of fellowship. The apostle Paul urges the Thessalonian Christians to continue to "encourage one another and build each other up" (1 Thess 5:11). To *encourage one another* here carries the sense of strengthening each other's faith so we are not tempted to lose heart or fall away.[16] The idea of strengthening is reinforced by the charge to "build each other up." We are built up not by our own efforts, but by the encouragement of other believers.

The writer of Hebrews was concerned that some believers were neglecting to meet together (Heb 10:25). He implored these believers not to

---

14. O'Carroll, "Kanohi ki te kanohi," *Pimatisiwin*, 441. See also: O'Carroll, "Kanohi ki te Kanohi," PhD diss.

15. Tan and Gregg, *Disciplines of the Holy Spirit*, 169–70.

16. Marshall, *1 & 2 Thessalonians*, 141.

neglect fellowship, and to consider "how we may spur one another toward love and good deeds . . . encouraging one another" (Heb 10:24–25). The basic idea of *encourage* here is that followers of Jesus should strengthen and stimulate one another's faith.[17] We are called to provoke one another "to energetic effort in love and good works" (Heb 10:24 NTFE). We are called not simply to keep meeting, but to consider the needs of others. Mathis reflects on this appeal in a very personal way: "Know each other. Get close. Stay close. Go deep. And consider particular persons, and interact with them, such that you exhort and inspire them to love and good deeds specifically fitting to their mix."[18]

When we go through hard times, it is easy to become remote. Our heads drop, our confidence takes a knock. Fear can keep us isolated. In times like this it is important for us to fellowship, to reach out for help or to have someone step in to support us. As Max Lucado puts it,

> Christ distributes courage through community; he dissipates doubts through fellowship. He never deposits all knowledge in one person but distributes pieces of the jigsaw puzzle to many. When you interlock your understanding with mine, and we share our discoveries, when we mix, mingle, confess and pray, Christ speaks.[19]

There is something precious about the encouragement of a brother who genuinely knows me and loves me, and who has earned the right to speak. I have often found such times essential for drawing closer to God.

I remember losing my job, a role that I had been in for many years. I recall the shock and the blow it was to my confidence. Over time I was further impacted by the uncertainty of my situation, and I was feeling anxious about the future. My friend, a Christian brother I have known since university, some thirty or so years, picked me up and took me out for a meal. He sat and listened as I poured out my concerns and my worries. Then he shared with me some of the things that had helped him when he had gone through a similar situation years before. He had taken the time to think of what he could say and do to help me in this low time. He encouraged me to try and relax and trust God and shared some good advice about perspective, and steps to take moving forward. Words that might have come across as mere bumper-sticker platitudes in the mouths

---

17. Guthrie, *Letter to the Hebrews*, 216.
18. Mathis, *Habits of Grace*, 147.
19. Lucado, *Fearless*, 144.

of others were, instead, a balm from the lips of a loving brother who had permission to speak into my situation and life. The food was good too.

To draw on Bonhoeffer's words, I had become "uncertain and discouraged" by myself, and my brother was able to speak "divine words" from a sure heart to my wavering gloominess. Christ, in the word of my brother, spoke to weakness in my own heart. The Christ in my own heart is weaker than the Christ in the word of my brother; my own heart is uncertain; my brother's is sure.[20] I appreciate the courage and strength I have received during such tētahi ki tētahi encounters.

2. Presence and Comfort

When my father died it was a shock, and I was heartbroken. I remember a brother came around to get me out of the house. We went out for a steak meal. I didn't feel like speaking, so we ate in silence. Then we went to a movie, *Green Lantern*. It was awful. Then my mate dropped me off. It must have been terribly awkward for my friend. Actually, I know it was. We have talked about it in the years since.

It might be easy to see this evening as a failure on my friend's part. There was no visible lift in my spirits, no revitalizing words of wisdom to draw me from the depths of my grief. But he had been there. And he has been there many times since. I have always appreciated the Māori saying and value he kanohi i kitea (a face seen).[21] In times of grief, I may not recall what you say, but I remember seeing your face. In my time of need, I saw you were there. Nothing can replace seeing the face of a whanaunga or friend in a time of grief.[22]

It is easy to pull back from people who are suffering. What should I say? Should I go around or not? Then we find we have left it too long, and now it is even more awkward. Sadly, we often end up putting it all in the "too hard" basket and avoiding them. To this end, I have found Philip Yancey's writing invaluable for supporting those going through hard times: "It is not our words or insights that they want most; it is our mere presence . . . it matters little what we say—our concern and availability matter far more."[23]

20. Bonhoeffer, *Life Together*, 23.
21. Mead, *Tikanga Māori*, 361.
22. Mead, *Tikanga Māori*, 133.
23. Yancey, "Helping Those in Pain," 92.

Loving presence. I have had brothers sit with me in the silence of my grief, and grapple with me in my questions about God in hard times. I have sat silently beside a young sister as she lay in a hospital bed, speaking only as she led the conversation. I can be led by the Holy Spirit in silence and speaking as I seek to support those suffering. I may not know what to say, but my physical presence and availability can communicate God's love and minister grace for my brother in his time of need.

3. Challenge and Confession

Tan and Gregg maintain that healthy Christian community requires challenge: "Each of us needs accountability, correction, and good advice from others in order to grow."[24] The first part of Prov 27:6 (KJV) reads, "Faithful are the wounds of a friend." True friends will bring challenge to one another, as "they tell each other things they need to hear even if they are painful."[25]

The loving challenge of a brother confronts my wrong thinking and unhealthy behavior. It affords me an opportunity to experience the conviction of the Holy Spirit, graciously calling me to repent and get back on track. James exhorts believers to "confess your sins to each other and pray for each other" (Jas 5:16). Willard speaks of the discipline of confession as a practice that occurs in fellowship whereby "we let trusted others know our deepest weakness and failures."[26] Bonhoeffer shares on the power of confession in Christian fellowship:

> Since the confession of sin is made in the presence of a Christian brother, the last stronghold of self-justification is abandoned. The sinner surrenders; he gives up all his evil. He gives his heart to God, and he finds the forgiveness of all his sin in the fellowship of Jesus Christ and his brother.[27]

Willard asserts that the highest level of fellowship, which "involves humility, complete honesty, transparency, and at times confession and restitution," is maintained by the discipline of submission.[28] The Christian life is one of *mutual* submission (Eph 5:21), but there is also a place

---

24. Tan and Gregg, *Disciplines of the Spirit*, 170.
25. Keller and Keller, *Way of Wisdom*, 166.
26. Willard, *Spirit of the Disciplines*, 187.
27. Bonhoeffer, *Life Together*, 112.
28. Willard, *Spirit of the Disciplines*, 189.

for seeking the help of certain brothers and sisters due to their depth of experience, character, and maturity. Willard explains further:

> In submission we engage the experience of those in our fellowship who are qualified to direct our efforts in growth and who then add the weight of their wise authority on the side of our willing spirit to help us do the things we would like to do and to refrain from the things we don't want to do.[29]

When I was a much younger man, I was in a long-term relationship that was threatened due to my deep anger issues and explosive temper. I knew I had to sort my life out with God. I was introduced to a wonderful older man, an elder in our church. He opened his home to me, sat with me and listened, empathized with me, and shared openly and honestly about his life. And as I gained courage, I shared deep secrets, the ugliest and most painful parts of my life, and he did not flinch. He provided gentle but robust challenges to my thinking, calmly confronting many of the misbeliefs I had long held as axiomatic truths. He spoke words of hope. He prayed with me. Free from judgment, and safe in his acceptance, I began to heal.

I submitted to my older brother as he sought to serve me and love me. After some months of meeting with him, the woman I loved saw the change in me and graciously gave me another chance to take her hand. We recently celebrated twenty-five years of marriage. I cannot imagine life without her.

I am here today because my tuakana gave up his evenings to sit with me and challenge me, and to guide me back onto the narrow path of a life following Jesus. Guilt and shame can isolate us. Before long we begin to stray a bit from the godly path, to wander, to drift further from the presence and ways of God. In our isolation from God and others, we become susceptible to lies and harmful thinking. It becomes easy to rationalize our sin, to make excuses for our poor behavior.

Lydia Kicker notes that we all have a natural tendency to drift, and that in our fallen human nature we tend to drift away from, not toward, all that is wholesome and holy. We don't drift into good habits and good relationships; rather, we generally drift and slide toward the unhealthy and unholy. I appreciate Kicker's thoughts on halting this internal drift: "The best defense against the drift is not me. The best defense against that is we not me. It is the us, not the you. We is the best defense against

---

29. Willard, *Spirit of the Disciplines*, 189–90.

the deceitfulness of sin in you."[30] As I join my "me" to the "we" of loving fellowship with fellow Christians and the Holy Spirit, I can halt the drift toward selfishness and sin and find my way back to the embrace of God and his whānau.

Final Reflections

I was once reading about men's health in New Zealand and came across an article interviewing Ricky Sione of Tala'aga Counselling who was speaking on the importance of community and friendships. Sione used a boxing analogy, saying a boxer has a couple of people in their corner, such as a coach or a medic, who play specific roles in their life. So, whatever happens in the ring, they can always come back and trust who is in their corner. He then encouraged us to find who is in our corner, and whose corner we are in.[31] It leads me to ask: Who is in my corner? And in whose corner do I stand ready to encourage and support?

Who is in your corner, the person you can come back to, the people you trust? Whose corner are you in? God works through our brothers and sisters in Christ as "a primary means to transform us and help us deal with our sin, sickness, and cultural idolatries."[32]

God has gifted us one another in his church. This is not simply for camaraderie (although we can find friendship and connection), or to overcome loneliness (although we are able to experience love and acceptance). Rather, as Mathis puts it, we are to be for each other "a priceless means of God's grace . . . an indispensable means of his divine favor."[33]

In dark periods and lonely times, such tētahi ki tētahi, one-another fellowship as I have described has been an incredible means of grace for me. My prayer is that you too may know God's grace and presence as you catch up with your fellow brothers and sisters in fellowship, turning your faces to one another in loving care and welcoming embrace.

---

30. Wave Church, "You Belong."
31. Madden-Smith, "There's a Friendship Recession," paras. 31–33.
32. Tan and Gregg, *Disciplines of the Holy Spirit*, 161.
33. Mathis, *Habits of Grace*, 148–49.

Bibliography

Bonhoeffer, Dietrich. *Life Together: The Classic Exploration of Christian Community*. Translated by John W. Doberstein. New York: HarperOne, 2009.

Davids, Peter H. *The First Epistle of Peter*. New International Commentary on the New Testament. Grand Rapids: Eerdmans, 1990.

Guthrie, Donald. *The Letter to the Hebrews: An Introduction and Commentary*. Tyndale New Testament Commentaries. Leicester, UK: Inter-Varsity, 1983.

Hillyer, Norman. *1 and 2 Peter, Jude*. New International Biblical Commentary 16. Peabody, MA: Hendricksen, 1992.

Keller, Timothy, with Kathy Keller. *The Way of Wisdom: A Year of Daily Devotions in the Book of Proverbs*. London: Hodder & Stoughton, 2019.

Lewis, C. S. *Beyond Personality: The Christian Idea of God*. London: Bles, 1944.

———. *Letters to Malcolm: Chiefly on Prayer*. New York: Harcourt, 1992.

Lucado, Max. *Fearless: Imagine Your Life Without Fear*. Nashville: Thomas Nelson, 2009.

Madden-Smith, Zoe. "There's a Friendship Recession and It's Hurting NZ Men." 1News, Sept. 24, 2022. https://www.1news.co.nz/2022/09/24/theres-a-friendship-recession-and-its-hurting-nz-men/.

Marshall, Howard I. *1 & 2 Thessalonians: A Commentary*. Vancouver: Regent, 2002.

Mathis, David. *Habits of Grace: Enjoying Jesus Through the Spiritual Disciplines*. Wheaton, IL: Crossway, 2016.

Mead, Hirini Moko. *Tikanga Māori: Living by Māori Values*. Wellington, NZ: Huia, 2003.

O'Carroll, Acushla Deanne. "Kanohi ki te Kanohi—A Thing of the Past? An Examination of Māori Use of Social Networking Sites and the Implications for Māori Culture and Society." PhD diss., Massey University, 2013. http://hdl.handle.net/10179/5323.

———. "Kanohi ki te Kanohi—A Thing of the Past? Examining the Notion of 'Virtual' Ahikā and the Implications for Kanohi ki te Kanohi." *Pimatisiwin: A Journal of Aboriginal and Indigenous Community Health* 11 (2013) 441–55. https://journalindigenouswellbeing.co.nz/wp-content/uploads/2014/02/09OCarroll.pdf.

O'Donohue, John. *Anam Cara: Spiritual Wisdom from the Celtic World*. New York: Bantam, 1997.

Sacks, Jonathan. *To Heal a Fractured World: The Ethics of Responsibility*. New York: Schocken, 2005.

Tan, Siang-Yang, and Douglas H. Gregg. *Disciplines of the Holy Spirit: How to Connect to the Spirit's Power and Presence*. Grand Rapids: Zondervan, 1997.

Wave Church. "You Belong." Oct. 19, 2016. https://wavechurch.com/you-belong/.

Wesley, John. "Sermon 24—Upon Our Lords Sermon on the Mount 4." ResourceUMC. https://www.resourceumc.org/en/content/sermon-24-upon-our-lords-sermon-on-the-mount-4.

Willard, Dallas. *The Spirit of the Disciplines: Understanding How God Changes Lives*. Sydney: HarperCollins, 1988. Kindle.

Yancey, Philip. "Helping Those in Pain." *Leadership* 5 (1984) 90–97. https://www.christianitytoday.com/1984/04/helping-those-in-pain/.

11

Encountering God in the Whenua (The Land)

Manakinui Te Kahu and Philip Halstead

Have you ever visited a place where the boundary between this world and the spiritual world was porous or thin, where the sacred and profane united, where you tasted something of the inherent sacrality, interconnectedness, and communality of creation?

Māori, as the indigenous population of Aotearoa (New Zealand), understand that humans are intrinsically and deeply connected to the land and each other. This awareness is often lacking in the Western world. Phil Halstead therefore wanted to find out more about Manakinui Te Kahu's unique and profound connection to the place he comes from and often visits when he desires to draw close to God. This chapter comprises a conversation between Manakinui and Phil about the value of the land as a living presence to be revered and communed with.

To go to the land for an encounter with God, or in search for new insights and guidance, simultaneously means to go inward to our deeper self and outward to the Creator of grasslands, forests, mountains, oceans, rivers, and deserts. This chapter introduces some important Māori values and practices and invites us all to

> *engage in pilgrimages to places where we engage with the powerful wisdom of the earth, allow this to ignite our soul, and connect us more profoundly with God and with our deepest and wisest selves.*

> Northland, Aotearoa (New Zealand). It has a smell to it. It smells of Manuka bark and ocean salt. It smells of toitoi grass and cow poo. The dirt holds the Mauri (life force). It is rugged but beautiful at the same time.
>
> —Manakinui Te Kahu[1]

> Long ago, before there were churches, it was normal for people to practice their religion out of doors. In the Hebrew Bible, Abraham meets his God under an oak tree and Deborah prophesies under a palm. In the New Testament, Jesus prays in the temple at Jerusalem, but also in the hills of Galilee. Nature was an acceptable place of worship, as it still is in many parts of the world.
>
> —Mary Low[2]

Kia ora! This is what we say when we greet each other in te reo (the Māori language). It means "may you be of life."[3] From these islands of Aotearoa (New Zealand), I (Manakinui) say to you, the reader, kia ora, may you be of life. Before we dig into this kaupapa (topic), you will notice the strong focus of te reo Māori. I whakapapa Māori (I have genealogical connections to Māoridom). I ground myself here and I am tāngata whenua (the people of the land). I am also passionate about seeing what God wants for us as Māori. Along the journey, Phil also holds insight and perspective as Pākehā (a European descendant now residing in Aotearoa). These cultures are different but reside on the same whenua (land). Given this kaupapa is about the whenua and how it ties into our connection with God, we think that it is important for you to know we are writing from the context of Aotearoa. We want to create space for

---

1. This is Manakinui Te Kahu's description of the geographical area in which his family's whenua (land) lies.

2. Low, *Celtic Christianity and Nature*, 1.

3. In addition to greetings like hello, good morning, and good afternoon, kia ora is also used to say thank you.

Māori theologies to be more vivid. With that context comes the intricate weaving of worldview, tikanga (protocol/custom), and language. These strands create a conversation that is vibrant, colorful, and engages the senses in a way that only Aotearoa can. So, we ask that you read our chapter in light of this context. This kōrero (conversation) serves to ground us in God and the given context that we find ourselves in so that we can be of life. So, yeah, kia ora!

The Kōrero

Phil: Kia ora Manakinui. It's a joy and a privilege for me to be able to kōrero (converse) with you. Over the years we've known each other I've heard you mention your relationship and connection with your family's whenua, how you travel regularly to it and encounter God in and through it. I've always been fascinated by this and wanted to hear and learn more from you. So, thank you for this opportunity! Is my thumbnail description of what you do correct?

Manakinui: Tēnā koe Phil, ōtira ki a koutou e pānui ana. (Hello Phil, and to everyone reading.) Yes, that's right, I do meet God on my whenua. Mātoa is that place. It is located in the beautiful Bay of Islands. It is in the heart of Ngāpuhi iwi (the Ngāpuhi tribe) and is located across from Te Tii (a Pā site, which was a Māori village or fort). Our Ūkaipō (mother, source of sustenance) has Manuka and Tii tree clothing its hills, and glistening pounamu-colored oceans of Waiatua (waters of god) on our doorstep. Just a small, two-bedroom homestead. Mātoa is our home. Mātoa is our whenua.

Phil: Oh, Mātoa sounds exquisite. Could you share a story about travelling to Mātoa and encountering God there?

Manakinui: Every year we would journey up north for the summer—Christmas, New Year, whānau time. Nana and Papa were the reason we would journey or pilgrim to the far north. Sometimes we would travel from Palmerston North to Mātoa through the night to avoid the traffic. That equates to a tiring ten-hour journey. But once we hit Redcliffs Road, we knew we were home. We had arrived at Mātoa.

One God encounter I had there was in 2014. That summer was really wet. It rained for most of the time we were at Mātoa and most of us were simply spending time on our electronic devices. I was unsure about where I was going in my life. It was my first year out of high school and I had no idea what to do. I remember sitting at our family table looking out at the ocean. The clouds cloaked the land, and a heavy mist was hiding the beautiful ocean from us. The environment reflected the way I was feeling: no clear view and no perspective. In that moment, I remember God speaking to me through the land. I felt God was saying, "The mist will fade away and you will be able to see the ocean again." This is exactly what happened. The mist faded away, I could see the ocean again; my trust in God strengthened and I was able to step into the unknown with the knowledge that God would bring clarity to my next steps.

Earlier that same year my Papa had passed away. He was a humble leader in our whānau (extended family or community). He would offer clarity when things seemed murky, and wisdom when presented with many paths. I guess in my moment of discernment, God spoke through Te Taiao (the milieu that surrounds and supports us), when Papa was no longer around to speak.

Phil: I'm very sorry to learn of the passing of your grandfather, a humble leader. What a lovely description and legacy of clearly an exceptional human being.

Manakinui: Kia ora.

Phil: In my experience, the passing of a significant family member is a rite of passage where we consider what our loved one stood for and we often embrace his or her values. It's interesting how God spoke to you through Te Taiao when your beloved grandfather was no longer able to be God's herald for you. It must have been incredible to see God remove the mist like that. The power and timing of the Creator is truly wondrous to behold.

While I realize that we can't force God's hand or tie God down to a formula, can you elaborate on how the spiritual practice of encountering God on your whenua works? For example, are there preparatory tasks that you undertake, such as reading the Bible? Is it a case of developing a posture of anticipation and expectancy that God would speak? I'm thinking here of Paul exhorting Timothy to "train [himself] to be godly" (1 Tim 4:7) and Agnes Sanford exhorting the attendees at a meeting in Anaheim, California, during a long drought to pray for rain. They prayed and within hours rain arrived and it rained for five days straight![4] There seems to be an expectation to work at spiritual practices. Is this your

---

4. Sanford, *Creation Waits*, 10.

experience? Or is it more the case that your task is to get to the land and then God will speak to you as you simply go about your business?

Manakinui: Good question. I think it's a mixture of both. While I believe that there's always space in our lives for self-discipline to help grow our intimacy with God, I also consider that there's always space for God to show up in the unexpected and in the ordinary. When we are on Mātoa, we go about our lives, but there is also a quiet expectation for God to show us something. In short, our tikanga are spiritual practices that help us navigate our ordinary lives, and in the ordinary, we always listen for the extraordinary small voice of God to speak to us through the environment or through whānau.

Phil: I guess in the early days you travelled to and stayed at Mātoa because that is what your parents did. Was there a time or an occasion when you took ownership of the spiritual practice of travelling to Mātoa to encounter God?

Manakinui: The practice became real for me when both my grandparents passed away. My Nan passed away two years after my Papa passed. Papa and Nan were our ahikā (family that stoked the home fires) and faithful followers of Jesus. They didn't grow up with te reo, but they did carry a sense of identity in te ao Māori (holistic worldview; the connection between people and nature). It was actually Papa who, with other kaumātua (Māori elders), fought for the land in the court systems. After succeeding, he moved up north and lived on the land, a year before I was born.

Things changed when Nana and Papa passed away. Suddenly, my parents' generation became the kaitiaki (guardians) of the whenua. Mowing the lawns or clearing the path down to the beach became part of our lives. I remember a project we did just before Papa passed away. He always wanted to lay down a better driveway toward the homestead. Due to the rain and erosion, the driveway needed fixing. Papa wanted the job to be done well. So, dad, my brothers, and I got on to it. We gathered shingle and all the necessary tools and did the mahi (work). We flattened out the parking bay, laid down the larger shingle and then the finer rock, formed the channels for the water flow, and cleaned up all the clay. It was hard mahi, but the look on Papa's face made it totally worth it. In his cancer-ridden state, he walked out to see the fruit of our mahi. He cried. And that made me cry. He was happy that we were looking after the whenua and taking up this responsibility. This also meant that God could continue to speak through the land. He mea wairua (It's a spiritual thing). This is when going to Mātoa started to feel spiritual to me.

Phil: Again, my commiserations.

Manakinui: Kia ora.

Phil: You used the word *pilgrim* as you described travelling up to Mātoa. A *pilgrimage*, as I understand the term, is to travel to a holy space with a spiritual purpose in mind. It involves intentionality, organization, and separating yourself from the ordinary to encounter the extraordinary. Where some folks may make a pilgrimage to Ffald y Brenin in Wales or to Jerusalem, you and your whanau make regular pilgrimages to Mātoa!

The concept of pilgrimage also reminds me of Eugene Peterson's classic book *A Long Obedience in the Same Direction* in which he describes the people of Israel making a pilgrimage to Jerusalem three times per year (Exod 23:14–17; 34:22–24). As they walk up to Jerusalem, they would likely sing, possibly in succession, the Psalms of Ascents (Ps 120–34).[5]

Does this resonate with you at all, Manakinui? Do you have any traditions that you habitually perform as you prepare or travel to Mātoa to encounter God? Or is the trip itself preparatory?

Manakinui: I'm going to say yes and no, if I can. *Yes*, because there is a preparation that happens with us. Much like Israel shifting their hearts toward Jerusalem or the temple mount, there is a shift in our hearts to return home. So yes, in this sense returning to Mātoa speaks of pilgrimage. Returning home for us is very much a preparation one goes through to encounter God.

And *no* because our journey to Mātoa has no spiritual distinction. We pack our bags and check our tire pressure much like for any other trip. The distinction here is that we are going and/or coming home. Perhaps sometimes the journey, and all necessary preparations, don't quite compare to arriving at the destination and saying, "I'm home."

I'd like to parallel where we find ourselves now in relation to Jesus's return. We are on the pilgrimage, the journey as faithful followers of Christ. But a part of me looks forward to the day where I can say, "I'm home."

Phil: Thank you. Could you elaborate a little further on preparing your whenua for you and others to encounter God?

Manakinui: There is definitely a kaupapa that I can think of that connects with your question. It connects again to Papa passing away. We had to prepare our urupā (cemetery). Although our whenua doesn't have

---

5. Peterson, *Long Obedience*, 18–22.

a marae (gathered meeting place for the tribe/community), a whare tipuna (the meeting house located on the marae; a house of ancestors), or a whare karakia (the church/house of prayer), we do have an urupā (burial site). It is difficult to get to. We must drive on private property to get to it. We must go through a set of fences in between the gorse and thistles. That's the thing with gorse, its purpose was to be used as a hedge over in Germany where it's cold. However here in the northland heat, it grows out of control and takes over. Preparing our urupā is a spiritual practice. It causes me to think, "How can I weed the 'gorse' out of my life?" Or maybe an intergenerational question is, "How do I deal with the 'gorse' that was planted in our whenua long ago?" In any case, we cleaned that urupā up and made it fit for a burial for our Papa. For me it was one of those before and after shots—the difference was remarkable. This experience came to bear fruit when we could get our Nan right next to where Papa would be buried. Because of that mahi, she was able to say "I'll see you soon dear" one final time.

I look at our urupā now and the gorse has returned. That reflects how we have not been consistent in going up for working bees. And the same questions stand: "How consistent am I in my own life?" "How is the gorse that someone else planted affecting me today?" The land watches us and is a witness to us.

Phil: "The land watches us and is a witness to us." That's a powerful image. God's loving gaze never leaves us. Am I correct in saying you expect God to speak to you through the land and when you're on the land? Gorse is a wild, non-native bush with sharp thorns. It's invasive and hard to control. It takes over the land and prevents it from being used for its designed purpose. Gorse symbolizes how some ideas—the influence of the media and busyness, for example—can overtake us. These influences need to be weeded out so that the word of God can be heard?

Manakinui: That's helpful.

Phil: You've also mentioned that you can smell the land and that God speaks to you through it. You don't seem to speak of the land as if it's an inanimate object. Can you elaborate further about your relationship with the land? Does Mātoa feel like holy ground to you?

Manakinui: Yeah, maybe. When you say, "holy ground," I think of Israel. I guess you could call it a sacred normality: a thin line between tapu (sacred) and noa (common) and the dance in between. You see, in te ao Māori, we weave together three concepts: Mana Atua (God), Mana Tāngata (Humanity), and Mana Whenua (the land). Mana Atua refers to the authority that lies within the divine; Mana Tāngata refers to the dignity that we as humans hold; and Mana Whenua refers to the respect the land holds. Each concept connects with the others as God intended. I believe you can have a relationship with God without the whenua aspect, but I don't think that's living in the fullness of God's design.

Phil: As I listen to how you connect your whānau and the whenua with Atua, I'm reminded of the concept of "thin" places where heaven and earth come together in sacred spaces. Iona is a known thin place. A few years ago, my wife made a pilgrimage there. A constant chorus of prayers have been prayed in Iona for centuries and apparently heaven is palpable there. Could you say a little more about the role of the land as it helps you to connect you with God?

Manakinui: Munther Isaac raises a unique set of issues pertaining to the land of Palestine, specifically the land being a "fifth Gospel."[6] After outlining a typical reading of Palestine and its ideal placement within God's narrative, Isaac then considers how a modern-day Palestinian Christian must uphold the holy nature of that land by adhering to the promises of God.[7] What Isaac means is that the land is the context to God's mission on earth and the goal of his mission. Isaac reimagines land within a Palestine context with the intent to fuse land and people as one:

> Christians must remember that the people of the land are as important as the land itself when it comes to narrating the biblical story and the story of the land over the centuries. Christians who visit the land must have a connection not just with old stones of old churches, but, more importantly, with the "living stones" of the land—the community of faith where God in reality dwells. The presence of God by his Holy Spirit in the midst of the community of faith in the land is what makes this land, as indeed any other land, holy. The people of the land are an integral part of the witness of the land. The testimony of the land apart from the people of the land is an empty testimony. If the land is the fifth Gospel, then the people in the land are . . . the Sixth Gospel.[8]

Phil: Does the quote mean, among other points, that the land carries memories of all that has transpired on it? This might include altars

---

6. Isaac, "Ecclesiology," 169.

7. Isaac, "Ecclesiology," 166–67.

8. Isaac, "Ecclesiology," 169. Isaac references Mitiri Rehab's work "Towards a New Hermeneutics of Liberation."

being built on it to help us remember and recite the history of the place. As I think of it, something like that is done here as part of the Pilgrimages Aotearoa whereby people meet with local Māori to learn about the land, its history, and the stories connected with a particular piece of land.[9]

Manakinui: Very much so! Our people have memory that is connected to land. We remember battles, moments of reconciliation, and new seasons. In learning about the land, you in turn learn about the people—the tangata whenua. Each tribe and hapū (subtribe) have their own stories to tell. Radio New Zealand has recently done some fine work on retelling the history of the land in places like Taranaki.[10] While some of the history is grim, recounting the stories prevents them from being forgotten. Persons today can visit these places, hear the stories, and learn from them.

Phil: I'm reminded of the Old Testament scholar Paul Williamson arguing that the Pentateuch and other biblical texts "emphasize not only the land's status as Yahweh's gift or inheritance to Israel, but also the covenant responsibilities inextricably bound up with it."[11] Or in the words of Randy Woodley, "My theology begins with the land. . . . Our responsibility as Indigenous people is to be keepers of the land. That means the whole of all the ecosystems and all the human systems. . . . That is my job on earth."[12] Off the top of your head, can you recommend a resource that people who wish to develop a theology of the land could investigate?

Manakinui: Yes, I recommend looking at K. K. Yeo and Gene L. Green's book *Theologies of Land: Contested Land, Spatial Justice, and Identity*. The book is both profound and concise. In it, Yeo asks seven key questions that make it possible for people to craft their own theology of the land. Examples include, "Why do theologies of land matter to you or your people?" "How do you view the relationship between land and spirituality? "What is the role of the Bible in the theologies of land?"[13]

Phil: What would you say to people who have no whenua? Through no fault of their own some of these people may have lived in rental properties all their lives or perhaps they are refugees, for example. How might

---

9. See https://pilgrimagesaotearoa.nz/.

10. See, for example, RNZ, "NZ Wars: Stories of Waitara."

11. Williamson, "Land," 640.

12. Randy Woodley is a theologian and Cherokee descendant. Woodley, "Community of Creation," paras. 2–3.

13. Yeo, "Theologies of Land," 138–41.

they participate in the spiritual practice you're describing of meeting God in and through the land?

Manakinui: This is a good question and one that I am frequently asked in the Te Ao Māori class that I teach. For me, it highlights a sense of disconnection from the whenua and one's whānau. This separation may exist for a variety of reasons such as migration to find better opportunities, historical amnesia (i.e., forgetting family histories), or a sense of wanting to create one's own way. Relatedly, our own choices can quickly pull us away from our whenua and whānau, and these choices can affect the generations to come. I feel that the noise of these reasons can quickly become louder than the still small voice of Atua.

If I were to ask you the question, "Are you grounded/connected to whenua?" and you answered no, I wonder what your next immediate thoughts would be? Similarly, if I were to ask you the same question and your answer was yes, I wonder what you'd think. Do the different responses elicit different feelings? By thinking of your identity and self in terms of relationships and connections (even beyond whenua) your worldview begins to shift.

My advice for people who may not be connected to whenua and whānau is to start looking and keep looking. Ask yourselves, "What are some practical steps I can take that actively connect me to whenua?" Keep listening to your whānau history. Become deeply articulate and knowledgeable of your whenua. This relationship may soon mirror your relationship with God. Stepping into relationship with creation beckons us into a deeper relationship with our Creator.

Phil: Kia ora. Given our conversation to date, I realize my next question is a strange one, but why Mātoa? I imagine you've met God in other geographical places. I know that God speaks to you via the Bible. But whenever possible you choose to go to Mātoa to hear from God. Why?

Manakinui: I knew I had to keep coming home, keep returning to the whenua, keep repeating the pilgrimage, just like I must keep coming back to God. Whenever I can, I hoki ki te whenua (return to the land). In early 2023 I got married. Something we wanted to do as a whānau was have a time of karakia (prayer), a rite of passage to be joined with my now wife, Leah Pania. We gathered on the whenua where my whenua (placenta) is buried. Āe (yes), whenua means land, but it also means afterbirth or placenta. In te ao Māori, you would bury your placenta where your whenua is as a sign of gratitude and respect to the earth from whence you came. Anyway, we gathered at this place, and the whānau just began to pray over me, sharing karakia and Scripture with me such as Ps 91 and Ps 139. Mum reminded me of the time she prayed for us and committed us boys to God. This was a moment where multiple experiences aligned at Mātoa. To trust in God no matter where he takes us. My brothers also prayed for me, two of my closest friends who would help usher me into a new chapter in life. I needed it. It was a special moment. I can still feel the warm sun on us, the cicadas buzzing around us, and the Tūī and Kōtare singing in the distance. He mea wairua (It is a spiritual matter). I felt prepared to step into marriage after that.

Phil: How special. So, the ritual of coming home helped you to complete the ritual of marriage and integrate your story with the story of your ancestors, the land, and God. And this blessing completed the transition into the next chapter of your life.

Manakinui: Āe.

Phil: If you were to list a few key benefits of your spiritual practice of encountering God in the whenua, what would you say?

Manakinui: One is a sense of groundedness. When I arrive at Mātoa, I am home. I feel stable. I have always associated that feeling of home with being in relationship with the Creator. Mātoa stores the memories of our whānau experiences. I walk where my forebears walked. It is the context in which our whānau shared and share our lives while witnessing to God. I would like to think God honors that. God is a part of what I would call our collective memory that we carry at Mātoa, as well as remembering alongside the whenua itself. Even now I still picture my Nana and Papa looking out on the moana (ocean) praying, washing dishes, or even napping, and it was well with their souls. Seeing how we treat each other and how we relate to the whenua itself. Groundedness is not only something I carry as an individual, but it stretches across generations. Groundedness is tūrangawaewae (a place of standing for myself, my ancestors, and those to come).

This leads to my next point: humility. The feeling of tūrangawaewae is realizing how small I actually am. While God's creation can give us perspective anywhere on the globe, this is particularly true for me at Mātoa. It is with these cicadas, it is with these pods of dolphins in the bay, it is with these people that I feel part of God's created order. Life tends to draw my attention from God. Whether it's study or work there is a constant pull to focus just on myself. Only when I come home do I know my place in the greater story. I then experience humility toward God. That God is so great and extends beyond our collective smallness, beyond all that we can fathom, and that he is in control. In my smallness, I hear that still, small voice, "It's ok my son, it will all be ok." I don't have to carry work or study by myself. I talk with my whānau about all the issues I face. My Nana and Papa would echo what God has already said. Talking about my issues with my whānau always seems to happen on Mātoa. Maybe that's because that's where I always saw them, or maybe my tūrangawaewae was and is connected to both them and Mātoa. Ko Mātoa ko rāua, ko rāua ko Mātoa (They are Mātoa, and Mātoa is them). Even if that does not work, I take solace in the moana allowing it to wash my āwangawanga (anxieties) away.

Being at home, I receive a state of mauri tau (energy that is settled). To feel settled in the grand design of things. There is the benefit of a sense of connectivity, of feeling grounded, of receiving rest. Despite my worries or anxieties, God is present with me providing assurance of who God is in the stillness of the whenua. I mentioned earlier about being down by the moana when facing life's challenges. I would sit on our small little beach and listen to the waves. The beautiful thing is our moana is very sheltered and tidal. The tide goes way out into the bay of islands and comes way in, to our whenua. Watching the tide would mirror the anxiety I was facing; anxieties come and go like the tide. We don't have huge waves that pound our whenua, nor do we have an expansive view of the Pacific but our moana massages the whenua gently with its small waves, much like it does with our concerns about our lives. From there I feel I can breathe again. Not only do I breathe the fresh air to revive my body, I also feel a sense of vitality in my wairua (spirit). I feel a sense of relief in my connection to both God and his created order.

And then, of course, there's the expectation and reality of encountering God. To go to and be on the land where I am most comfortable, most at home, and most connected with my family and history, is to be empowered to set aside my ego and enter mauri tau (being at peace, having arrived). In this space, I put aside my day-to-day activities, assume a contemplative stance, adopt a posture of expectancy, and become more receptive to God. And God speaks.

Phil: Thank you very much Manakinui. This has been a life-giving conversation. I'm reminded of Scripture exhorting Israel to remember. Remembering builds faith. God remains the same. God spoke and God will speak again. Mātoa speaks of what matters: God, family, relationships, history, the land. Kia ora. May I leave the final word to you?

Manakinui: I would like to finish with a mihi (a formal thank you) if I could. This is a way that Māori acknowledge different spaces and people that all contribute to this kaupapa.

Tuatahi, ka mihi au ki te Matua nui te toi o ngā rangi. Nāu te rangi me te whenua koe I hanga. Nāu anō te whenua te moana au kua kōrerotia nei. Ka tuku au ngā mihi whakawhetai, ngā mihi whakamoemiti ki a ia. Nāna I tukuna tāna tama kōtahi kia whakaora ai tātou te ira tāngata. (First, I want to acknowledge our Father creator of the heavens. He created the heavens and the earth. He also created the land and ocean of which I have talked about in this piece. He sent his one and only son so that we, as humanity, may have life.)

Tuarua, ko ōku tīpuna kua kōrerotia nei. Nei rā te mihi okioki kia a kōrua mō ōu kōrero, ōu aroha ki au, otira ki a mātou e ora ana. E mau ana au I ngā mahara I ngā kōrero whakapono. Haere atu rā ki ngā ringa manaaki o tō tātou Matua nui I te rangi. (Second, acknowledging my nana and papa who have passed on. May you rest on, and your stories and love continue to rest with me and those who continue to live on. I will always remember my faith talks. Go on to the caring hands of our Father in heaven.)

Tuatoru, kia koe Phil, kōrua ko tō hoa rangatira a Angelika. Ko kōrua kē e karanga ki au ki te tautoko te kaupapa nei. Mihi nui ki a kōrua ki te whakawhāriki te kaupapa nei hei painga mō te hunga e pānui ana. Kia piki te wairua, kia piki te māramatanga i a rātou. Mihi aroha ki a kōrua. (Third, to Phil and Angelika. You both put out the call for me to support this cause. Much love to you both for weaving this mat together and gathering all the various authors for this book. So that their spirits and knowledge may be encouraged. Again, much love to you both.)

Whakamutunga, ki tōku whānau ki Mātoa. Kore kau ngā kupu e whakatinanahia te whakaaro nei. Ka tūturu te whakataukī nei, Toitū te whenua, whatungarongaro te tangata. Haumi e hui e taiki e. (Last, to my family at Mātoa. There are no words that can capture my thoughts for you all. The following proverb stands true: The land remains even though the people will fade.)

Bibliography

Isaac, Munther. "Ecclesiology and the Theology of the Land: A Palestinian Christian Perspective." In *The Church from Every Tribe and Tongue: Ecclesiology in the*

Majority World, edited by Gene L. Green et al., 153–72. Majority World Theology. Carlisle: Langham Global Library, 2018.

Low, Mary. *Celtic Christianity and Nature: Early Irish and Hebridean Traditions*. Edinburgh: Edinburgh University Press, 1996.

Peterson, Eugene H. *A Long Obedience in the Same Direction: Discipleship in an Instant Society*. Rev. ed. Downers Grove, IL: IVP, 2000.

Rehab, Mitri. "Towards a New Hermeneutics of Liberation: A Palestinian Christian Perspective." In *The Biblical Text in the Context of Occupation: Towards a New Hermeneutics of Liberation*, edited by Mitri Raheb, 11–28. Bethlehem: Diyar, 2012.

RNZ. "NZ Wars: Stories of Waitara." YouTube, Oct. 28, 2019. https://www.youtube.com/watch?v=fW2ozpWlCC8.

Sanford, Agnes. *Creation Waits*. Plainfield, NJ: Logos International, 1977.

Williamson, Paul R. "Land." In *Dictionary of The Old Testament: Historical Books*, edited by Bill T. Arnold and H. G. M. Williamson, 638–43. Downers Grove, IL: IVP Academic, 2005.

Woodley, Randy. "Community of Creation." Center for Action and Contemplation, Oct. 31, 2023. https://cac.org/daily-meditations/community-of-creation/.

Yeo, K. K. "Theologies of Land: Contested Land, Spatial Justice, and Covenantal Identity." In *Theologies of Land: Contested Land, Spatial Justice, and Identity*, edited by K. K. Yeo and Gene L. Green, 132–56. Crosscurrents in Majority World and Minority Theology. Eugene, OR: Cascade, 2020.

12

But *How* Do We "Taste and See That the Lord Is Good?"

Feasting as Spiritual Practice

Michael J. Rhodes

Around the world, people celebrate by fellowshipping around a beautifully decorated table, eating and drinking together, and celebrating God's goodness through a delicious, plentiful meal. While eating and drinking are ordinary daily activities, Scripture frequently calls God's people to ritual and spiritual practices of feasting. Why is that so? Because feasting is an opportunity to literally taste and see that the Lord is good. Feasts can become sacred and transformative rituals that help us to cultivate wakefulness, feel fully alive, experience joy, and live our human life to the full. As we mindfully engage our senses—see, smell, touch, and taste our food with pleasure—we nourish not only our body, but also our spirit and soul. For Israel in the Bible, feasts also shaped the people of God to inhabit a sacred calendar. The meals helped them remember and even reenact the story of their life with God.

Michael Rhodes encourages you through this chapter to take time to cherish each other, feast on the Eternal as you return with open arms and thankful hearts to your Maker, rehearse the grand

> story of Jesus's rescue of his people in the rhythms and cadences of your sacred meals, and to taste and see that God is good.
>
> We were given appetites, not to consume the world and forget it, but to taste its goodness and hunger to make it great.
>
> —Robert Farrar Capon[1]

"O TASTE AND SEE that [Yahweh] is good. Happy are those who take refuge in him" (Ps 34:8 NRSVUE)! The psalmist here shares the perspective of the entire Bible: the good life, the happy life, is found only under the sheltering wings of "God the Father Almighty, Maker of heaven and earth."[2] Because the LORD is not only the Creator, but the just, righteous, and holy King, the good life, the happy life, is also a life lived walking along the path of the LORD's good way.[3] Because "righteousness and justice are the foundation of [God's] throne" (Ps 89:14 NRSVUE), "Happy are those who keep justice. Who practice righteousness at all times" (Ps 106:3, author's translation).

The belief that the life worth living is the one lived *with God* and *in line with God's way* serves as a starting point for the journey of spiritual formation. What makes this belief a starting point rather than an end point is simply that we have such a hard time *living* it. Spiritual formation recognizes this gap between what we theoretically believe and the way we live, and invites us to begin to bridge that gap, in part through concrete practices of spiritual formation.

As a Bible scholar and ethicist, I have spent years exploring the role formative spiritual practices play in the journey of discipleship.[4] But early on in my scholarly journey, I was caught off guard by one particular biblical practice that has come to dominate my imagination. That practice is *feasting*.

While we might casually refer to any meal that includes lots of food as a feast, according to Fu and Altmann, a feast is "a central social event oriented toward abundant display and communal consumption with

---

1. Capon, *Supper of the Lamb*, 189.
2. Apostle's Creed.
3. Indeed, this is the theme with which the book of Psalms opens.
4. See, for instance, Rhodes et al., *Practicing the King's Economy*; and Rhodes, *Formative Feasting*.

ritualizing tendencies."[5] In other words, feasts are meals we (1) eat together that (2) include food and drink that differ in quantity or quality from our normal food practices, and that (3) often include ritual elements.

Even with a more careful definition of feasting, though, we may be surprised by the idea that feasts play a central role in spiritual formation. In this chapter, I will first explore how the biblical feasts served as discipleship practices within the biblical world. I will then share a few ideas for how their feasting might inspire us to embrace a feast-formed spirituality in our own communities. This will be followed by a few stories of my own community's attempt to embrace a feast-formed way of life.

Setting the Table

Before we get to the meals themselves, we need to "set the table" metaphorically by reminding ourselves of the background to Israel's feasts. Yahweh liberated his people from Egypt and brought them to Mt. Sinai so that they might become a community that lived life *with him* and *in line with his way*. God's purpose, originally promised to Abraham, was that such a community would serve as a conduit for Yahweh's blessing to all the families of the earth (see Gen 12: 1–3). Yahweh gives them guidance on how to do this in the form of the law. This law offered to usher them into a life lived in line with God's good, just, righteous, holy, happy way. And standing at the center of that law is Yahweh's command that Israel embrace feasting—"You shall rejoice" (Deut 16:14 ESV)!

The feasts, then, stand at the center of Yahweh's answer to the question, "*How* do you taste and see that the Lord is good?" The answer is, in fact, fairly simple: you learn to taste and see God's goodness by *feasting* on that goodness together. Again and again, the Torah commands Israel to rejoice by celebrating multiday feasts with God and alongside the full community (Deut 16:14–15). Indeed, three times a year Yahweh commands the Israelites to embark on a "destination celebration" by journeying to the sanctuary and embracing and engaging in a multiday, joy-filled feast.

As Deut 14:22–27 makes clear, the people embrace ludicrous, outrageous joy at these meals by eating from a ludicrous, outrageous menu. The LORD requires the people to bring a tithe of their crops and the firstborn of their livestock to the sanctuary. But remarkably, the moment God receives this well-deserved tribute, he gives it right back to his people as

---

5. Fu and Altmann, "Feasting," 15.

ingredients for a full-fledged festival. The LORD commands the people to use their contributions to buy whatever they deeply desire, to *eat* their tithes and offerings together before the LORD, and to rejoice! "You and your household" (v. 26 NRSVUE).

The Israelites had been suffering as slaves in Egypt. In the promised land they lived as vulnerable subsistence farmers who depended on the rain to survive.[6] The LORD's over-the-top invitation to an enormous feast taught Israel to trust God's generous goodness. Israel tasted—quite literally—the goodness of God through the gift of these communal meals.

We can identify at least four aspects of Israel's formative practice of feasting. First, feasting fosters the virtues of gratitude toward God and delight in him as our generous King. As the frequent commands to rejoice at the feast in Deuteronomy make clear,[7] the LORD provides the feast as a pathway to joy. The little phrase "you shall eat there *before the LORD*" (Deut 14:26 ESV; italics added) reminds us that the feast directly connects Israel's experience of this joy with their experience of the LORD's presence. At the meal, the people learn to identify their deepest joys with their present relationship with the divine King. The feast thus cultivates gratitude for God's gifts of both his presence and provision.

Second, feasting is a ritual that reminds us of the surprising goodness of all that God has made. Those with eyes to see recognize that the food on the festal table is simply miraculous. How else do we explain that when the grain of wheat falls to the ground it bears a crop? How else to explain the mystery of the new life growing in the sheep's womb every spring? Deuteronomy 14:22–29 puts "wine" and "strong drink" (v. 26 NRSVUE) on the table. But how in the world does it get there? Who can explain the miracle of fermentation? Feasting in God's presence reminds us that there can be only one explanation. As Robert Farrar Capon puts it, "The bloom of yeast lies upon the grape skins year after year because He likes it; $C_6H_{12}O_6 = 2C_2H_5OH + 2CO_2$ is a dependable process because, every September, God says, 'That was nice; do it again.'"[8]

Indeed, central to the feast is the act of eating, an act in which we enact the reality that our bodies are bound together with the earth

---

6. Of course, vulnerable, daily bread was also part of Israel's journey of spiritual formation (cf. Deut 8:1–20). For a discussion of both fasting and feasting as part of Deuteronomy's spiritual formation toolkit, see Rhodes, *Formative Feasting*, 137–40.

7. Nine out of twelve of the Torah's commands to rejoice are in Deuteronomy, and nearly all are in direct relation to feasting and food; see Anderson, *Time to Mourn*, 19.

8. Capon, *Supper of the Lamb*, 85.

and other creatures. We are enriched and sustained by the good world brought inside our bodies. As Shannon L. Jung puts it, "Eating is how the world enters into us and how we become part of the world. . . . Food is revelatory of the goodness and joy of the earth. . . . God comes to feed us, to fill us, to love us. We know grace first through our bodies."[9]

Third, the food Israel feasted on was also the result of the Israelites' own cultural and economic engagement with God's creation. It is the people of Israel that put the grain of wheat in the soil, help the newborn lamb make its way into the world, and store the fruit of the vine in hope that God will once again work his wine-making and other miracles. While we moderns often imagine our feasts beginning at the supermarket, it was obvious to the Israelites that their feasts began on their farms, months ahead of time.[10] Because of this, feasting offers the Israelites a chance to taste and see the goodness of work amidst God's good world as well.

Fourth, because the work of the feast is communal work, and because the guest list of the feast includes the orphans, widows, refugees, and Levites, the food on Israel's festal table is both received as a gift from God and arranged on the table as a sort of potluck celebration for all.[11] Each and every member of the community symbolically contributes a plate to the party. "All shall give as they are able, according to the blessing of the LORD your God that he has given you" (Deut 16:17 NRSVUE). These joyful feasts, therefore, also bind each and every individual together as a family; to eat the feast is to taste and see the Lord's goodness *together*. At a feast, "one either *is* kin, or one *becomes* kin."[12]

"This Torah Shall Be in Your Mouth"

The feast thus offers a multifaceted practice of spiritual formation designed to shape the Israelites to "taste and see that the Lord is good." But feasts also sought to shape the community for faithfulness in line with Yahweh's just, righteous, and holy way. Exodus 13:7–8 explains that the Israelites will eat the Feast of Unleavened Bread as a reminder to them

---

9. Jung, *Food for Life*, 45.

10. And *years* ahead of time in the case of alcoholic beverages. See Smith, "Feasts and Their Failures," 1219–21.

11. For an extensive argument for and deployment of this metaphor of the potluck as central to the kingdom of God's socioeconomic vision, see Rhodes et al., *Practicing the King's Economy*.

12. Braulik, *Theology of Deuteronomy*, 51.

and their children of what the LORD did for them when they came out of Egypt. "For," Moses says, "it will be for you for a sign on your hand, and a reminder between your eyes, *in order that the law of the LORD will be in your mouth*" (Exod 13:9a, author's translation). When Israel sits down at the table, they find themselves feasting on the law.[13]

How does this happen? For the sake of space, let me consider just a few of the many examples that could be mentioned here. First, the law's requirement that the Israelites do justice for refugees, debt slaves, and the poor is explicitly grounded in Israel's experience of the exodus: "A refugee you will not oppress. For you yourselves know the heart of the refugee, for you were refugees in the land of Egypt" (Exod 23:9, author's translation). But of course, future generations would *not* know the "heart of the refugee" through their own experience. By requiring future Israelites to ritually reenact the exodus from Egypt at the Passover Feast, or the wilderness wanderings by living in booths during the Feast of Tabernacles, the law sought to train the hearts, heads, and bodies of future Israelites to remember their forefathers' and foremothers' oppression in Egypt and subsequent liberation by Yahweh. In this way, the feasts also shape each generation to enact the kind of justice that overflows from the community's experience of injustice and their gratitude toward the God who rescued them from it.[14]

Second, much of Yahweh's just, righteous law is bound up in treating one's neighbor as kin. As we have seen, the feast created opportunities for the orphans, widows, refugees, and the poor to *become* kin through the shared meal. This, too, is a way that the feast invites the people to *swallow* the rest of Yahweh's law. For instance, in Deut 14:22–29, right after inviting the people to feast on their tithes, Yahweh tells the people that in the third year they will instead *keep their tithes* in the village to serve as emergency food aid for the orphan, widow, refugee, and Levite. Having become family at the feast, the people of God find themselves formed for

---

13. Rhodes, *Formative Feasting*, 196.

14. The way the Passover places Yahweh's Torah in the Israelites' mouths by reenacting their sacred history may, in fact, be part of a broader pattern. A number of scholars suggest that Israel's sacred calendar, moving from Passover through the Feast of Weeks and culminating in the Feast of Booths, symbolically requires the Israelites to reenact the journey out of Egypt and into the promised land. For extensive arguments making this point, see MacDonald, *Not Bread Alone*, 82; and Culp, *Memoir of Moses*, 147–51.

the world's first law requiring regular contributions to ensure that the vulnerable eat all year long.[15]

Finally, these feasts would place the law in Israel's mouth because instruction in the law would occur at the table. Parents would tell the children the story of Passover as part of that festival's liturgy. Deuteronomy 31:11–12 calls the people to have the entire law read aloud every seven years at the Feast of Booths. The text makes clear that all are to be assembled for this festal reading of the law: "men, women, and children, as well as the [refugees] residing in your towns" (v. 12 NRSVUE).

A text like Neh 7:73—8:12 gives us a glimpse of what this might have felt like. On that occasion, "all the people gathered together" and "told Ezra the scribe to bring the book of the law of Moses. . . . Accordingly, Ezra the priest brought the law before the assembly, both men and women and all who could hear with understanding" (8:1–2 NRSVUE). Ezra is assisted by Levites who "helped the people to understand the law" (8:7 NRSVUE). While the conviction that the law brings initially causes the people to weep, Nehemiah clarifies:

> "This day is holy to the LORD your God; do not mourn or weep." . . . "Go your way, eat the fat and drink sweet wine and send portions of them to those for whom nothing is prepared, for this day is holy to our LORD, and do not be grieved, for the joy of the LORD is your strength." . . . And all the people went their way to eat and drink and to send portions and to make great rejoicing, because they had understood the words that were declared to them. (8:9–10, 12 NRSVUE)

I expect Yahweh knows that many of his people, not least modern Christians, tend to think of his law as stuffy, legalistic, and constraining, rather than the life-giving, liberating, expansive invitation to justice and righteousness that the law itself claims to be.[16] So Yahweh places the community's largest dose of Torah study smack-dab amid their most joyful feast. Apparently an extremely large spoonful of feasting helps the medicine of the law's righteous and just requirements go down!

---

15. See Baker, *Tight Fists or Open Hands?*, 248.

16. Note, too, that the law is read at the Feast of Booths in the year of release, when the people would already be celebrating their liberation from debt.

But That Is All *Old* Testament

My focus on Israel's feasts may have led some to think, "Well, yes, but that is all *Old* Testament stuff."[17] While it is true that Christians do not replicate Israel's sacred calendar, there is every reason to believe that we should have our own festal practices shaped and inspired by it.

To take just a few examples, in Luke 7:34 (NRSVUE), Jesus comes "eating and drinking." Indeed, his feasts were apparently so rich that his enemies could accuse him of being a "glutton and a drunkard." Their distaste for Jesus's indulgence in food and drink is matched by their distaste at his generously inclusive guest list; he is not just a "glutton and drunkard," but "a friend of tax collectors and sinners!" At these meals, Jesus invites all, and especially the marginalized and oppressed, to a kinship-creating feast.

And of course, Jesus's Last Supper celebration of the Passover meal becomes the model for the church's primary feast: the Lord's Supper or Communion. At the Lord's Supper, we feast in remembrance of Jesus's death and enact an embodied proclamation of that death before a watching world. We do this as we anticipate Jesus's establishment of God's kingdom at his return.[18] Standing at the center of the church's life, then, is a meal that is not only modelled after the Torah's feasts, but stands in direct, albeit complicated, continuity with one of those feasts.

The book of Acts makes clear that the early church picked up on this festal theme:

> All who believed were together and had all things in common; they would sell their possessions and goods and distribute the proceeds to all, as any had need. Day by day, as they spent much time together in the temple, they broke bread at home and ate their food with glad and generous hearts, praising God and having the goodwill of all the people. And day by day the Lord added to their number those who were being saved. (Acts 2:44–47 NRSVUE)

If our Lord Jesus and the early church celebrated regular feasts and meals together and were inspired and shaped by the Torah's festal instruction, perhaps we should follow in their footsteps.

---

17. This is, in actuality, a terrible way to relate to the Old Testament for all sorts of reasons, but here I can only focus on the question of what to do with Israel's feasts.

18. 1 Cor 11:26. See also my further reflections on the Lord's Supper as a formative feast in Rhodes et al., *Practicing the King's Economy*; and Rhodes, *Formative Feasting*.

Formative Feasts Today

What might this look like today? I expect the church could spend decades exploring what a feast-shaped spirituality might look like and still only scratch the surface. Just ask yourself: What would it look like for the way we eat together to be transformed by the Bible's vision of feasting? As you reflect on that question, allow me to respond and conclude with three ideas from my own experience.

Feasting at Home

Christians can practice the feast in their homes.[19] Inspired by the Old Testament feasts, we can cultivate joy in God and one another by regularly indulging in rich food and drink that is lovingly prepared. We can invite others to join us both in preparing and eating the meal, and we can think critically about welcoming those others most often *excluded* from our lives, and thus our feasts.[20]

The non-farmers among us might have to work hard to remind ourselves that the bounty on our tables did not begin at a grocery store, but in the dark mysterious corners of creation. That bounty was then transformed through the skillful application of human culture and competency exercised by farmers and field hands, butchers and bakers, truck drivers and shelf stockers. We can work to remind ourselves of this reality by slowing down, preparing food together as part of the feast itself, feasting in line with the seasons, and prayerfully remembering the many hands that helped bring God's good, transformed creation into our kitchens.

Do you need some inspiration? If so, you may wish to check out Robert Farrar Capon's explosive meditation on the experience of cutting an onion in *The Supper of the Lamb*. Because, according to Capon, if you do pay attention to the onion, then

---

19. By the time of the New Testament, Passover itself is celebrated by household, and Acts 2:46 makes clear that the earliest Christians celebrated feasts in homes.

20. For instance, the fact that economic segregation has been on the rise in American neighborhoods, workplaces, and schools for thirty years suggests that, in American contexts, Christians will have to work hard to create household feasts that bring people together across class lines. But the biblical feasts demand nothing less. For an overview of studies demonstrating this dynamic see Mijs and Roe, "Is America Coming Apart?" 7–9.

> you have seen at least dimly that the uniquenesses of creation are the result of continuous creative support, of effective regard by no mean lover. He *likes* onions, therefore they are. The fit, the colors, the smell, the tensions, the tastes, the textures, the lines, the shapes are a response, not to some forgotten decree that there may as well be onions as turnips, but to His present delight—His intimate and immediate joy in all you have seen, and in the thousand other wonders you do not even suspect. With Peter, the onion says, "Lord, it is good for us to be here." "Yes," says God. "Very good."[21]

Passovers provided parents with opportunities to tell the sacred story. The early church conducted their entire church service over a meal. Why should our household feasts not become places where we share God's story—and the way our story has been caught up within it—with one another? Why not begin our feasts with a song in praise of the one "from whom all blessings flow?"[22] Why not pause before dessert and spend time thanking the Lord of Hosts for filling our glasses with wine and our hearts with joy?

Those looking for inspiration in this direction might consider the beautiful liturgy to be prayed before a feast in the book *Every Moment Holy*,[23] or sharing together a conversational form using the ancient practice of examen through questions like: "Where did I sense God's presence today?" "Where did I feel that God was absent?" "What am I most grateful to God for today?" "What am I least grateful to God for today?" Of course, children are particularly adept at slightly modified versions of these questions!

Whatever else we do at our feasts we must do two things. First, attend to our Lord who not only "sustains all things by the word of his power" (Heb 1:3, author's translation) but also personally hosts the feasts of his people (Matt 18:20). Second, attend to our companions at the feast, and actively recognize that God has brought us to the table to bind us together as kin.

For my part, one place I have tasted and seen the goodness of the Lord is in the household feasts hosted by my parents. For over twenty years they have served as leaders in an international community group at their church. As a result, our holiday meals often included friends from

---

21. Capon, *Supper of the Lamb*, 17.
22. Ken, "Praise God."
23. McKelvey, "Liturgy for Feasting with Friends."

China, India, Latin America, and elsewhere. At my father's insistence, all were invited to share something of their experience of God, something of their gratitude to the Creator. For guests who were brothers and sisters in Christ, these conversations created sibling connections. For those of different faiths or none, they were quiet forms of a hospitable witness.

I have not just seen my parents feast with their international friends but also the way their feasts have overflowed into shared lives of mercy and justice. My father's constant efforts to help newcomers find work and regular visits to Ahmad on hospice, my mother constantly showing up amidst the joys and pains of daily life, Xiu and Li's radical hospitality to newly arrived Chinese immigrants, Jing's fervent prayers for my family, Ella's openhanded hospitality to newcomers, and the group's regular gatherings around the bedside of her husband, Carl, as he died of brain cancer are all examples of this (names changed). Being close and connected in these ways, which includes the shared feasts, taught them to receive life from God as a gift, and to share their lives in costly ways with one another as family.

Feasting Alongside the Christian Year

Christians might practice feasting by engaging in the annual liturgies associated with the Christian calendar, whether as households or as a church. Just as Old Testament feasts welcomed feasters to ritually reenact Yahweh's deliverance from Egypt and the journey to the Promised Land, embracing the church's festival calendar invites us to ritually enter the story of Jesus. An added bonus is that the Christian calendar weaves seasons of fasting, another important spiritual practice, together with seasons of feasting. So, for instance, in many traditions, the season of waiting in Advent gives way to the celebration of the Incarnation at the Feast of Christmas. On the twelfth day of the Christmas season many Christians celebrate the Feast of Epiphany, often with ritual practices that reflect the story of the arrival of the magi.[24] Likewise, the fast of Lent gives way to forty days of celebration in Eastertide, and finally the Feast of the Ascension, in celebration of the risen Lord's return to the Father.[25]

---

24. The way the Christian calendar gets worked out varies across traditions, cultures, and geographies. For a fascinating look at Latino celebrations of Dia de Los Reyes (Three Kings Day) see Lee, "Why Latino Christians Treasure January 6."

25. Different traditions do all of this somewhat differently. I am an ordained minister in the Evangelical Presbyterian Church, but often draw on resources from the

In our home, we celebrate the Feast of Epiphany with several other families from our church. All the considerations of the previous section would apply here, but we have also been delighted to draw on some of the various traditions around Epiphany. An example here is that everyone removes one shoe before entering the home. The resulting limp reminds us all of the long journey of the magi to meet the Lord. We also prepare food from as many different cultures as we can muster because the arrival of the magi reminds us that the King of the Jews draws even us gentiles to his generous throne. We tell the Epiphany story and sing Christmas songs one last time between courses. The feast forms us for joy and gratitude to the One who "comes to make his blessings flow, far as the curse is found," as the carol "Joy to the World" puts it.[26]

To take another example, around Christmas and Easter we have often thrown large, public feasts. One iteration of our Christmas feast included upward of a hundred people, spiced wine, a full potluck, raucous Christmas carols, and a rousing recounting of the Christmas story. Homemade shakers are expected and shouting at key moments encouraged. Another iteration of this event took place at the local Irish pub and included fundraising for clean water in loose partnership with the Advent Conspiracy.[27] The bartender, not a Jesus follower himself, always said it was the best night of the whole year.

Some might wonder whether food and drink, public dancing, and extravagant singing should really all go together. I would argue that is exactly what the Israelites would have heard God calling them to when Yahweh called them to make their pilgrimage to the sanctuary and feast before the Lord. For Israel, the best party and the high point of their worshipping lives coincided; when "God had made" the saints in Nehemiah's day "rejoice with great joy," the "joy of Jerusalem was heard far away" (Neh 12:43 NRSVUE). By contrast, we often spend our holidays slipping out of worship services to get to the "real party" somewhere else. What if Christians, inspired by the Old Testament feasts, found ways to place serious celebration with God and one another back at the center of our worshipping life? We might become a community that knows the goodness of God deep in our bones because we have tasted that goodness on the plate and seen it in the faces of our brothers and sisters at the table.

Anglican communion. See, for instance, Church of England, "Calendar."

26. Watts, "Joy to the World."

27. Advent Conspiracy, "About Advent Conspiracy."

Feast at the Lord's Supper

Finally, I suggest that we follow in the early church's footsteps and at least occasionally celebrate the Lord's Supper as a full meal. Our brief exploration of feasts in the Bible should make clear that part of the way meals do what God intends them to do is by being *actual meals*. The worship, joy, trust, and gratitude God wants from us does not take place merely in our heads. Because God wants our whole bodies, he invites our whole bodies to a meal that enacts worship, joy, trust, and gratitude through an actual celebration over actual food and drink. Moreover, meals bind us together because we work together to prepare them, sit down and share the joy of the food together at the table, and clean up together afterward.

By contrast, most Christians celebrate the Lord's Supper *exclusively* as a ritual meal, and with liturgies that emphasize our individual isolation. We are encouraged to bow our heads in introspective prayer. In many churches, we come up front to receive the tiny wafers and cups of grape juice in single file lines that feel more like drive-thru lanes than place settings at a table. In my tradition, we further distance what is happening from what happens at a meal by referring to the bread and wine as "elements." I can assure you that nobody has ever asked me to come to dinner because they were serving "elements"!

I do not mean to suggest that the Lord's Supper is thereby deprived entirely of its power to, as Calvin put it, "send us to the cross of Christ" and "exercise us in the remembrance of Christ's death."[28] No, indeed! Paul bears witness that when we gather at the Lord's Supper, the Lord Jesus is in our midst.[29] By God's grace, Jesus offers himself to us at the table and through us offers himself to the world.

But I *do* mean to suggest that, by celebrating the Lord's Supper with miniscule, ritual portions and apart from any kind of actual table that brings us together, we deprive the Lord's Supper feast of much of what we might call the creational power that God clearly intends for the sacrament to draw upon. To put it another way, if God thought the saints in the Old and New Testament needed to taste the goodness of God with their tongues and alongside their neighbors, why would we settle for less?[30]

---

28. Calvin, *Institutes of the Christian Religion*, 109.

29. 1 Cor 11:32; although of course, Paul's specific point in this passage is that Jesus is present in (pedagogical) judgment!

30. Some people from traditions like mine that fence the table may raise concerns about this practice, but there is no reason why bread and wine cannot be set apart and

So, here is my two-part proposal: first, churches should seriously consider celebrating the Lord's Supper every week, using their current liturgy. Second, at least four times a year, churches should celebrate the Lord's Supper as part of a full meal. This could be done in all sorts of ways; we have, for example, embedded a full meal celebration of the Lord's Supper in our Easter feasts. My former pastor Robby Holt coordinated with elders to enable their church to celebrate the Lord's Supper as part of a full meal in their church's home groups as part of their Easter season celebrations. At my friend Marlon Foster's church, the congregation gathers for a large potluck meal *after* the services at which they celebrate the Lord's Supper.

These special eucharistic feasts would be particularly powerful opportunities to gather churches together, especially across the lines that typically divide us. They could also be hosted in conjunction with parachurch partners that minister to the marginalized. Under such circumstances the Lord's Supper would serve as the Spirit's vehicle for fostering kinship connections between strangers. Perhaps such kinship connections would spill over into lives of justice, mercy, and holiness together. In other words, such feasts could allow all to taste and see that the Lord is good and instill the Lord's just and righteous way deep in our hearts by way of our tongues.

Welcome to the Table

The Bible's rich depictions of feasts are mouthwatering. My hope is that by taking them seriously we might begin to reinvigorate our own feasting practices. I have barely scratched the surface of what this might look like, and the suggestions I have made are more allusive than conclusive. Meditating on biblical meals and celebrations invites us to a lifetime of creativity and improvisation in search of a life formed by the Lord's feast. My prayer is that readers of this chapter will be inspired to set off on such a quest, knowing that while all our feasts fall short, they also in a small way express our anticipation of that day when

> the LORD Almighty will prepare a feast of rich food for all peoples, a banquet of aged wine—the best of meats and the finest of wines. On this mountain he will destroy the shroud that enfolds all peoples, the sheet that covers all nations; he will swallow up

---

fenced within a broader meal that all share.

> death forever. The Sovereign LORD will wipe away the tears from
> all faces; he will remove his people's disgrace from all the earth.
> The LORD has spoken. In that day they will say, "Surely this is
> our God; we trusted in him, and he saved us. This is the LORD,
> we trusted in him; let us rejoice and be glad in his salvation."
> (Isa 25:6–9)

Bibliography

Advent Conspiracy. "About Advent Conspiracy." https://adventconspiracy.org/.

"Apostle's Creed." Grace Invercargill. https://www.graceinvercargill.co.nz/about-2/the-apostles-creed/.

Anderson, Gary A. *A Time to Mourn, a Time to Dance: The Expression of Grief and Joy in Israelite Religion.* University Park: Penn State University Press, 1991.

Baker, David L. *Tight Fists or Open Hands? Wealth and Poverty in Old Testament Law.* Grand Rapids: Eerdmans, 2009.

Braulik, Georg. *The Theology of Deuteronomy: Collected Essays of Georg Braulik.* Translated by Ulrika Lindblad. North Richland Hills, TX: D & F Scott, 1998.

Calvin, John. *Institutes of the Christian Religion: 1536 Edition.* Translated by Ford Lewis Battles. Rev. ed. Bibliotheca Calviniana 1. Grand Rapids: Eerdmans, 1995.

Capon, Robert Farrar. *The Supper of the Lamb: A Culinary Reflection.* Modern Library Food. New York: Modern Library, 2002.

The Church of England. "The Calendar." https://www.churchofengland.org/prayer-and-worship/worship-texts-and-resources/common-worship/churchs-year/calendar.

Culp, A. J. *Memoir of Moses: The Literary Creation of Covenantal Memory in Deuteronomy.* Minneapolis: Fortress Academic, 2019.

Fu, Janling, and Peter Altmann. "Feasting: Backgrounds, Theoretical Perspectives, and Introductions." In *Feasting in the Archaeology and Texts of the Bible and the Ancient Near East*, edited by Peter Altmann and Janling Fu, 1–32. Winona Lake, IN: Eisenbrauns, 2014.

Jung, L. Shannon. *Food for Life: The Spirituality and Ethics of Eating.* Minneapolis: Fortress, 2004.

Ken, Thomas. "Praise God from Whom All Blessings Flow." Hymnary, 1674. https://hymnary.org/text/praise_god_from_whom_all_blessings_ken.

Lee, Morgan. "Why Latino Christians Treasure January 6." *Christianity Today*, Jan. 6, 2022. https://www.christianitytoday.com/ct/2022/january-web-only/three-kings-day-dia-reyes-spanish-magi-herod.html.

MacDonald, Nathan. *Not Bread Alone: The Uses of Food in the Old Testament.* New York: Oxford University Press, 2008.

McKelvey, Douglas Kaine. "A Liturgy for Feasting with Friends." The Rabbit Room, Nov. 24, 2016. https://rabbitroom.com/2016/11/a-liturgy-for-feasting-with-friends/.

Mijs, Jonathan J. B., and Elizabeth L. Roe. "Is America Coming Apart? Socioeconomic Segregation in Neighborhoods, Schools, Workplaces, and Social Networks, 1970–2020." *Sociology Compass* 15 (2021). https://doi.org/10.1111/soc4.12884.

Rhodes, Michael J. *Formative Feasting: Practices and Virtue Ethics in Deuteronomy's Tithe Meal and Corinthian Lord's Supper*. Studies in Biblical Literature 176. New York: Peter Lang, 2022.

Rhodes, Michael, et al. *Practicing the King's Economy: Honoring Jesus in How We Work, Earn, Spend, Save, and Give*. Grand Rapids: Baker, 2018.

Smith, Monica L. "Feasts and Their Failures." *Journal of Archaeological Method and Theory* 22 (2015) 1215–37. http://dx.doi.org/10.1007/s10816-014-9222-y.

Watts, Isaac. "Joy to the World." Hymnary, 1719. https://hymnary.org/text/joy_to_the_world_the_lord_is_come.

Part 5

Transformed Through Prayer and Conversations with God

13

Karakia and Īnoi

LYNDON DRAKE

In our modern times we often liken rituals and set routines to thoughtless repetitive acts and boredom. We think that formalized liturgical prayers lack creativity or imagination and do not seem to reflect our personal thoughts and emotions. However, in this century where we are not only faced with our personal stories of pain, vulnerability, anxiety, and loss but also with global calamities, wars, and natural disasters, daily prayer liturgies can fill us with hope and ground us in the familiar and dependable. They present alternative perspectives and possibilities and provide a sense of constancy and certitude amid the disruptions of life and events that are beyond our control.

In this chapter, Lyndon takes us back in history and shows us that while a defined morning and evening karakia were not formalized among Māori prior to the translation of the Book of Common Prayers, karakia was routinely used in everyday life, and the use of set prayers were important in premissionary Māori culture. Consequently, it was not so much the translation of the Bible, but the provision of set Christian prayers that gave a liturgical expression of Christian life and belief that proved profoundly transformative for Māori. May this form of daily prayer and commitment to order and structure in worship help you to pray without ceasing and enrich your spiritual life.

My whakapapa connects me to Te Haahi Mihingare, the Māori Anglican Church. Te Haahi Mihingare predates the introduction of colonial rule and traces its origins back to the invitation from Te Pahi and Ruatara extended to Samuel Marsden, who preached the first sermon heard in Aotearoa at Rangihoua in the far north.

This first moment, which we still regard as the start of the church in Aotearoa, was not the point at which Christian faith and worship really began to flourish. For many years, the missionary endeavor struggled to gain traction. Māori, for some time, were welcoming in their hospitality to missionaries but resolute in being unpersuaded about the adoption of Christianity. There was not a linear progression from Marsden's sermon to mass Christian conversion. Instead—and many people are still surprised to discover this—the turning point in the missionary encounter with Māori was closely tied to the translation of a group of prayers into te reo Māori.

These prayers, which were a Māori version of the English-language Book of Common Prayer services of Matins and Evensong (Morning and Evening Prayer), were spiritual practices that did not arise merely as a pragmatic strategy of missionary endeavor. They were instead formative practices with a theologically informed and historically tested pedigree. Liturgical daily prayer was also both culturally and contextually appropriate, and when Māori encountered them, they were a key point in Māori adopting faith in Jesus Christ, taking this spiritual practice widely across Aotearoa. Morning and Evening Prayer offered Christian content appropriate to existing Indigenous practice and embodied in the Māori language and form the entirely novel concept of salvation.

In what follows, I propose that one reason central to the conversion of Māori to Christianity was that this pattern of daily prayer, morning and evening, speaks to a desire which can be culturally located but which is also, to some degree, common to humans more generally.

Human beings are worshipping beings. We flourish when we are oriented outside ourselves, toward te Kaihanga o ngā mea katoa, the Creator of all things. Humans, at our best, instinctively reach for a pattern of life which is rightly oriented toward God. Hence, daily prayer is not a contingent innovation but can be detected in many cultures. The innovation the missionaries offered, and which Māori gladly accepted, was the provision of Christian content to existing Māori patterns of karakia.

In fact, the practice of daily prayer long predates the origins of Māori and our arrival in Aotearoa, extending back millennia. Karakia has, in a sense, been part of a rightly ordered life for most Christians and, when we also include the time before Christ, for most Jews around the world and through history. Some form of regular religious practice has been part of most cultures in history. Hence, it is not surprising to find that it played such a central role in the history of the revelation of Christ as Savior in Aotearoa too.

I offer this reflection as an encouragement not merely to regard the history of the reception of the Christian faith in Aotearoa New Zealand as a kind of historical curiosity. It is historically significant, it is unusual and remarkable, and it is worthy of our attention in those senses. But I think it can also be understood as a pointer to a different way of functioning as Christians.

All too often my own experience of participation in the life of the Christian church in Aotearoa New Zealand has been one of historical amnesia that makes it challenging to see a wider perspective on Christian life and belief. I have often encountered a narrative, particularly outside the historic mainstream denominations, of an imagined Christian past in the Pākehā world, in which Pākehā New Zealand was a Christian endeavor (Pākehā means a person of European descent now residing in Aotearoa). The very genuine decline of Christian allegiance in the country is then framed against that rose-tinted view of the historical past. In this narration, there was an individualized piety, with egalitarian churches where hierarchy was absent or at least minimal, and the aspirations of Christian faith were identifiable by extemporaneous expressiveness in worship and life.

The enemy of Christian belief and practice, in this narration, is "religion." Religion, in a truly neo-Lutheran sense, can be identified by its use of rituals, a commitment to order and structure in worship and church organization, and any whiff of recognition of expertise among the trained pastors and ministers of the church. The decline of the church is blamed on religion. The remedy is to push further into an egalitarian view of ministry and church leadership, to emphasize extemporaneity and expressiveness, and to guard against any pattern or practice of worship which is not continuously novel.

One defect of this narration is that decline is most evident in precisely those parts of the church which hold these anti-religion views. Another is that, as Michael Crudge has shown in the past, Pākehā New Zealand was never particularly active in Christian adherence.[1] Lastly, it is a narrow view that excludes much of what we know about Christian faith and practice from other countries and times.

For the purposes of this chapter, however, I want to particularly highlight the way such a view ignores Māori Christianity and the mission history of Aotearoa New Zealand. Among Māori, Christian adherence really did at one point include the vast majority of people, in both weekly Christian worship and devout Christian life. The greatest missional success of the church in this country took place before many Pākehā even lived here. What is more, its form was almost the exact opposite of the prescription that I still hear commonly held out for the New Zealand church.

In Māori History

In many Māori communities, it is possible to refer to the "Rāwiri," and expect that people will understand what is being referred to. The reference is not to a particular person called David but to Te Pukapuka Inoi, the Prayer Book—or more specifically, to the 1662 Book of Common Prayer in its te reo Māori translation. This central Anglican liturgical text includes a liturgical variant of the Psalms, which, due to the traditional attribution of many of them to David, became known by that attribution.

Even though the 1662 English Prayer Book uses English language that now sounds archaic (although very beautiful), the te reo Māori used in the translation has not dated as much. While the language used is not entirely modern, it is still entirely understandable. As a consequence, it remains in widespread use.

It is important to carefully distinguish the terms *karakia* and *īnoi*. Both can be used for prayer, but karakia has a broader semantic range than īnoi. Karakia can refer to incantations, invocations, and what might be termed "prayers." What is more, it has come to be used widely in Māori religious settings for a religious service, rather than a specific individual speech act. Hence a karakia (service) might well include a number of karakia (invocations) and īnoi (prayers or petitions).

---

1. Crudge, Mike, Frances Nelson, and Rosser Johnson. "Communication, church and society: A story of qualitative enquiry." *Ecclesial Practices* 3, no. 1 (2016): 94–119.

So the Book of Common Prayer, as it is called in English, became Te Pukapuka o Ngā Īnoinga me ērā atu Tikanga in Māori (The Book of Prayers and other Practices).

The popularity of the Rāwiri is almost impossible to overstate. As Hirini Kaa notes, "By 1842, up to 47,000 copies in various bibliographical guises had been printed and distributed across Aotearoa—astonishing considering the total Māori population was estimated to be around 80,000 at the time."[2] This was both a greater distribution than that of the Bible,[3] and of enormous relevance in a Māori world where every activity required karakia.[4]

My personal copy was printed in 1859, and the frontispiece is annotated by "R. H. Rhodes Feb 1873 ChCh Canterbury NZ." As Rhodes was a second-generation English immigrant, it is notable that even in 1873 a devout English person might expect to worship in the Māori language (and in Christchurch at that, hardly the most brown city in modern New Zealand!).

I also have in my possession an 1848 copy of Ngā Waiata a Rāwiri (the Psalms of David), the liturgical translation of the Psalms laid out for chanting collectively. This is the same kind of book of Psalms that most Prayer Books have, including the English Book of Common Prayer. My copy is annotated in pencil by its owner, whose name in the front I have not been able to decipher. Many of the Psalms contain notes by them such as "2 ata" for Waiata 9, and "4 ahiahi" for Waiata 22, identifying the use of the Psalms in morning and evening karakia.

Copies of these books are commonly available and attest to the widespread use and practice of daily prayer, not merely to the enthusiastic publishing efforts of the missionaries. The books were used and prized by Māori, and the prayers adopted widely with real spiritual commitment. It was only the Waikato invasion that turned the tide against Christianity and meant that many Māori set aside the prayers.

---

2. Kaa, *Te Hāhi Mihinare*, 145.
3. Yates, *Conversion of the Māori*, 127.
4. Buck, *Coming of the Māori*, 476.

Contemporary Use

Despite that, some of the individual karakia within the overall book have entered into almost universal use, including in the present day. An example is the grace:

> Kia tau ki a tātou katoa te atawhai o tō tātou Ariki, o Īhu Karaiti, me te aroha o te Atua, me te whiwhinga tahitanga ki te Wairua Tapu, āke ake ake. Āmine.
>
> May the grace of our Lord Jesus Christ, and the love of God, and the fellowship of the Holy Spirit be with us all, now and forever. Amen.

You can hear this said (often with a small grammatical error in vernacular use: "a Īhu Karaiti," which is to my ears an indication of a slight misunderstanding) at marae (gathered meeting place for the tribe/community) and other hui (a ceremonial or social gathering) in numerous places, although it is becoming rarer as opposition to Christian karakia in Māori settings grows more widespread. The point is that while very few people using this set form will know that it originates in the Rāwiri, the remnant use among contemporary Māori is a vivid demonstration of the memory of an earlier, almost universal Christian practice among Māori centered in the Rāwiri and Morning and Evening Prayer.

Among many Māori communities, particularly in Te Tai Tokerau (the North) or Te Tai Rāwhiti (the East Coast), the Rāwiri continues to be a living part of spiritual life and practice. This is evident, for example, at tangihanga (the revered Māori ceremony or funeral rite for the dead), marae hui, and other events, which typically involve karakia from the Rāwiri. It is not uncommon to find Māori, especially those of an older generation, who have committed large parts of these karakia to memory, and who join in when someone begins to pray. Because of the orality of karakia, people using these prayers do not always connect them to the Rāwiri, although the connection is certainly explicit at some marae. Instead, it has become part of the oral culture of northern and eastern marae communities, even as knowledge of the overall Rāwiri has faded.

Alongside this, more modern forms of the Morning and Evening karakia have been developed which, while not having such a widespread following, are part of the liturgical life of many whānau.

Karakia and Īnoi

It is key to note the way Rāwiri gave Māori novel content and form appropriate to, and comprehensible within, the framework of existing cultural-religious practices. This offered both expressive and formative opportunities to Māori, vital in embracing the Christian faith and in expressing the faith as a daily practice. While a defined Morning and Evening karakia were not formalized among Māori prior to the translation of the BCP, the idea of karakia being routinely used in everyday life (rather than confined only to a weekly gathered service), and the use of set prayers, *were* important in premissionary Māori culture. As a consequence, it was not so much the translation of the Bible, but the provision of set Christian prayers that gave a liturgical expression of Christian life and belief that proved profoundly transformative for Māori.

In translating the BCP Morning and Evening Prayer services, the missionaries gave attention to a pattern of spiritual life which—given the widespread use of daily liturgical prayer across such a range of time and cultures—also seems to address a matter of common humanity. The Christian prayers were not identical, though, to pre-Christian karakia. While karakia in general use offered a way to invoke certain spiritual realities, the inclusion of īnoi (intercessions or requests) in Christian prayer offered another mode of engagement, where requests to God had potential for outcomes without the potential risk involved in non-Christian karakia.

While the form and cultural setting made the adoption of Christian karakia a congenial opportunity, the formative content of the prayers is something which is also often overlooked in modernist rejection of set prayers. Praying the same prayers will not, of course, always provoke the same emotional response. It is also true that praying set prayers might sometimes mean that the person praying is feeling entirely different emotions from those feelings and thoughts which the prayer expresses.

But this begs the question: what is prayer for? If, for example, prayer is at least in part to offer worship to God, perhaps it is in fact useful to have a way to do so when our own thoughts and feelings fail to be rightly oriented toward worship. Set forms of prayer can both liberate us to express those things to God which we do not at a given moment feel but which, in our better selves, we know we ought to feel and which rightly belong to God.

What is more, as human beings we are not simply expressive agents. We do not have only some unchangeable inner being, which we must express outwardly in our spiritual practices. All thoughtful people are aware of dissonances between different aspects of our inner lives, and of gaps between the kind of inner person we aspire to be and the kinds of thoughts and actions we experience ourselves to be.

One insight, commonplace for most of Christian history but largely forgotten in modernist thought, is that when we pray or indeed carry out any habitual activity, while we do express ourselves, we are also forming ourselves. In other words, daily prayer is worthwhile at least in part because it changes us to be the kinds of people we wish we were in our more enlightened moments.

Memorization

This is also related to the practice of memorization. Memorization and recitation offer ways to internalize a formative which are related to, but distinct from, an exercise of the will to change. In the church setting I grew up in, spontaneity and extemporaneous prayer were highly prized as markers of spiritual life and depth of piety. Alongside this, any spiritual change sought was expected to come from the combination of an exercise of the will and the miraculous intervention of the Spirit. No Christian, of course, would deny that both are essential. But they were often placed in contrast to ritual and rote practice as if ritual was opposed to piety and progress in Christian devotion and life. This again finds a counterexample in Māori practice.

Anyone who encounters Māori Christianity, at least in its more long-standing forms, will immediately notice the substantial use of recitation in karakia. I am often struck by the extraordinary feats of memory and communal recitation of karakia by Ringatū people, for example, but even in Mihingare contexts it is entirely normal to make use of set prayers, and long ones at that. Perfection in both the memorization and precise form of recitation are considered highly important, an art that must be mastered. Conformity to the ideal of the community, rather than individuality and personal expression, are highly prized.

This, in part, is because such practices are very familiar in the Māori world. As Tā Apirana Ngata wrote some considerable time ago:

> I learnt one outstanding feature in the education of a Māori, that he must know a thing in one lesson; in two lessons, if his teacher is indulgent. To learn a song in one lesson, words, air and all

its graces seemed an impossible feat. But it was demonstrated in many cases within one's knowledge. There were illiterate elders among my relatives in the sense that they read with great difficulty and could barely sign their names to paper. But they could memorise genealogies, land boundaries and strange songs with ease. They took no written notes, showed in fact from the commencement of any narration or recitation that they were committing to and holding the matter by an effort of memory. In that way they acquired the expression, the intonation, the rhythm, all the graces which reveal the meaning of the composition in its many shades. Words received their full signification from the stance of the bodies, the play of the eyes and the movements of the heads of the singers.

There were the song leaders, who attained to that position by a process of selection in practice. A fundamental feature of recitation or singing in Māori is that there must be no hitch of any kind. So a leader must not only know his matter, but must also remember it in all its phases. A fault was an aituā, a presage of ill-fate, even of death.[5]

In contrast to Ngata's reference to memorization of the first encounter with a new song, Joan Metge reports that in forming memorization, others in the past used "constant repetition," "repeating . . . over and over," and "returning periodically to an earlier point" as techniques.[6] Regardless of method, it is evident that the perfect memorization and recitation of oral material form a common part of Māori life. All of this was culminated for use within oral settings of the memorized material. In the case of waiata, for example, "rote learning was clearly not an end in itself but the first step toward the goal of meaningful performance."[7]

In fact, despite substantial and widespread demand for printed Prayer Books, revisions were challenging to implement because of the practice of "Māori taking the words of the text to heart, learning to recite from memory."[8] Similarly, while set prayers might seem unappetizing to some modern Westerners, within some Māori contexts they are perhaps even to be considered essential: "A feature of a karakia utterance was that its power and efficacy depended upon accurate repetition of set phrases. . . . It was essential that nothing should be omitted and nothing

5. Ngata, *Ngā Mōteatea*, xxxv.
6. Metge, *Tauira*, 257.
7. Metge, *Tauira*, 257.
8. Kaa, *Te Hāhi Mihinare*, 156.

added. To make a mistake was considered a serious ill-omen and disaster was expected to follow."[9]

We should also be attentive to the mix of orality and textuality that occurred in mid-nineteenth-century Māori society. Another feature of literary practice (not unique to nineteenth-century Māori but certainly prevalent) was the interplay of oral and textual forms through reading documents aloud followed by group discussion.[10] In other words, the importance and frequent use of set forms of prayers was not necessarily at odds with extemporaneous and expressive aspects of Christian worship and shared life. Certainly, they were not at odds among Māori in the nineteenth century.

Books were prized and popular. Textual culture rapidly developed among Māori in the mid-nineteenth century, with many Māori-language newspapers, for example. Māori agency in the co-option of textuality has not always been appreciated, partly because historians have not always possessed the linguistic competency to read them, and because Māori never abandoned orality in their adoption of textuality. It has not always been obvious to outsiders how these two have functioned together. But the use of texts, the memorization and recitation of them, and the formative influence they had can be seen in history in Aotearoa New Zealand.

Missional Impact and Potential

The historical popularity among Māori of the daily office (Morning and Evening Prayer) offers us a window into spiritual practices that focuses not on the personal benefits of a particular practice, but on the communal and missional impact. In the history of Aotearoa New Zealand, I have argued, the most effective missional practice of the church has been Morning and Evening liturgical karakia. This is indeed because I see the spiritual practice of set daily prayers as personally beneficial. My observational and theological view is that set prayers are formative and expressive of what we ought to be as humans and offer a coherent framework for other more spontaneous acts of worship and spiritual engagement.

My main reflection here, though, is that practices were also extraordinarily effective in missional terms. They benefited the progress of the Christian faith and led to human flourishing among Māori. I have no

---

9. Irwin, *Introduction to Māori Religion*, 43.
10. Paterson, "Māori Literary Practices," 92.

reason to doubt that the spiritual practice of daily liturgical prayer has the potential to produce similar effects in the present day.

In fact, I can attest that the most evangelistically effective work I have ever personally undertaken was the offering of daily morning prayer online during the COVID lockdowns. I know of more converts to Christian faith from those very simple liturgical karakia, with no intention of evangelism, than of anything else I have personally done in my life and ministry.

I commend the practice of daily prayer to readers because it will form you, give you a wonderful and appropriate way of relating to God, and because it will lead to the growth of the kingdom of Jesus Christ.

Bibliography

Buck, Peter. *The Coming of the Māori*. 2nd edition. Wellington, NZ: Whitcombe and Tombs, 1950.

Crudge, Mike, Frances Nelson, and Rosser Johnson. "Communication, church and society: A story of qualitative enquiry." *Ecclesial Practices* 3, no. 1 (2016): 94–119.

Irwin, James. *An Introduction to Māori Religion: Its Character Before European Contact and Its Survival in Contemporary Māori and New Zealand Culture*. Special Studies in Religions 4. Bedford Park, Aus.: Australian Association for the Study of Religions, 1984.

Kaa, Hirini. *Te Hāhi Mihinare: The Māori Anglican Church*. Wellington, NZ: Bridget Williams, 2020.

Metge, Joan. *Tauira: Māori Methods of Learning and Teaching*. Auckland, NZ: Auckland University Press, 2015.

Ngata, Apirana, ed. *Ngā Mōteatea: The Songs; Part One*. Translated by Pei Te Hurinui Jones. 3rd ed. Auckland, NZ: Auckland University Press, 2004.

Paterson, Lachy. "Māori Literary Practices in Colonial New Zealand." In *Indigenous Textual Cultures: Reading and Writing in the Age of Global Empire*, edited by Tony Ballantyne et al., 80–98. Durham, NC: Duke University Press, 2020.

Yates, Timothy. *The Conversion of the Māori: Years of Religious and Social Change, 1814–1842*. Studies in the History of Christian Missions. Grand Rapids: Eerdmans, 2013.

14

Experiencing More of God

Mick Duncan

We are not the only ones who long for a more intimate relationship with God. From the very beginning of the Bible to Revelation we read of a God who delights in spending time with us, and we also read of people like David who deeply thirst for closeness with God. The very heart of Christianity is about an intimate relationship with our God and Maker. So, how do we get closer to God or cultivate an intimate friendship with the One who stills our thirst and satisfies the needs of our soul and being?

To address this important question Mick Duncan shares insights from his personal story and prayer life. Mick's desire for intimacy with God translated into a pursuit and action. The philosophical dictum ex nihilo nihil fit or "nothing comes from nothing" applies here. You can only get closer to a person when you spend time together. In this chapter, Mick expands on the topic of prayer and talks about the importance of coming to God as you are and approaching this dialogue with God in an honest and transparent way. To do that you might want to engage in emotionally expressive prayers which includes shouting, protesting, crying, and pleading. Prayer as an authentic conversation with God can therefore be verbal, loud, raw, and real. Choosing various topics and establishing a weekly structure for prayer can further enhance your relationship with God.

The Backstory

AS A CHILD OF the hippie drug counterculture, I often hit the road, hitchhiking with my dog Poet from place to place. We finally ended up in Christchurch in the South Island of New Zealand. To my utter amazement, every lunchtime in the main city square, a tall wizard dressed in black would get up on a stool and keep the crowds spellbound with his incantations, interpretations, and political rants. While the wizard was in full flight, a short, shiny-white, Bible-carrying preacher would stand on his soapbox and preach sin, hell, and Jesus. These daily high-noon showdowns at the square were too good to miss and so I became a regular.

During one of these times, I was approached by a Christian who asked where I was staying. I informed him, "Wherever . . . with friends or on the streets." He urged me to follow him to his car and within fifteen minutes we pulled up outside an old concrete house. I followed him down the corridor of this cold house, through the kitchen and into his bedroom. The stranger then pulled out a suitcase and proceeded to fill it with his stuff. On zipping it up, he turned to me and declared, "The rest is yours as well as the room." With that, he was gone, and I was left with a bed, a wardrobe, some clothes, a table, a side lamp, and a Bible!

I had never owned a Bible before and such a demonstration of love certainly inspired me to pick it up and begin reading; it was to prove dynamite, simply blowing my old life away. In the hippie drug counterculture, I blamed the world's woes on the "system." Reading the Bible introduced me to another cause: mini-me! While absolutely clear about structural and systemic evil, this book was also forthright in declaring my sin sickness. I learned that at a deeply mysterious level an aggressive virus had attached itself to every part of who I was (Ps 51:5), attacking and transforming me into a weapon that would be used against myself and other people.[1] To put it crudely, these biblical antiviral missiles were now attacking the virus from my innermost being as well as challenging the tall and lofty thoughts I had about myself. I had no words or framework

---

1. This and other descriptions of sin can be found in Plantinga, *Not the Way It's Supposed to Be.*

to explain what was happening to me, but I was certainly becoming aware that sin was an assassin. Acknowledging these new truths helped me to reach a new stage of awareness.

Through reading the Bible, I heard an announcement of God returning to God's people, as God always said would happen, in the person of God's second self, Jesus Christ. The Gospels declared that through the agency of God's Son, God would establish a new ruler, a king over all the earth, who would come to restore everything to himself. Intuitively I knew this required me to submit and pledge my loyalty. Would I shift the allegiance at the core of my being to Jesus? Would I give up everything to make that commitment? As a staunch Kiwi,[2] who was fiercely independent and did not like anyone telling me how to live my life, I knew this was asking too much. So, I threw the Bible away.

Months later I was sorely tempted to pick the Bible up again. I was reminded of all the verses I had read that promised a greater level of freedom and transformation. I needed that. And to be honest, I also knew that I was ready for a new leader in my life; if you like, I needed a king. My self-leadership had turned out as a disaster. So, on Easter Monday morning in 1976, I got down on my knees and pledged loyalty to King Jesus. I gave him my solemn pledge, a sacred oath, to align my life with his purposes from that point on—no matter the cost. I placed myself on his side. But would the King accept me? This was the thought of doubt that invaded my thinking. However, I soon experienced his welcome at the core of my being; he pardoned past sins, flooded my heart with a sense of peace, and filled my life with God's third self, the Holy Spirit.

Intimate Prayer

Almost immediately, I reorientated my life around prayer. Intuitively, I understood that prayer is relational. It is not just an activity but a dialogue that involves another person. I therefore decided to create spaces in my day where I would be in conversation with this new King. These spaces became holy ground. Nothing and no one could encroach. If friends came knocking inviting me to a film or party, I simply said I had a prior appointment. I became very regular at turning up. And Jesus seemed, at least to me, to be ever so present. I was enjoying him.

---

2. The word *Kiwi* is a common and affable nickname to describe people from New Zealand. It is also "a small flightless bird that is endemic to New Zealand." See Chant, "Why Are New Zealanders Called Kiwis," para. 2.

This was my spiritual practice and life for several years. And then I became a pastor. At the tender age of twenty-five I found myself pastoring a small Baptist church. It was then that my prayer life took a turn for the worse. I fell into the temptation of co-opting Jesus as a way of achieving in ministry and only later realized that I had treated him as a means to an end. I was appalled by this development and decided to create several other times and spaces in my week to focus on him and do nothing church-related, such as preparing sermons and the like. You might ask what some of these spaces looked like. On Monday mornings I candidly talked with Jesus about my anxieties. On Tuesday mornings, I prayed for family and friends. On Wednesdays, again in the early morning, I asked for a fresh new infilling of the Spirit. Thursday mornings, I talked with Jesus about my ministry and mission. On Friday morning, it was a celebration of praise and thanksgiving. Saturday mornings, it was flexible. On Sunday, it was coming to the quiet and being still in the presence of God. Because each of these spaces was so special, I could not wait to get to the following week to repeat them over again. In other words, I built into my rhythm of prayer a psychology of anticipation.

Furthermore, during each day, after these early morning spaces, I indulged in casual conversational prayer. For example, when driving to a meeting it is tempting to turn the radio on or listen to a podcast (both good things). But more and more, I kept the switches off and put the devices aside to converse with God. Come evening time, it was the prayer practice of examen, where I replayed the tape of the day and reflected on the events in my day where a confession of sin was needed. Other episodes required a prayer of intercession for another, or thanksgiving over something received.

Slowly I recaptured that ground where all centered around him. Searching for him, delighting in his presence. Loving him, desiring him, and being intimate with him. I appreciate that these words may, for some, come close to "Jesus is my boyfriend" language. But Mark Galli, a former editor of *Christianity Today*, is surely right to remind us that there is a romance of God.[3] Scripture describes this romance further; the prophet Isaiah writes, "My soul yearns for you in the night; in the morning my spirit longs for you" (Isa 26:9a). Echoing Isaiah, the psalmist declares: "As the deer pants for streams of water, so my soul pants for you, my God. My soul thirsts for God, for the living God" (Ps 42:1–2a). And again, "You,

---

3. See Galli, "Monomaniacs for God."

God, are my God, earnestly I seek you; I thirst for you, my whole being longs for you" (Ps 63:1a). "Whom have I in heaven but you? And earth has nothing I desire besides you" (Ps 73:25). The apostle Paul joins this chorus of intimacy: "What is more, I consider everything a loss because of the surpassing worth of knowing Christ Jesus my Lord" (Phil 3:8a).

These are the words of love describing a desire for God that is not unlike falling in love. This is how I experienced Jesus upon my conversion. But as a pastor, I slowly and incrementally drifted into a need-type love. Upon my conversion I said, "I want to be with you because I love you." Upon becoming a pastor this became, "I am with you because you are useful to me." I am not denying the need of Jesus in ministry. The Johannine Gospel cuts to the quick, and states that without him we can do nothing (John 15:1–5). So, let there be need-love. However, at a deeper heartfelt and affection-filled level let there be gift-love, where we gift all that we are to God and God to us so that we almost lose ourselves in tender moments of intimacy, one between the other.

Expressive Prayer

There is a power in prayer but first let there be powerful prayers. By this I mean, express yourself! Lovers express themselves with strong emotions, passionate pleas, tears, clenched fists, and protests. Moses argues with God (Exod 32:11–14) and the apostle Paul pleads with God (2 Cor 12:7–10). In the latter, Paul pleads three times that an ailment be taken from him. The Greek renders pleading to someone who gets up close and personal. It even hints at admonishing. In a sense, Paul is praying, "Come on God!" To which God stridently replies, "My grace is sufficient for you, for power is made perfect in weakness." What is intriguing about this open and emotive conversation between Paul and his God is the timing of God's response. Was it after Paul's first plea? If so, and without hesitation, Paul pushes back and pleads twice more. If after the second plea, Paul persists with a final plea. If after the third time, we still have Paul beseeching and, if you like, nagging heaven. What a way to pray! It is daring and Paul does not give up. It is fair to say that God had the final word, but up until then there was a lot of pleading and a great many words.

Scripture is replete with individuals who express themselves in conversation with God. Take Jonah, for example. God summons him to go to the city of Nineveh to "cry against it; for their wickedness" (Jonah 1:2

KJV) to which Jonah replies, "yeah nah,"[4] and heads off in the opposite direction (v. 3). Via a very circuitous route, including whales and the like, God eventually gets his man into Nineveh. As soon as Jonah begins preaching to the people of this capital city, which is part of an incredibly cruel empire, they acknowledge their despicable practices and beseech God to have mercy on them, which God does. Jonah feared this might happen so, again, angrily disputes with his God and finally concludes that it would be better if he, Jonah, would be dead than alive (Jonah 4:1–5). To say the least, Jonah's prayer life was expressive, and emotionally so.

In Moses we have a pray-er who unapologetically and unashamedly urges God to change his mind. Implicitly at least, Moses is suggesting that God's original course of action is wrong and that a wiser way forward is to forgo Plan A, and adopt Plan B, the one being put forward by Moses (Exod 32:11–14).[5] And God is so persuaded!

In similar fashion, the patriarch Abraham feels compelled to argue, if not bargain God down from a certain course of action—namely, the destruction of Sodom and Gomorrah. He gets God to concede that if fifty righteous people are found in the city, then God will halt the judgment that was originally intended. Emboldened by this, Abraham then goes for forty righteous people, then thirty, then twenty, and finally ten (Gen 18:16–32).

Have you ever attempted to bargain God down? I recall taking a prospective missionary out for lunch just prior to his departure for overseas. As I got out of my seat to pay the bill, an audible whisper (from heaven) summoned me to give the missionary $500 to which I quickly replied, "no!" I mean, at that stage we only had about $3,000 in the bank and giving $500 would have made a massive dent. As I got close to the counter, again the summons, "Give $500," to which I replied, "$250." Upon getting to the counter, I heard again: "Give $500!" In this instance I had tried to bargain God down and it clearly was not working. As I paid the bill I reluctantly asked if I could also take out $500. They said no, which brought a huge sigh of relief from me. This was immediately expunged when they informed me that just around the corner was a bank. And so, with heavy

---

4. "Yeah nah" is a noncommittal way of saying "No."

5. Of this passage Terence Fretheim writes, "Human prayer (in this case, intercession) is honored by God as a contribution to a conversation that has the capacity to change future directions for God, people, and the world." See Fretheim, *Exodus*, 287. Similarly, John Goldingay notes that "God combines a capacity for planning and for serendipity, [and that] the biblical story as a whole suggests that God is more inclined to serendipity." See Goldingay, *Israel's Faith*, 165.

feet, I trudged up to the bank, withdrew the money, and far from being a cheerful giver, almost threw the envelope at the missionary.

The above conversations with God are verbal, loud, raw, and real. Paul, Jonah, Moses, and me in my own small way, are all having what can be termed an "argy-bargy" with God; where the pray-er is not afraid to launch into quarrelling and wrangling with God. The pray-ers express themselves, and so does God. We read of so many people in the Old and New Testaments who felt they could say and do whatever in God's presence or in the company of Jesus. This says something about the God we worship. God creates room for us to move.

These days, it is not uncommon to hear from God's people that their prayer lives are boring. Maybe we are too nice with God, too quiet, too mystical, too childlike, or too scared of God. Moses, Paul, and their ilk went to mature adulthood when praying. In no uncertain terms do they tell God what they think. They are not afraid to try and sell their ideas on God. They remind us that in our praying there can be times of shouting, protesting, crying, and pleading. As stated at the beginning of this chapter, there is the power of prayer but let there also be powerful prayers.

Two-Way Prayer

The encounters that Abraham, Moses, Jonah, and Paul had with God were two-way encounters. These men of God are not the only speakers; God responds and also communicates. In the case of the first three, God speaks first, but by no means stops there. In Paul's case, the apostle speaks up and then God replies. In fact, throughout the whole Bible, God is again and again communicating. God is very much a talker. And yet, these days God's people often say that they don't really hear God speaking to them. How shall we explain this? Some might posit that since we now have the written word in Scripture we do not need as much of God's spoken word in the context of conversation and prayer. Israel, however, while possessing their own written Scriptures, still experienced God regularly speaking to them.

At the time of writing this chapter, I have been enjoying Billy Graham's little memoir on old age and nearing death. Under a section titled "When God Speaks" Graham writes, "I have never heard the voice of the Lord audibly, but the Lord has spoken to me many times throughout my life."[6] He then recounts the many different ways God speaks in the Bible. The operative words here being *many* and *different*. This, too, can be our testimony! It can be a dream in the night, or a vision in the day. It may be an inaudible whisper, or a deep gut impression. One can also talk of being stirred up or even admonished by another person and then of course there are the angels. The Bible has over three hundred references to these angelic beings, and they, too, are messengers from God.

A Pathway Toward Intimate Prayer

What, then, might be the pathway to hearing from God and experiencing him more as a talker? Before continuing, let it be said that God is God, and as such, God can do whatever God chooses. But as noted above, God seems to be very responsive to our intercession, praying, and conversations. It is almost as though, when we turn up, not just at a certain time but more importantly as the person we are, God is there and responds. As we express ourselves, so does God. Talk and God will talk.

Rowan Williams, the former archbishop of Canterbury, in his book *Being Christian* has a section on praying where he draws from the writings of John Cassian, a fifth-century monk. Williams writes, "Prayer, he [Cassian] says, is a promise, a pledge: when I pray, I say to God, 'You're there for me: I am going to be here for you.'"[7]

Prayer begins with God. God is here. God desires us. God is for me. God has expressed this and more in Jesus Christ. If God is here and I am here we are here together. Further, I am going to be here for God. I am going to turn up, be fully present to the moment, and express myself, be it in shouting, tearful lament, protest, adoration, or intimate desire. And so begins the dance of reciprocity. Each responds in kind.

You (the reader) may be wondering what the first steps in this dance might be? An initial, small, but significant step is to capture your recent history and do some memory work. Think about the last two months. Pick out and name events and episodes that have caused angst, confusion, and anxiety. As you revisit those moments, I invite you to do your grief work. This is where you allow yourself to live again into the feelings of the remembered event or episode. Take your time here before moving to the next step. Set aside a time and place in each of your weeks where

---

6. Graham, *Nearing Home*, 73.
7. Williams, *Being Christian*, 75.

you can take the bits and pieces of your recent remembered past and express your thoughts and feelings to God. Because you work with recent events, the feelings are still raw and it is exactly this rawness that will enable you to be fully present to the moment when talking to God. All that is needed is for you to turn up and be real.

Jesus's instruction on prayer is to go into your room and shut the door (Matt 6:6). The room is to be a secret chamber, where you can be unashamed and almost say and do whatever you wish in Jesus's company.

Prayer is not something we do per se, it is someone we talk to and listen to—namely, Jesus. By way of one final next step, when face-to-face with Jesus, I imagine it so. This Jesus is not located in some distant corner of the universe. And nor is he in the next room. Rather, Jesus is as close as Jesus can be. With my imagination and with my mouth I utter the words, "I am here, you are here, we are here together." Theologically, heaven is not "up there" and earth "down here." Rather, heaven and earth are parallel dimensions. In this sense, heaven is right next to each one of us, and even though there is a veil between heaven and earth, which one day will be lifted, this King of heaven sees us, hears us, and in turn can whisper to us. When Jesus asks, "Are you ready for me?" I use the gift of Scripture that reminds me *where* Jesus is, and the gift of imagination to believe he is very near, as close as he can be.

Bibliography

Chant, Sarah. "Why Are New Zealanders Called Kiwis? (And Why You Shouldn't Eat a Kiwi!)" New Zealand Travel Tips, Jan. 9, 2023. https://nztraveltips.com/why-are-new-zealanders-called-kiwis/.

Fretheim, Terence E. *Exodus*. Interpretation: A Bible Commentary for Teaching and Preaching. Louisville: John Knox, 1991.

Galli, Mark. "Monomaniacs for God." *Christianity Today* 63 (2019). https://www.christianitytoday.com/2019/05/monomaniacs-for-god/.

Goldingay, John. *Israel's Faith*. Old Testament Theology 2. Downers Grove, IL: IVP Academic, 2006.

Graham, Billy. *Nearing Home: Life, Faith, and Finishing Well*. Nashville: Thomas Nelson, 2011.

Plantinga, Cornelius, Jr. *Not the Way It's Supposed to Be: A Breviary of Sin*. Grand Rapids: Eerdmans, 1995.

Williams, Rowan. *Being Christian: Baptism, Bible, Eucharist, Prayer*. Grand Rapids: Eerdmans, 2014.

15

Journaling Conversations with God

Robyn Mellar-Smith

Journaling is a popular spiritual tool that has been used by many generations to draw closer to God. It provides an opportunity to pause, reflect upon, and evaluate one's journey and to formulate new goals and visions. Devotional journaling often includes insights and reflections that surface from a person's spiritual readings, prayers, special moments of intimacy or encounters with God, and/or questions and wonderings. Historical journaling is used to document the lessons that were learned from life's journey. These journals are very personal and intimate in nature and commonly referred to as diaries. To record insights gained from listening to God's voice, prophetic dreams, or other revelatory experiences a person might want to practice revelatory journaling, and this chapter introduces us to a version of this kind of journaling.

Imagine you could ask God any of your questions and God responded with clear and understandable answers. Suppose you could write to God, share your thoughts, concerns, and wonderings, express your feelings, and vent your frustrations. And suppose that God would actually interact with you and offer you divine

> *perspectives and answers. This happened to Robyn Mellar-Smith and it can happen to you as you engage in the spiritual practice of journaling conversations with God. As you read through this chapter, we encourage you to put pen to paper and start your own dialogue with God.*

A Desire to Grow in My Faith

IN 2005, SOMEONE SUGGESTED that I start seeing a spiritual director as a way of strengthening and growing my faith in Christ. At that time, I was a busy home-schooling mother who had been endeavoring to follow Jesus Christ for about twenty years but was feeling stale in her faith. Jeanette Bakke, in her book *Holy Invitations*, writes that "spiritual direction is the name given to a particular kind of helping relationship whose primary objective is to discern how God is inviting someone to be, to live, to appreciate, and to act in the midst of life."[1] This spoke to me. I knew that I needed help discerning God's invitation to me, but I did not know where to start and how to go about it. So, the suggestion of having a companion on this journey, someone who was more mature in her or his faith in Christ, was very helpful.

The first spiritual director I visited was Sister Patricia. She was an elderly Catholic nun who had vast experience in companioning others and helping them to grow in their relationship with God. When we first met, she asked me to commit thirty minutes each day to the spiritual practice she would teach me; otherwise, she explained, she was not willing to become my spiritual director. I agreed to her terms and started the practice which I call "journaling conversations with God." This practice has totally revolutionized my life. In the same session Sister Patricia asked me what I did in my current devotional time or how I practiced "spending time with God." I replied that every day I read through a few chapters of the Bible, reflected on what I had read, and prayed for people. She said that while those spiritual practices were good, they must not be done in the thirty minutes that I was setting aside where I engaged in this new practice based on her instructions.

---

1. Bakke, *Holy Invitations*, 11.

Journaling Dialogues with God

Instead, Sister Patricia instructed me to sit in silence and solitude, light a candle, open my journal, say "Here I am, Lord," and then write down what I felt God was saying to me. A few months after I began this daily practice, people started to ask me what was going on in my life because they could see that I had changed. The people around me were noticing that my worship leading was more relaxed at church and that I was suddenly less performance oriented. At the same time as I was sitting in silence with God in this way, I was also reflecting on Scripture from the Ignatian perspective, and the Gospels came alive to me. My new journaling practice culminated in Jesus calling me into Baptist ministry. I shared about this sense of call first with my husband, then with my pastor, and with Carey Baptist College, when I applied to train there. Each of them affirmed the call of God on my life, that I had received through my journaling conversations with God. This enabled me to navigate moving our family to Auckland and completing a degree while working as an intern at a church. I then received a call to be the pastor of Epuni Baptist in Lower Hutt in 2009.

Could I have received the call to ministry if I had not been practicing these journaling conversations with God? I am sure that I could have; however, it would have been very difficult for me to believe in God's call on my life without hearing from God personally and directly via my journaling conversations.

Can anyone hear God through journaling conversations with him? I am not sure. There does seem to be a link between one's ability to hear God and the spiritual gifts described in 1 Cor 12:7–11. The Spirit gives gifts of words of wisdom, knowledge, and prophecy. Thus, the ability to hear from the Spirit in one's heart may be a gift that, if received, makes it easier to hear from God. Still, I also believe hearing from God can be practiced and, therefore, I encourage you to start journaling conversations with God and see where this journey might take you.[2]

Breaking Down the Practice into Easy Steps

I engage in this prayer practice first thing every morning when my mind is uncluttered and alive. I light a candle, give thanks to God for keeping

---

2. Jesus seems to encourage us to seek this. See John 10:27, "My sheep listen to my voice; I know them, and they follow me."

me through the night, and commit my time to God. Then, I open my journal, ask God to speak to me, and I write to God about whatever is on my mind. If I feel that he is speaking something back in my heart, I will write what I believe he says in quotation marks, to distinguish it from what I had said to him. Obviously, what I feel he says will often come from my own mind or soul and not from the Spirit, but I do not spend much time worrying about that initially. I simply write down what I think he is saying, as if I'm chatting to a friend, and at the end of the conversation, I review it.

Here is a recent example that might give you an idea of how this practice unfolds for me. As you will see, this is a particular conversation, pertaining to a specific time in my life. It is not a blanket instruction or model to follow for everyone, which is why I rarely share what I feel God is saying as any sort of teaching for anyone else.

Robyn: Thank you, dear Lord, for today.
Spirit of God: "Peace, Robyn."
Quiet space where I imagine myself sitting in his presence.
Spirit of God: "Stillness, child."
Robyn: Yes, Lord, I have been reading too many novels—using them as a form of hiding maybe?
Spirit of God: "Peace, child. Come back to you and me, Robyn."
Robyn: Yes, Lord.
I imagine us walking on the beach together.
Spirit of God: "Quiet, Robyn. The quiet will heal you, child."
Robyn: Yes, Lord. Thank You.
Spirit of God: "Peace, child."
Robyn: Peace, Lord.

As you see, I was not reflecting on Scripture in this interaction although I often do. I was stilling myself, sitting with an awareness of God's presence, speaking to him, and listening for his reply. I want to encourage you to just start somewhere. This practice has become easier for me over time, and I imagine it will be the same for you.

Hearing the Voice of God

How do I hear God? It is difficult to describe. It is not an audible voice in my ear. I quiet myself. I write what I am thinking and address it to God or formulate a question I have for God. As I am writing, a thought or image appears in my mind that seems to be a response to what I have written. There is no impersonal force grabbing my arm and making me write anything—it is more like a gentle whisper in my soul.[3] As mentioned before, I write down what I feel the Spirit of God is saying and enclose it in my conversation in quotation marks and then I respond myself to this in my writing. I do not overthink or complicate this process, but I do reject any voice that is contrary to Scripture. I also spend a reasonable amount of time sitting in quiet with God, and I have noticed that this amount of time has grown over the years.

I recommend regularly seeing a spiritual director while developing a practice like this, as trying to hear God's voice can be very subjective. Having said this, it is very important that a spiritual companion believes that it is possible to hear the Spirit of God in your heart today, as some do not hold to this belief. I was fortunate because Sister Patricia had trained in the Ignatian tradition and was fully convinced that God would speak to me in conversational prayer as I reflected on the Gospels and yes, God did.[4]

Anything that you hear needs to be compared to and aligned with Scripture since the Bible is our guideline here. For example, God would not tell you to kill someone or hurt someone. God is love and these actions are against God's nature. So, if a person heard such destructive words, it would not be God speaking but the person's own inner voice or some other interference from outside. You might ask how much the powers of darkness can interfere in such conversations (Eph 6:12)? I am not sure. I personally do not spend too much time worrying about that, but instead I try to focus on God as much as possible, trusting that God will help me to discern the voices I hear. I have found much more interference in these conversations from the critical voice inside my head than from any demonic forces.[5] It is impossible to outline in this chapter all aspects of learning to hear the voice of God.[6] My intention here is to describe a practice that has helped me immensely to grow in my personal faith in Christ and offer you some guidelines.[7]

3. See 1 Kings 19:12 for the place of a gentle whisper in the life of the prophet Elijah.

4. There are many good books on Ignatian spirituality. One that has been helpful to me on my prayer journey is Silf, *Landmarks*.

5. Emily Nagoski and Amelia Nagoski helpfully call this voice "the mad woman in the attic." See Nagoski and Nagoski, *Burnout*, 190–92.

6. For examples of good books on this topic, see Smith, *Voice of Jesus*, and Willard, *Hearing God*.

7. Other books that I have found useful in helping me reflect on what God might be saying to me are: Aronis, *Developing Intimacy with God*; Silf, *Landscapes of Prayer*;

I have found it important not to complicate matters and overthink trying to hear the Spirit of God. This practice has a lot to do with becoming still and calming down my hyperactive mind, and this takes time. If I am upset, my own mind often interferes too much, although this too has improved over time with practice. If I am startled by what I feel God is saying, or how what I might be hearing could affect the lives of other people, I will consult trusted friends about the content and actions I might take in response to it. But usually, I do not share the content of this intimate dialogue with others because it is largely a private matter between God and myself. Having said that, when I first started journaling my conversations with God, I did need some feedback from another spiritually minded person. In this time, I found that God spent a lot of time telling me how much he loved me. I was very sin-focused back then, and I thought I must have been mishearing God. Consequently, I phoned my pastor to describe what I felt I was hearing repeatedly. My pastor laughed and told me to continue with the practice and that this was exactly the sort of thing that God might say.

Reflecting on My Journey with the Practice

Over the years, I have found that God speaks to me mainly about my own heart, and by doing so he is drawing me closer to him. In Matt 6:5–6, Jesus explains to his disciples that the call to prayer is a private one, to be done mostly in secret. Some people have published their conversations with God. I respect that as their personal choice. However, I have found my dialogue with God to be very private and sacred and therefore decided that these conversations are not for the public eye.

In recent times, I have sometimes tried to draw what I feel God is saying. I use paper and crayons and have found that using images and colors in my journaling with God has enhanced and improved my ability to comprehend what God is saying. God's ways to communicate with us are so much bigger than anything we can imagine and there is always the possibility that I misunderstand what he is trying to tell me.[8] Many years ago, I attended Evangel Bible College at Gateway Christian Church in Hamilton, New Zealand. Pastor Don Barry was our lecturer, and he taught a course on hearing the voice of God. Don taught us that there are

---

Green, *Weeds Among the Wheat*; and Thibodeaux, *Reimagining the Ignatian Examen*.

8. See Isa 55:8–11.

three ways that we can misappropriate what God is saying.[9] First, we can mishear the original words. This is very easy to do as God is spirit and we are fallible human beings.[10] Second, we can misinterpret God's message. Think, for example, of the apostle Peter's vision in Acts 10:9–17 where Peter thought the vision was about impure and unclean food and to be taken in a literal way. Only later did he realize the symbolic meaning of the vision and understood that God has no favoritism but accepts people from every nation who fear him and do what is right. And third, we can apply what we hear wrongly. We can rush off and act in response to what we have heard, instead of waiting on God for more detailed instructions.

If it is so easy to misunderstand the message of God to our hearts, why then would we try to listen to God? I believe that we have a compassionate and loving God who consistently reaches out to us and wants to communicate and connect with every one of his children in many ways. When we listen to and then hear God's voice on a regular basis, we are constantly reminded that we are not alone, but rather that God loves each one of us and wants to make himself known to us. When we hear God's instruction and receive guidance and direction, both through reading his word and by hearing the whispers of his Spirit, we are more and more transformed into the image of God's Son, Jesus Christ. Practicing journaling conversations with God will not necessarily protect us from suffering nor stop us from experiencing difficult and challenging times. However, these daily conversations with God will increase our understanding that he is with us amidst our troubles and increase our trust, faith, and hope in the Bible's promises that God will work things together for good. As we submit to him, he will work things out for his glory (Rom 8:18–30).

Through the spiritual practice of journaling my conversations with God, which I have largely practiced daily since I first visited Sister Patricia, God has transformed my life. He has healed many emotional wounds, led me to train for ministry, and given me a felt sense of connection with him through very difficult times. Each one of us struggles with the feeling of being separate and alone. Being able to connect with God in this way each morning (and occasionally using the practice at other times of the day) has at times enabled me to feel and sense his presence strongly. Consequently, I have been able to relax more and know and trust God's

---

9. Don outlines these three as (1) Revelation, (2) Interpretation, and (3) Application. Don Barry, email to author, April 4, 2022.

10. Many Christ followers don't try to hear God's voice, because they are so fearful that they will get this wrong.

loving care, guidance, and provision. The more I trusted him, the more I was able to let go of my need to manipulate my circumstances and surroundings. I am more inclined these days to watch what God is doing.

Moreover, as God has faithfully spoken to me again and again, God has healed many of my personal wounds and dealt with my sins. God has also increased my awareness and understanding of myself and helped me to make sense of my protective patterns and reactions. Further, God has spoken to me about other people's actions and helped me to understand their motives and ways of relating. This has filled my heart with peace and made me less defensive. There is still work to be done but I am on the path of healing moving toward wholeness. Through very dark and difficult times, God's guidance that I have received and voice that I have heard through this practice has been like a rope that I have held onto and a rock in a stormy sea that I am grounded on. Having heard God's clear call on my life and his invitation to certain roles has helped me persevere when things got difficult. It has given me a sense of being in the right place at the right time even when the circumstances were challenging and messy.

A Final Word

There is a truism that we become what we repeatedly do. Our habits influence and shape our personal development and character. My life has been changed beyond measure through my daily practice of journaling conversations with God. As I sit in quiet with God each morning, write my thoughts to God, and record what I feel God is saying to me, my life continues to be transformed. This practice has given me a stronger sense of belonging to God, grown my character to be one exhibiting more fruits of the Spirit, and given me a sense of the Spirit's leading through the ups and downs of life. I am sure that this could be your experience, too. I encourage you to begin journaling your conversations with God.

Bibliography

Aronis, Alex B. *Developing Intimacy with God: An Eight-Week Prayer Guide Based on Ignatius' "Spiritual Exercises."* Milton Keynes, UK: 1stBooks, 2003.
Bakke, Jeannette A. *Holy Invitations: Exploring Spiritual Direction.* Grand Rapids: Baker, 2000.
Calhoun, Adele Ahlberg. *Spiritual Disciplines Handbook: Practices That Transform Us.* Downers Grove, IL: InterVarsity, 2005.

Green, Thomas H. *Weeds Among the Wheat: Discernment; Where Prayer & Action Meet.* Notre Dame: Ave Maria, 1984.

Nagoski, Emily, and Amelia Nagoski. *Burnout: The Secret to Unlocking the Stress Cycle.* New York: Ballantine, 2019.

Silf, Margaret. *Landmarks: An Ignatian Journey.* London: Darton, Longman & Todd, 1998.

———. *Landscapes of Prayer: Finding God in Your World and Your Life.* Oxford: Lion, 2011.

Smith, Gordon T. *The Voice of Jesus: Discernment, Prayer and the Witness of the Spirit.* Downers Grove, IL: InterVarsity, 2003.

Thibodeaux, Mark E. *Reimagining the Ignatian Examen: Fresh Ways to Pray from Your Day.* Chicago: Loyola, 2015.

Willard, Dallas. *Hearing God: Developing a Conversational Relationship with God.* Downers Grove, IL: InterVarsity, 2012.

16

Prophetic Listening and Discernment

A Practical Introduction to Hearing God's Voice

Tim Palmer

Many people know how to talk to God, thank God for the many blessings, express their feelings, share their concerns, and commit their own needs or requests for others into God's hands. However, when it comes to a dialogue, a two-way conversation, or to listening to God's voice, they struggle. God speaks to us in many different ways, but like young Samuel we often don't recognize God's voice and need to learn how to listen to our heavenly Father. True listening to God is connected to both a stance of openness, receptivity, and expectation, and the practice of discernment. In order to grow spiritually we need to learn to hear God's voice because only then can we know the mind of Christ and find transcendent wisdom which includes understanding, personal guidance, deeper knowledge, appropriate exhortation, and comforting consolation.

But how do we hear God's voice? How do we practice prophetic listening and how do we discern whether what we hear is truly from God? These are the questions that Tim Palmer discusses in this chapter as he introduces us to four simple and profound exercises in prophetic listening that encourage believers of all ages to hear God's voice and develop their listening skills as a regular spiritual practice. The second part of this chapter explores the topic of discernment regarding prophetic listening and considers not only individual but also collective practices.

Vocal Instability

MY ADOLESCENT YEARS PROVIDED many embarrassing moments. One day as I shouted my friend's name across the crowded school courtyard, my unstable pubescent voice warbled out of control like an untrained yodeler. I attracted much more than my friend's attention! There was nowhere to hide from the stares and laughter of onlooking peers. Embarrassing moments are not confined to the school grounds. In the church grounds also, I am reminded of loud, trembling "prophets" that have invited negative attention. In recent church history, rediscovered charismatic gifts like the gift of prophecy have attracted criticism and controversy, perhaps due to immaturity and inexperience. The underdeveloped prophetic voice with its familiar sounding phrase of "thus says the Lord" of those claiming to hear from God, has at times warbled out of control, to the embarrassment of the church body.

However, these awkward situations should not cause us to avoid prophetic activity. Instead, they ought to strengthen and improve our prophetic practices. As an evangelical who identifies with charismatic experiences, it is my conviction that the Trinitarian God still speaks to his people today, through a variety of different means, all of which are subject to the ultimate authority of Scripture.[1]

This chapter introduces a series of simple exercises in prophetic listening to develop the regular spiritual practice of listening to God for people of all ages. The second part of this chapter explores discernment, as we move from an individual focus toward collective practices. This includes criteria for discerning the validity (or otherwise) of a human interpretation of such divine experiences. These themes will be considered in regard to the Bible, particularly 1 Corinthians, church history,

---

1. This chapter assumes the continuing function of the gifts of the Holy Spirit and does not seek to defend this position against cessationist views. For helpful further discussion on this subject refer to Grudem, *Are Miraculous Gifts for Today*.

and contemporary practice. The goal of this chapter is to help identify safe parameters in which spiritual practices may be encouraged.

An Introductory Exercise for Children, Teenagers, and Adults

My journey to discovering God's voice began as an eight-year-old when my mother introduced me to a simple prayer-journal exercise. I was encouraged to read one chapter of the Bible each morning and then complete a set of prayer prompts.

Practical Exercise One

I invite you to pause here for a few minutes and try this simple prayer exercise for yourself:

- After reading a passage or chapter of the Bible, pause for a few minutes; reflect on the Scripture you have just read.
- Complete the following sentence starters with pen and paper:
    - Father God, I love you because . . .
    - I am sorry for . . .
    - Thank you for . . .
    - Please help me . . .
    - Today I am praying for (name of a person) . . .
    - Favorite Bible verse from my daily reading . . .
    - What are you telling me today?

Reflecting on Exercise One

These seven simple phrases help cultivate relationship with God. They include adoration and worship, confession, gratitude, petition, intercession, reading of, and listening to God's voice through Scripture. By introducing her children to this exercise, my mother wanted us to learn how to hear God's voice, expressing concern that it seemed difficult for many adult Christians. She wanted to normalize the experience of an authentic relationship with Jesus from a young age.

Since then, I have shared this practice in many church settings. Initially I introduced it to children, but soon discovered that adults needed this practice too. I still need it. There are many complex issues in life, theology, and church for us to wrestle with. Amidst this, we need to maintain the childlike simplicity of our relationship with Jesus.

Reading my childhood prayer notebooks is amusing. There are entries where the eight-year-old confessed that he was sorry for getting grumpy at Mum for making him go to bed early. He expressed remorse for hurting another classmate (sorry Joe!) and he prayed sincerely for his friends to discover Jesus. There are also some profound insights and truths that are beyond his developmental age. The interesting thing I noticed when I was rereading these prayer journals is that spiritual awakening occurred. My Bible reflections began to extend, the intercessory prayer lists grew, and the prophetic listening section expanded from sentences to paragraphs. God began to speak. Or perhaps, more accurately, God is always speaking but I was still learning how to listen to his voice and recognize it. Jesus reminds us that as his sheep we will hear his voice and know him. Prophetic listening begins with a simple, childlike posture of expectation that he is always reaching out to us and that we will hear the words of Jesus.

I intentionally began this chapter with the description of this spiritual practice of prophetic listening before delving into definitions and details. In my observation, an initial overemphasis on theory can detract from active growth. Our sincere desire to "get it right" by consuming more information can be a barrier to prophetic listening. However, both are essential. One helpful approach, therefore, as attempted in this chapter, is to weave together action and reflection for the expansion and deepening of understanding. Before we approach the next practical exercise, let us consider how the word *prophecy* could be understood in the church.

Prophecy in Hindsight

The word *prophecy* carries a vast array of both biblical and secular connotations. As the term prophecy is not exclusive to the Christian church, its definition is further complicated by association with mysticism of other religions, various cults, and other practices. In this chapter, the word prophecy is used in a very broad sense, with the general meaning of God's words expressed through humans. C. M. Robeck Jr. acknowledges several different aspects of prophecy, all of which are legitimate: "Prophecy has been alternatively identified as (1) an oracle, spontaneously inspired by the Holy Spirit, and spoken in specific situations; (2) a form of expositional preaching from a biblical text; or (3) a public pronouncement of a moral or ethical nature that confronts society."[2]

In the Old Testament God used prophets and the gift of prophecy to reveal his thoughts, plans, and purposes to his people. Old Testament prophets were considered to be God appointed and gifted by the Spirit.[3] Within their words we find several different categories of prophetic oracles such as indictment, judgment, instruction, and aftermath, as well as apocalyptic and messianic prophecies.[4] The majority of Old Testament prophecy is not primarily foretelling but "forth-telling of the will of God."[5] God's perspective on current issues was also presented as a way of transforming the nation by moving people toward repentance, worship, and social justice. However, it is also clear from Scripture that not all prophets were from God, hence the need for testing prophecies.

Although the Old Testament's example of prophecy conveys an important biblical backdrop, it does not provide an adequate model for the New Testament or for contemporary understanding. Jesus refers to John the Baptist as the last and greatest of the Old Testament era of prophets (Matt 11:9–17). He goes on to explain that the "least in the kingdom of heaven is greater than he" (v. 11), alluding to the vast implications of Christ's new covenant and the infilling of every believer with the Holy Spirit which happened at Pentecost after Jesus's death.

These profound words of Christ, along with the outpouring of the Holy Spirit at Pentecost, reshape the landscape of prophetic perspectives. Multitudes are now sharing sacred mountaintop moments. This New Testament understanding of prophets and prophecy is demonstrated through Paul's First Epistle to the Corinthians.

---

2. Robeck, "Prophecy, Gift of," 728.
3. See Deut 18:15–18; Zech 7:12; 1 Pet 1:21.
4. Walton and Hill, *Old Testament Today*, 238–42.
5. Vine et al., *Vine's Complete Expository Dictionary*, 492.

A Gift for All Believers in 1 Corinthians

Paul urges the Corinthians to "pursue love and strive for the spiritual gifts and especially that you may prophesy" (1 Cor 14:1 NRSVUE). His later comments indicate that this spiritual gift is available to every believer (vv. 5, 24, 31).[6] In 1 Corinthians, within the vital context of loving unity, prophecy is encouraged and corrected. Prophecy benefits individuals and the whole church by "upbuilding and encouragement and consolation" (v. 3 NRSVUE). Gordon Fee argues that these three words "set forth some parameters" indicating that prophecy primarily is "not the future, but the present situations."[7] The church is built up, unbelievers are convinced, and believers learn and are encouraged (vv. 5, 24–25, 31).

Other New Testament passages would indicate that the prophetic role is limited to some individuals.[8] The implied response to Paul's rhetorical "are all prophets" (1 Cor 12:29) question is no. At this point, Fee's insights are helpful as he makes a clear distinction, with prophets simply referring to "frequent speakers" of prophecies, while general prophecy is "potentially available to all."[9]

Paul's phrase that we can "all prophecy one by one, so that all may learn and all be encouraged" (1 Cor 14:31 NRSVUE) is like a personal invitation delivered from the pages of God's word. Believers of all time, including you and me, are urged to nurture this gift. It is consistent with the words of Jesus "my sheep hear my voice, . . . and they follow me" (John 10:27–28 NRSVUE).

As Jesus declares this, it is only natural to assume that if we hear his voice and speak those words, we are indeed speaking God's words. Hence, "all can prophesy." It is my conviction that this kind of prophetic encouragement is available, beneficial, and necessary for all believers. The practice of prophetic listening is simply taking time to hear God's words with the desire to share and encourage others. The next practical exercise encourages us to practice prophetic listening and recognize what God is saying through prophetic pictures and visions.

As a teenager, I was intrigued by Scripture's invitation to "eagerly desire" this gift of prophecy, and secondly by the idea that "all can prophesy." The famous Pentecost day proclamation from the prophet Joel,

---

6. This view may differ according to various definitions of prophecy.
7. Fee, *God's Empowering Presence*, 219.
8. Rom 12:6; 1 Cor 12:29–31; Eph 4:11.
9. Fee, *God's Empowering Presence*, 170, 244.

"Your sons and daughters will prophesy, your young men will see visions," echoed in my heart (Acts 2:17b). In my youthful naivete, I expected and anticipated that it would be normal to have prophetic words and visions. I can't recall the setting I first experienced an exercise like the following practical exercise, but I have developed it over the years and found it helpful in many settings.

Practical Exercise Two

This next practical exercise encourages us to practice prophetic listening and recognize what God is saying through prophetic pictures and visions. I invite you to pause for a few minutes and try this simple prayer exercise now.

- Close your eyes. Imagine Jesus walking into the room right now.
  - What is his appearance like? What kind of clothes is he wearing?
  - What is he doing?
  - What Scripture does it remind you of?
- Jesus walks toward you and stands in front of you, face-to-face.
  - What does it feel like to imagine yourself looking into his eyes?
- Imagine that he is holding something symbolic in his hand to give you.
  - What do you think Jesus wants to give you today?
  - What do you think Jesus would say to you in this moment?
- After visualizing this encounter with Jesus, you might want to pick up pen and paper or use your journal and write down the answers to the questions above.

Reflecting on Exercise Two

This exercise has often resonated well with children, teenagers, and visual learners. I have been profoundly moved by the way God has spoken to individuals through engaging in this exercise. One young person in her teenage years (now training to be a doctor) first felt compelled to pursue medicine after God had spoken clearly to her at an Easter camp. An adult was moved to tears as, for the first time, they sensed Jesus simply say they were loved and forgiven. A teenager approached me after a youth service to let me know that Jesus had told them to step back from an unhealthy relationship. Some shared different ways Jesus had been revealed to them personally, as a gentle shepherd, as a radiant king, as a suffering savior, as a healer, and as a friend. There were visions of one who holds hearts, preserves tears, lifts our burdens, provides an undistorted mirror, erases sin, repaints a masterpiece that was damaged, carries a compass to navigate difficulty. Words and pictures were received that nobody else had prompted. For many people, these have been life-transformative encounters with Jesus.

Prophecy and Discernment

Experiences like the ones described above can be encouraged and nurtured. At the same time, these moments of insights and encounters with God raise some questions: How much authoritative weight should these experiences carry? What biblical boundaries are offered? And how do we determine the validity, or otherwise, of a subjective prophetic experience? It is therefore important to consider some discernment guidelines alongside prophetic listening.

In 1 Corinthians, prophecy is to be "eagerly desire[d]" (14:1) but all things should be conducted "decently and in order" (14:40 NRSVUE), which involves discerning or weighing what is said (14:26–29). Earlier in the epistle (12:10) the gift of prophecy seems to be "paired" with the gift of discernment of spirits.[10] Although Paul provides no clear indication here of how to test the spirits, David Garland in his commentary lists seven criteria that could be inferred from the wider context of discussion within 1 Corinthians: the tradition of Jesus; the preaching of Christ crucified; Scripture as interpreted through Christ; the apostles' teaching; sacrificial love; the promotion of healthy community; preventing others from stumbling; leading outsiders to faith.[11] We could apply these same questions to our prophetic listening practices.

---

10. Fee suggests that discernment in 1 Cor 12:10 is linked with and explained by the instructions in 1 Cor 14:26–29. Fee, *God's Empowering Presence*, 171.

11. Garland, *1 Corinthians*, 664.

In a related passage, the Thessalonian church is also urged not to "despise" prophecy (1 Thess 5:19–21 NRSVUE) but rather to test it. Paul advises to "hold fast to the traditions" (2 Thess 2:15 NRSVUE), or in other words, doctrinal soundness.[12] In light of this, our prophetic listening experiences should be consistent with sound doctrine.

A thorough examination of these issues is provided by Wayne Grudem, who makes a distinction between the general potential of all believers to prophesy and those who regularly fulfil this function as "prophets."[13] Grudem parallels Old Testament prophets who spoke "God's very words" with the canonical words of the apostles of Christ.[14] Those words were authoritative to the extent that they became part of Scripture. However, a "prophet" in the New Testament church or contemporary setting *does not* equate with "one who speaks God's very words" with the weight of scriptural authority.[15] General prophecy, which would include our prophetic listening practices, would be distinguished as "human words to report something God brings to mind."[16] This helpful explanation ensures that we do not overemphasize or elevate our experiences inappropriately.

Prophecy and Discernment in Church History

Similar concerns have led to the development of discernment practices over the centuries.[17] Historical figures such as Montanus, Priscilla, and Maximilla had begun to claim that their prophetic revelations came directly from the Spirit and were superior to Scripture in significance. Understandably, these were anathematized by the church who became increasingly suspicious of spiritual gifts.[18] By the fourth century and onward, the practice of spiritual gifts within the church appears to have diminished significantly, though there were some notable exceptions such as St. Francis of Assisi, Vincent Ferrer, and Francis of Paola. These

---

12. Fee, *God's Empowering Presence*, 61.
13. Grudem, *Gift of Prophecy*, 161–81.
14. Grudem, *Gift of Prophecy*, 27–33.
15. Grudem, *Gift of Prophecy*, 40.
16. Grudem, *Gift of Prophecy*, 71.
17. Collins, *Gifts of the Spirit*, 92–93.
18. Collins, *Gifts of the Spirit*, 93.

luminaries were also reported to have practiced some form of prophecy and miraculous signs.[19]

The desert fathers had developed a discernment framework, modelled on the temptations of Jesus.[20] This discernment heritage was later further developed in the Western church and enabled the church to discern orthodoxy from heresy.[21] After the Reformation, discernment practices primarily centered on doctrine. However, questions of spiritual discernment were aroused again during the eighteenth- and nineteenth-century revivalist movements such as the Holiness movement in Methodism, the Great Awakenings, and Pentecostalism.[22] There was an increasing focus on outward signs of grace that could be attributed to the work of the Holy Spirit. Jonathan Edwards, for example, identified five "positive signs" including: recognition of Jesus Christ as Savior, repentance, increased regard of Scripture, conviction of Christian truth, and greater love for God and others.[23] This development highlights our need to recognize Christ-like living as a goal of spiritual experience. Prophetic listening should encourage and lead toward Christ-like character and action.

A healthy emphasis on Christ-like character has developed in Pentecostal and charismatic movements, such as those presented by Michael Sullivant in his book *Prophetic Etiquette*. Within the context of prophetic ministry, Sullivant devotes entire chapters to the subjects of love, integrity, humility, and compassion. He urges believers to engage in solid biblical and theological training, whereby experience is "pulled through the grid of orthodox theology."[24]

Another Vineyard pastor, James Ryle, presents a threefold test for discerning prophecy: the Lordship of Jesus Christ, the Bible, and the fruit of the Spirit.[25] He instructs that the theme or spirit of a prophetic message must always glorify Christ (John 16:13–15; 1 Cor 12:3; 1 John 2:22–23), be subject to the final authority of Scripture (2 Tim 3:1–17; Heb 4:12), and produce evidence of the Holy Spirit's transforming work (Gal 5:22–23). We will apply some of these concepts in our next practical prophetic listening exercise.

19. Collins, *Gifts of the Spirit*, 98–106.
20. Yong, "Discernment, Discerning the Spirits," 232.
21. Yong, "Discernment, Discerning the Spirits," 233.
22. Yong, "Discernment, Discerning the Spirits," 233–34.
23. Yong, "Discernment, Discerning the Spirits," 234.
24. Sullivan, *Prophetic Etiquette*, 150–52.
25. Ryle, *Hippo in the Garden*, 220–26.

As my prayer life developed through journaling, I began to write with a four-colored pen. My personal notes and prayers were handwritten in blue, and I changed color to black to write the words I sensed God was saying to me. As I devoted more time to prophetic listening, I utilized the two remaining colors. Green became a record of visions and pictures, and I used the red pen to write prophetic words for other people. Initially, the purpose of a color-coded journal was to help me find things more easily. However, I noticed a difference in my approach to prayer when I clicked my red pen. The simple stance helped shift my focus outward. I encourage you to spend some time now and do the following simple exercise.

Practical Exercise Three

Use a red pen to write down any prophetic words you receive as you listen to God on behalf of another person. The following questions will help you with this exercise:

- Holy Spirit, who would you like me to write to today?
- How do you want me to encourage, build up, or comfort that person?
- What Bible verse are you prompting for that person?
- What prophetic word or picture would you like me to share?
- How does this align with the truth of God's word?

Reflection on Exercise Three

Discernment based on a solid biblical framework is inseparable from prophetic listening because it is necessary to assess our subjective experiences. Notice that simple discernment practices can be built into the way we frame our basic spiritual practices. The biblical framework of encouragement, building up and comforting, prompting specific Scripture, and seeking alignment between prophetic impressions and God's truth are all important assessment tools. In this way, healthy discernment practices can be nurtured alongside and within our introductory prayer practices.

Another alternative perspective could be that discernment becomes a complex task and is an exercise for trained theologians. While this high-level perspective of discernment may be necessary for determining doctrine it may have a stifling or intimidating effect on those who want to embark on a journey of prophetic listening. Hebrews 5:14 describes a more accessible natural development of discernment, likened to a baby growing into adulthood. "Solid food is for the mature, who by constant use have trained themselves to distinguish good from evil." This seems to assume that all believers start off as beginners, with the potential to develop their spiritual senses toward maturity through practice and learning, whereby all can become competent at discernment.

Outward Facing Discernment

This third practical exercise also seeks to encourage others through an outward facing dimension to our prophetic listening. Similarly, discernment can include a proactive approach to doing God's work in our world. Kirsteen Kim considers discernment to be "the first act of mission," whereby we recognize the ongoing missional work of the Spirit and subsequently participate in that mission.[26] In my opinion, this view marks a significant feature that has been neglected in many discussions on the topic of discernment. It helpfully shifts the attention of spiritual activity (including experience and the shaping of doctrine) from an inward focus (both individually and within the church) toward an outward focus of the greater mission of God for which the Holy Spirit has anointed us. A proactive approach to discernment encourages an ongoing openness to the Holy Spirit's guidance, which we will explore further in the next prophetic listening exercise.

Human and Prophetic Words

Another important factor to consider in this discussion is the human element of spiritual gifts. Nigel Wright wrote that discernment has "as much to do with careful thought and theological analysis as with inspired guesses and sudden intuitions."[27] He does not necessarily view the human influence of prophecy negatively, acknowledging that the "product of careful thought and analysis" may be equally prophetic as spontaneous spiritual intuition.[28] Legitimate prophetic models may therefore present

---

26. Kim, "How Will We Know," 96. Kim attributes this to liberation theologian Samuel Rayan.
27. Wright, "Rise of the Prophetic," 122.
28. Wright, "Rise of the Prophetic," 120.

a range in style from Martin Luther King Jr. to Paul Cain, right through to an eight-year-old child using a prayer journal. This also reflects the Lukan idea of the "spirit of prophecy," as described by Max Turner, referring to a broader range of gifts including pastoral preaching, evangelization, glossolalia, dreams, visions, and wisdom.[29] From this balanced perspective, both the "supernatural" charismatic style of prophecy and the more conservative "natural" understanding of prophecy as prepared proclamation can be brought into the same discussion.[30] Another implication for our prophetic listening exercise is that general prophecy can be delivered in various forms and contain a combination of elements that are natural and supernatural, prepared and spontaneous, pondered and inspired.

These considerations can contribute to our view of discernment, as the framework for discernment is connected to our understanding of prophecy. Instead of striving to weigh up the divine, we see ourselves as humans identifying and endorsing the divine component of a message. Recognizing our active human participation in prophecy rightfully relegates the inflated authority of prophetic words. By simply acknowledging the human dimension of prophecy, we immediately resolve many contemporary problems. This is especially important where the divine aspect of prophecy has been exaggerated with absolute statements such as "Thus saith the Lord."

The prophetic voice stabilizes with maturity. For the prophetic listening practices, we do not need to stress about whether our impressions are divine or human or a mixture of both. But rather, as human beings, we celebrate moments that resonate with God's Spirit at work. With all of these ideas in mind, prophecy could be viewed less as a divine interruption of human activity, and more as a regular interaction of human and divine activity.

Practical Exercise Four

Consider the idea of prophecy as divine interaction with human activity, and Kirsteen Kim's perspective of discernment as the first act of outward mission. Then use your pen and paper to respond to the following questions:

---

29. Turner, *Holy Spirit and Spiritual Gifts*, 212.

30. Also see Fee's discussion on "teaching" and "prophecy" in Fee, *God's Empowering Presence*, 225.

- Father, Son, and Holy Spirit, where have I seen evidence of your activity recently?
- How are you calling me to move to join that work?
- What do you want me to hear or learn from that activity?
- Is there something you are calling me to say to encourage that work?
- What practical task are you inviting me to do to share in that work?

This exercise could be done as an individual, or as a collective discernment process in a church group.

Renewed Mission

God's voice moves us toward his mission. Prophetic listening enables prophetic action. Discernment, as Kim urges, "requires wide horizons—in view of the breadth of the Spirit's mission, openness—because of the unpredictability of the Spirit's movements, and humility—since the Spirit is the Spirit of Almighty God."[31] As we normalize prophetic gifts, we embrace the possibility of the supernatural activity of the Holy Spirit working through the natural, willing activity of human participation in God's mission.

Conclusion

Prophetic listening as a spiritual practice seeks to introduce and develop the gifts of prophecy and discernment to followers of Jesus of all ages. Prophetic gifts are to be eagerly desired and healthy discernment criteria provide a safe context where the Spirit is listened to and nurtured at all ages. These gifts can be used for individual prayer, personal prophetic encouragement, collective discernment, and outward-facing mission. Through the exercises listed above, prophetic voices that once wavered with immaturity can mature through healthy discernment practices.

A typical goal for discernment is to determine the validity or accuracy of a human interpretation of a divine experience. Therefore, basic scrutiny is required: does the prophetic word edify, encourage, comfort, and move those who hear it toward unity and the fruits of the Spirit? Does it glorify Jesus and testify to his lordship? Is it consistent with the teaching of the Bible?

---

31. Kim, "How Will We Know," 94–95.

A new perspective on prophecy and discernment also readily accepts the reality of human influence on prophecy. We are granted permission to acknowledge the limitations, faults, and immaturity of human endeavor, while at the same time affirming the recognizable work of the Holy Spirit. The question of discernment turns from "Is this valid?" toward "What is the Holy Spirit doing?" In doing so, the flame of prophecy is released from the overly mystical realm of occasional divine interjection for the exclusive few. Like tongues of fire, prophecy is now resting upon lives and lips in the everyday experience of all believers.

A childlike listener now stands on the mountaintop with Moses. The prayer journal of the juvenile dances in the language of deliverance with Miriam. Modern-day prophetic poets linger in the palace with David. Sons and daughters are hearing and speaking God's words as the mission of the church is restored. All flesh embodies the words and work of the risen Christ as the Spirit is poured out. Words reform action as God's people are renewed with bold expression of the gospel. Each of these prophetic words are understood as God's message spoken through humans. All of this happens as we take time to listen.

Bibliography

Collins, Pat. *The Gifts of the Spirit and the New Evangelisation*. Dublin: Columba, 2009.
Fee, Gordon D. *God's Empowering Presence: The Holy Spirit in the Letters of Paul*. Peabody, MA: Hendrickson, 1994.
Garland, David E. *1 Corinthians*. Baker Exegetical Commentary on the New Testament. Grand Rapids: Baker Academic, 2003.
Grudem, Wayne, ed. *Are Miraculous Gifts for Today? 4 Views*. Counterpoints. Grand Rapids: Zondervan, 1996.
———. *The Gift of Prophecy in the New Testament and Today*. Rev. ed. Wheaton, IL: Crossway, 2000.
Kim, Kirsteen. "How Will We Know When the Holy Spirit Comes? The Question of Discernment." *Evangelical Review of Theology* 33 (2009) 93–96.
Penney, John. "The Testing of New Testament Prophecy." *Journal of Pentecostal Theology* 5 (1997) 35–84. https://doi.org/10.1177/096673699700501003.
Robeck, C. M., Jr. "Prophecy, Gift of." In *The New International Dictionary of Pentecostal and Charismatic Movements*, edited by Stanley M. Burgess and Eduard M. van der Maas, 728–40. Grand Rapids: Zondervan, 1988.
Ryle, James. *The Hippo in the Garden: Hearing the Voice of God in the 21st Century*. Guildford, UK: Highland, 1992.
Sullivant, Michael. *Prophetic Etiquette: Your Complete Handbook on Giving and Receiving Prophecy*. Lake Mary, FL: Creation House, 2000.
Turner, Max. *The Holy Spirit and Spiritual Gifts: Then and Now*. Carlisle, UK: Paternoster, 1996.

Vine, W. E., et al., eds. *Vine's Complete Expository Dictionary of Old and New Testament Words*. Nashville: Thomas Nelson, 1997.

Walton, John H., and Andrew E. Hill. *Old Testament Today: A Journey from Original Meaning to Contemporary Significance*. Grand Rapids: Zondervan, 2004.

Wright, Nigel. "The Rise of the Prophetic." In *Charismatic Renewal: The Search for a Theology*, edited by Tom Smail et al., 117–22. London: SPCK, 1995.

Yong, Amos. "Discernment, Discerning the Spirits." In *Global Dictionary of Theology: A Resource for the Worldwide Church*, edited by William A. Dyrness and Veli-Matti Kärkkäinen, 232–35. Downers Grove, IL: IVP Academic, 2008.

17

Prayer

A Near-Death Experience

Sam Burrows

In the book New Seeds of Contemplation, *which is one of the great spiritual classics of our century, Thomas Merton writes, "If we could let go of our own obsession with what we think is the meaning of it all, we might be able to hear [God's] call and follow Him in His mysterious cosmic dance."[1] Relating this quote to the topic of prayer, we could say that if we could only let go of our ideas and preconceptions of what prayer is or is not, we might be able to truly dialogue with and encounter God and have a profound experience of the union we were created for. At times we need an experience of spiritual awakening to initiate this process of relinquishing previous understandings, practices, and versions of prayer. Such an awakening can remove the veil that clouds our vision and help us experience God's presence.*

In this chapter, Sam Burrows shares his own story of spiritual awakening, which resulted in the transformation of his prayer life. It describes a path that goes beyond traditional forms of prayer and allows God to become what we most desire.

---

1. Merton, *New Seeds of Contemplation*, 296.

> All of a sudden we just know: prayer is a conversation
> in which God's word has the initiative and we, for the
> moment, can be nothing more than listeners.
>
> —Hans Urs von Balthasar[2]

Near the end of Chuck Palahniuk's acclaimed 1996 novel, *Fight Club*, the narrator finds himself in the passenger seat of a car. The driver of the vehicle begins to deliberately swerve into oncoming traffic with the intention of bringing the passengers into a heightened sense of their own mortality. The threat of death is presented to them as they repeatedly experience narrow misses, headlights filling up the windshield time after time. As he approaches a head-on collision with a truck, the driver demands that everyone in the car answers his question: "What will you wish you'd done before you died?" "We've got five seconds to oblivion," he informs them, and the rest of the car quickly produces answers like "Ride a horse," "Build a house," and "Get a tattoo."[3] In these frantic seconds, the narrator evaluates his life and sees it with a new clarity. He realizes how much time he had wasted and how much attention he had given to meaningless pursuits like the continuous acquisition of furniture and home decor. The full car swerves away from the truck just in time, and it eventually makes its way into a ditch on the side of the road. The narrator wakes up twisted on the floor but with a fresh understanding of how alive he really is. "You had a near-life experience," the driver informs him in the wake of the experience.[4]

There is something mystical about the breakthrough into clarity that Palahniuk is trying to describe. In moments like this, where our existence is shown to be as fleeting and fragile as it really is, we are jolted into a clear blue sky about what is *really* important to us. Near-death experiences are therefore near-life experiences: we get close to what it really means to be alive, close enough to stare it full in the face. These moments are profoundly pedagogical on an existential level if we let them speak to us like this. There is something powerfully animating about confronting oneself with both the fragility and miracle of our existence.

2. Balthasar, *Prayer*, 15.
3. Palahniuk, *Fight Club*, 145.
4. Palahniuk, *Fight Club*, 148.

Among other themes, *Fight Club* is a narrative that rages against the somewhat numb and zombie-like acceptance of our day-to-day lives, where we find ourselves caught up in rituals and routines with their comforting familiarity. It is a book that reminds us that we often reduce and narrow the mystery of life to aspects such as furniture preferences and career advances. In *Fight Club*, Palahniuk protests against the systems and habits that keep us asleep, albeit in an aggressive and often nihilistic fashion. It might seem bizarre to begin a chapter on prayer with this dark, anarchistic nineties novel, but there is a fundamental awakening experience described here that I think is similar to what is at the heart of prayer.

Like many spiritual practices, prayer can become banal, repetitive, and frustrating. The familiarity of something as simple as prayer can often cause us to forget what we are actually stepping into when we engage in prayer. To pray is nothing short of opening ourselves up to the deepest and truest of realities. Since God knows us better than we know ourselves, since he created us and is familiar with all aspects of our being there is no point in presenting a façade or public self to him. Prayer is an intimate and real engagement with our Maker. When we pray, we commune from the deepest, most authentic, and truest part of our being with a God who is real. There is nothing false in him. To pray is to snap out of autopilot and inhabit this part of ourselves where we are fully known and safely held by God at the core of our being.

At its best, when we pray we see life for what it really is: a profound experience of grace and givenness. Our very existence is a gift. Prayer thus is the closest actuality we have to a near-death experience, because just like near-death experiences, praying brings us into contact with that which is most real and most alive within us. As we pray, we meet God as the Trinitarian life force pulsating at the core of everything. This realization has helped me to move out of a sense of obligation around prayer into a profound sense of wonder. My aim for this short chapter is simply to give you as the reader fresh language for the vivifying experience of prayer. It is my hope that you taste something of the awe-inspiring aspect of prayer for yourself.

My Experience

This shift in my thinking around prayer came about in an unexpected way and was something that I kind of stumbled upon. I had a challenging experience of the late-2021 Auckland COVID lockdown. As it dragged on, it became harder and harder for me not only to find energy to keep working, but also feel any sense of positivity. Through the isolation I felt depleted as every day seemed to blur into the next. Routine and discipline became nearly impossible and the thought of taking the needs of others into consideration on top of this was almost too much.

I felt totally depleted, and prayer therefore did not seem to be a viable option. Why should I try something that was bound to frustrate me even more and make me feel like more of a failure? I was just hanging in there by a thread and enduring. It was as if I was running up a hill and just had to put my head down and push through until this lockdown was over. In such a demanding time prayer was not a good match for a cynical and exhausted person like me—it was a practice suitable for a far more advanced saint. It felt like something done by those who knew how to thrive, not by someone who was simply holding on for dear life. And so, I continued to tick off the days as they passed, feeling half-dead rather than alive. In this phase I did not believe I could experience anything more than this. I had given up hoping for more.

My situation changed toward the end of the lockdown period. In a very mysterious and personal way God invited me to pray. It happened as I was listening to a podcast where one of my favorite preachers explained his morning routine, which consisted of reading a short passage of Scripture, spending some time in contemplation, and praying for others. As I listened to this podcast it was as though the speaker reminded me that things could actually be different and that there was much more for me to experience. Praying was a simple and joyful part of his every day life. In response to the podcast, I decided to give this practice a go.

In a very low-key fashion, I began to set aside a little space for God each day, usually as I was eating breakfast. It was nothing radical or impressive. I just read a short Bible passage and prayed for a few minutes. I also created a little list of people to pray for and just kept at it for a few days. Consequently, I found that I gave more attention to the state of my heart and to the character of God. As I made space within me to consider and love others, everything began to shift. First, a desire emerged to do more than just survive each day. Hope that there could be more than my current bland experience arose within me. I also wanted to know God at a much deeper level and commune with him in the difficulties I encountered. I began to believe that this was possible.

As I drew closer to God and trusted him in this process, God began to show me aspects within myself that I had allowed to gnaw at me and keep me inward looking and self-focused. I learned to differentiate faster and with greater ease between truth and lies. Rather than pushing down unpleasant feelings I entered into a dialogue with my fears and anxieties with the hope of this process leading to healing. Again and again God met me at my deepest level and revealed to me that I could trust him, I was safely held in his hands, and there was no need to control my life anymore. This realization resulted in some incredibly powerful experiences of forgiveness and grace. I had found something that was deeper than my own self-definition and had come to know more of what it means to be in Christ. I had learned anew, and in quite visceral ways, that nothing could take this new reality away from me as it was a gift and not caused by an act of my will or my own understanding.

The most profound result of this experience was that my eyes had been miraculously opened to the glory of the people around me, past and present. As I gently explored areas of grief that I had suppressed in my own life, God's Spirit illuminated for me a much greater spectrum and depth of relating to others. I was shown the beauty and glory in others that I had missed and, in a way, that I had never known before. My life itself totally changed through my communion with God. I suddenly saw with new eyes that all of life was grace. Instead of seeing prayer as something that was adjacent to or removed from life, it now became the means to see the reality and glory of life all around me. As I listened to the One who always speaks truth and beholds the world in love, my eyes could perceive the purest and truest version of everything. I was learning to see the world a little more as God does, and prayer became the place of entering more fully into life as it was intended to be. My previous understanding that prayer somehow took me away from experiencing life turned into the revelation that prayer is the space where new perspectives come into view and where I truly see what is real.

I had known all of this in my head, but suddenly I was experiencing it, and it was almost too overwhelming at times. As I let the Spirit speak, I heard reminders of joy. At times, God seemed to fill my heart with love for particular people. Frederick Buechner uses some beautiful language for this recognition. He instructs his reader,

> Listen to your life. See it for the fathomless mystery it is. In the boredom and pain of it, no less than in the excitement and gladness: touch, taste, smell your way to the holy and hidden heart

of it, because in the last analysis all moments are key moments, and life itself is grace.[5]

My prayer life changed drastically for me. I was no longer seeing it as something to do, but a way to reach something else, or *someone* else. I had tasted something that had given gravity and meaning to everything else. Life was suddenly vivid in its resolution and "fierce with reality."[6] Naturally, I wanted to stay as close as possible to this way of seeing and not lose sight of it. I had seen God's heart of love and learned that all is sacred because it was loved by the ultimate Other. Unlike my previous narrow-minded view of life that was conditioned by lenses of obligations and despair, I was now seeing everything in new dimensions. The best of life was continually unfolding around me, and the only logical and appropriate response to it was gratitude and praise. Prayer was no longer a task to complete, but a way of being. It became the path to stay close to the One who always takes me to new depths in understanding and keeps my eyes open to the miracle of existence. Inviting the Spirit to speak was no longer a chore, but rather an adventure and a refusal to settle for anything less than the best.

Spiritual writers like Hans Urs von Balthasar have long been describing prayer in these terms. In his book *Prayer* Balthasar writes,

> Man is the creature with a mystery in his heart that is bigger than himself. He is built like a tabernacle around a most sacred mystery. . . . To the never-ending joy and amazement of those who pray—man's ineffable relationship to the word of God is always two things at once: an entering-in to the innermost "I", and the turning-outward of this I to the highest "Thou." . . . Just as the part loves the whole more than itself, and loves itself most when it does so in the whole and not in its particularity, the created "I" loves and affirms itself at the deepest level by loving God's absolute, free "I" that manifests itself to him in the Word.[7]

I had certainly been shown more of my "innermost 'I'" as I had encountered the "highest 'Thou.'" I had not lost my life in a sacrificial, transactional sense, I had gained another quality of life altogether. My simple thesis here is this: prayer is the mechanism that allows us to embrace life in its fullness, because in prayer we attend to God who spoke and

---

5. Buechner, *Now and Then*, 87.
6. Scott-Maxwell, quoted in Palmer, "Fierce with Reality," para. 3.
7. Balthasar, *Prayer*, 22–23.

continues to speak life into being. Prayer is not just a spiritual exercise; it is the very way to get close and transformed by God. Prayer allows us to apprehend all of reality in an open, undefended way: in love. Prayer is communing with the Triune God through the Spirit who continually shows us new depths of what it means to be truly alive. While a classic near-death experience may indeed snap us out of our sleepwalking through life and bring everything into sharp focus, it really can only reveal what we already know but so often forget. Prayer goes further. Prayer is an act of hope through which we meet a God who always has more to offer and show us. It leads to an understanding of the mystery that runs through all of reality and speaks of him who holds it all together. Henri Nouwen describes it in the following words:

> When we learn to descend with our mind into our heart, then all those who have become part of our lives are led into the healing presence of God and touched by him in the centre of our being. We are speaking here about a mystery for which words are inadequate. It is the mystery that the heart, which is at the centre of our being, is transformed by God into his own heart, a heart large enough to embrace the entire universe.[8]

The popular concept of prayer is a pretty inoffensive one today. Usually folded under the larger category of spiritual practices, it can be lined up alongside contemplation, meditation, and mindfulness. In this sense, prayer is easily construed as something in which human beings are the primary agents and as something that is done as part of a self-care scheme and for its therapeutic benefits such as centeredness, inner calm, and a feeling of connectedness. But there is much more to prayer than this. Prayer brings us into contact with our Creator and the ultimate Other. We are not simply paying attention to our inner worlds but entering into dialogue with the very ground of all being and the source and life of all things. We are participating in the communion of the three persons within the Trinity. We are joining into this most amazing conversation. We are invited to hear the heartbeat that is at the center of the cosmos, and the whispers between the Father, Son, and Spirit. We are embraced here by the deepest form of reality. This is a truly staggering mystery! Prayer seen in this way is always too big for us and something we consistently grow into.

---

8. Nouwen, *Way of the Heart*, 87.

Theologian Kevin Vanhoozer defines prayer against therapeutic spirituality and inwardness, saying that true contemplation is "not, 'I think therefore I am' . . . but '*Here* I am!'"[9] It is not primarily something we do toward God, but it is about humans "*being spoken to* and their capacity to *speak back*."[10] It is communing with that which is so utterly other, holy and beyond us, yet at the same time so loving, so available and so for us.

Looking Again at Transfiguration

One of the most remarkable passages of Scripture that illustrates this understanding of prayer is Matthew's account of the transfiguration of Jesus (Matt 17:1–11). The experiences of the disciples in this account show us what it means to commune with God in a profound way. Jesus takes Peter, James, and John up a mountain and suddenly begins to shine with an unfathomable radiance. The glory which was so often hidden in him was made apparent in this moment in a very dramatic way. Incredibly, he is joined by Moses and Elijah; the Law and the Prophets became subservient to him. They are covered by a bright cloud and God speaks from this cloud, commanding them all to listen to his son. The disciples are rightly terrified and fall to the ground, which is the correct response. They are filled with fear, not because they believe God will destroy them in his fury, but because they are confronted by how different and beyond them all of this is. They are so overwhelmed with the glory and presence of God that it is all too much for them. Peter, James, and John are echoing the responses of many in the Old Testament that had similar experiences. People who encounter God realize just how out of their depth they are. They fathom how much they do not belong in the presence of something so far out of their own category of being that they want to cease existing in that space of intensity. Their beings cannot hold the enormity of the One who has made himself known to them.

But then Jesus touches them and says, "Don't be afraid" (v. 7). With this, Jesus is doing more than just reassuring them. He is reminding them that while their experience has shown them something deeply true about the beyond-ness of God, he is *for* them. Jesus is the bridge that allows us to know the unknowable, comprehend the incomprehensible, and put

---

9. Vanhoozer, *Remythologizing Theology*, 318.
10. Vanhoozer, *Remythologizing Theology*, 319.

language to that which cannot be articulated. The mystery has a name, God has a face, and we humans can now speak of that which we never could speak of with our own limited capacities. When you close the door and begin to pray, you are, by grace, entering into communion with this God. He has made it possible for mere humans, flesh and blood, people made from dust to be in his presence. Prayer is a miracle.

Will We Answer the Call?

Before God opened my eyes to these new insights and revelations, I had only experienced this sort of seeing in short bursts. I did not know it was something you could cultivate. Prayer had been hard work and always felt like an endurance sport. Before this encounter with God, I would never have agreed with this sentiment that you can truly commune with God and I certainly did not agree with it theologically. Nevertheless, this is how I felt. In the past my prayers were sporadic. On a functional level, I did not believe I was really communing with God. I was addressing God, asking of God and petitioning God, but I was not really opening myself up to an encounter with God. Prayer for me then was only a discipline, not a joy. I was sending spiritual smoke signals up to the sky that got no reply. I was somewhat hoping that they were seen and understood by a deity but I did not believe that God would actually listen to my prayers and respond.

My prayer times now are very different. They are special and full of expectation. I now start my prayer by first lighting a large candle and then lighting a small one to remind myself that all that I am rests on all that Christ is. I then listen to songs that remind me through sound and their effect on my body that I am taking part in something eternal. I am tapping into a reality that is beyond time and space, inhabited and upheld by a God who is for me. Next, I become aware that I am on holy ground, unable to comprehend fully what it means to commune with God. I spend some time contemplating the privilege of prayer itself, the privilege of knowing God in a personal manner. He is the one in whom we live, move, and have our being (Acts 17:28). I often become aware of my smallness and invite the Holy Spirit to be present and to speak to me and at the same time I am reminded how unqualified I am to do this. Compelled by this knowledge I get down on my knees and remind myself through my body posture that I am speaking to God who feels too awesome and beyond me to address with words. I then read a Psalm and a small section from the Gospels.

When we read the Gospels, we are seeing Jesus—the bridge, the window, the way to understand the Father or a God we could never understand through our mental faculties alone. I therefore read of this God-man, who was both divine and human, and contemplate this mystery, and gratefully dwell on everything this God-man, Jesus, did and spoke. I acknowledge again that in him all truth resides, and if I don't understand what I read I try to look closer in a posture of anticipation. Sometimes that means sitting with discomfort, sometimes with wonder, sometimes troubled by his teachings and sometimes overwhelmed by a felt tenderness that I would have never ascribed to God. With all these aspects and realizations that are now alive within me, I ask God to speak. There is nowhere to hide in front of him, and so all that I have read and contemplated also exposes me, showing me my defense mechanisms, the barriers, and the pride that I have erected to stay in control and secure my fragile self and identity. Often God does show me what is in my heart, for example the resentments I've been dragging around. Other times he fills my heart with an overflowing love for particular people. At times I have been shown the ways that I have been hard and unforgiving with myself, and I learn a little more to lower my guard and open my heart to the God Jesus reveals.

As you, the reader, read this chapter of mine I accompany you with a very simple hope. You do not need a near-death experience to wake up to the miracle of existence. You actually just need spiritual practices that bring you into contact with God, the Mystery himself, and a posture of openness, anticipation, and receptivity. Move away from preconceived and fixed ideas and be open to his always new and miraculous work. I listened to a podcast and heard the whispers of God and as I followed those whispers God showed up. My hope is that I reignited a passion for prayer as an encounter with God in you. Prayer is the place where we become fully alive, where our truest self emerges as we experience the love and acceptance of the One who created us; take it from me. In the words of A. W. Tozer, "If my fire is not large it is yet real, and there may be those who can light their candle at its flame."[11] May your candle shine brighter and brighter as you meet God through prayer.

---

11. Tozer, *Pursuit of God*, preface.

Bibliography

Balthasar, Hans Urs von. *Prayer*. Translated by Graham Harrison. San Francisco: Ignatius, 1986.

Buechner, Frederick. *Now and Then*. San Francisco: HarperCollins, 1991.

Merton, Thomas. *New Seeds of Contemplation*. New York: New Directions, 2007.

Nouwen, Henri J. M. *The Way of the Heart: Desert Spirituality and Contemporary Ministry*. New York: Seabury, 1981.

Palahniuk, Chuck. *Fight Club*. Sydney: Random House, 1997.

Palmer, Parker J. "Fierce with Reality: Living and Loving Well to the End." On Being, July 8, 2015. https://onbeing.org/blog/fierce-with-reality-living-and-loving-well-to-the-end/.

Tozer, A. W. *The Pursuit of God*. Harrisburg, PA: Christian Publications, 1948. Repr., Project Gutenberg, 2008. https://www.gutenberg.org/files/25141/25141-h/25141-h.htm.

Vanhoozer, Kevin J. *Remythologizing Theology: Divine Action, Passion, and Authorship*. Cambridge Studies in Christian Doctrine 18. New York: Cambridge University Press, 2010.

Part 6

Transformed Through the Arts

18

Practicing a Visual Spirituality
Fueling Your Eyes When Your Faith Depends on It

Mike Crudge

When was the last time the sparkling stars in a beautiful, still night sky, or a piece of art, or a genius invention took your breath away and transported you beyond yourself? Can you remember a time when a visual image awakened your sense of awe and wonder and swung the door wide open to the beauty and mystery of life and to the Creator behind it? Have you ever had an experience where what you saw with your eyes transformed you and deepened your relationship with God?

In this chapter, Mike Crudge shares his own faith journey and how he connects with God through practicing a visual spirituality. As a person who responds much more to visual images than to words and texts, he looks for images in the world around him that might be able to represent some aspects or characteristics of the Creator. As he engages in this practice and shares his experience and insights with others, his life becomes part of a more expansive story and he feels connected to something much bigger than himself. We hope that you might also discover a deepening of your relationship with God through this practice.

THIS CHAPTER IS POSSIBLY not for you. The fact that you have picked up this book probably means that some of the other chapters may be more for you. Do not stop reading, though, because what you find here might allow you to help someone else cut to the chase much sooner in their spiritual journey than I did. These might be people in your family, perhaps a child that never picked up books unless they really had to, or a friend who grew up in church but is not part of it anymore, or the Christian person you know who always seems on the fringe or edge of "normal" church life, but other than that seems quite ordinary.

I do not claim to have a spiritual practice to define and unpack here. What I offer is a particular landing place that invites moments that have transformed my body and spirit. It is a landing place that I need to visit from time to time and what happens there is what I now define as a spiritual practice. Let me create some context for my experience to show how sheltered I have been, as well as how limited many faith communities are.

While I have no regret or negativity for being born in 1974 in New Zealand, I do not think my own personal makeup—brain wiring, personality type, the what-makes-me-me—or, ultimately, my spiritual growth were best served by the Christian environment I was socialized into. This is no criticism of the rural Open Brethren faith community that shaped my family and I, or the suburban Baptist ones that had influenced my parents before my birth, or my own experiences after I left home when I was seventeen. I have learned a lot in all these settings and was cared for well. As a teenager, I was mentored and allowed to use my technical and musical interests and skills within the faith community, which kept me busy and engaged. I was not forced to do things like attending a youth group, which I would now define as activities that suck the life out of me. But, in the first twenty years of my life, I had no exposure to art or design as expressions of worship of God or mediums for greater spiritual connection, sustenance, and transformation. Both art and design were nonexistent in my Christian and spiritual formation, yet these are the very two things that connect me with God in ways that words and language never have.

In my introduction I referred to "normal" church life to describe the formula of our local church gatherings. As an example, I will use the Christian "tribe" I am currently part of and have been for thirty years: the Baptist churches of New Zealand, which I would define as being broadly evangelical with room for some variations of theology and expression (too much room for some, not enough for others). If you walk into any

Baptist Sunday church service (or catch it online) you will find a weekly formula, which is a form of liturgy even though the word *liturgy* is not used. The reason for this, I suspect, is based on historical associations to "boring" Anglican church services—which is fair sometimes, but also misunderstood. (Incongruously, many Baptist services are boring, too.) The formula in the Baptist church focuses on a loud sing-along to a live band, a sermon by a trained professional, bookended by small talk with people you see there a few times each month. And if it is like the church my own household is part of—Royal Oak Baptist Church in central Auckland—there is an excellent program for children run by exceptional volunteers which my six-year-old loves.

Another aspect I should mention is my desire for local. It takes us five minutes to walk from our house to the building our local church meets in. In our current time there are many things that take us away from our neighborhoods, such as work, university, and entertainment. I believe we should counter that trend by trying to be as local or "incarnate" as we can be with the features in life which we can more easily choose—for example, local school, local shops, local cafes, and local faith community. I am endeavoring to love my literal neighbors, but that is a different spiritual discipline (perhaps another chapter in a different book).

What I understand to be the intended purpose of our weekly religious gatherings (communal worship of God, edification of the saints, connection with the community, concern for others, confession—of faith and sin, affirmation of faith, etc.) seldom occurs for me in the context of my local church service. When I look around, I see other people having their own liminal moments and dreamy fuel-ups, but not me. I have concluded that the model of our church services works for some and not for others. There is a critical mass to keep this model working; there are enough sing-along/sermon/weekly-catchup people to keep it alive and viable—for now.

I am so embedded in this expression of church that it is culture for me. It took me twenty years within this culture to figure out the parts that did not work for me, and probably never will, and to find what helps me connect to God. I think I am not especially unique in my spiritual ways of connecting with God, so I wonder where others like me are hiding. Have they left the church, have they left the faith, have they not found the real Jesus yet? Is it possible to be broadly evangelical in New Zealand and have a visual approach to, and visual reliance on, spiritual formation and connecting with God? I think it is. I therefore want to spend the rest of this chapter describing what I mean by "visual reliance" (and I appreciate the irony of trying to do this with words instead of pictures!).

In 2017, I was asked to articulate "What helps me worship God." It was part of a chapel series at Carey Baptist College where I was working. I started by showing some images and short videos: a close-up of a glass office building reflecting the sky, a statue fountain in a cathedral garden depicting the encounter Jesus had with the woman at the well, several installations from various art galleries, a close-up photo of part of the "Bird's Nest" 2008 Olympic stadium, structures from outdoor sculpture parks, an aerial shot of a crowded underground-rail interchange, a museum's atrium, some historic and contemporary Christian art, an office building that looks like giant pants, the view from an airport gate looking out at a massive passenger plane, and an airline's promotional video clip of a flying Airbus A380. There were thirty-four photos or video clips which you can view online now.[1]

As you can see, they showcased an amazing array of creativity from around the world. I had stood in front of each of them in real life and sensed something of God. In each of these examples I had somehow felt that I had given something of myself to God, and that I had received something from God. My faith gained meaning and insight, and I felt transformed—sometimes in the moment, sometimes by ongoing pondering, drawing on the library of images in my mind. And for me this has become a spiritual practice.

The people who imagined the things in the thirty-four photos and videos and the people who made the ideas happen are absolutely amazing to me. They are truly remarkable humans. They fill me with awe and wonder. Through their work, my perception changed. I now see things differently, my eyes are opened to new things, my imagination is fueled.

In our world we see amazing things all the time, but we have lost our ability for awe and wonder. Imagine if Henry Ford could see the latest Mondeo, or Thomas Edison the LED lights that fill modern homes. I think they would be more than amazed. To us these things are normal and everyday occurrences. No one goes "wow" when they see a Ford Mondeo on the motorway, or when they flick on the light switch in their kitchen.

Artists remind us that there are no limits to the imagination. They communicate through their work what words cannot convey. Art teaches, reminds, and inspires us in ways other things in life cannot. Amazing

---

1. See Crudge, "Visual Spirituality."

things that humans create can provoke, broaden, and inspire my mind. The examples I have mentioned above, the real-life experience of them, for me, was about *seeing* something with open eyes, and making sense and meaningful connections from this visual experience.

You might be surprised but I cannot spell. This has never really bothered me, and most of the time I think *my* way of spelling words is better than the traditional way. Nevertheless, word processors and computers help me conform. Assuming the English language maintains a dominant position on this planet, I expect in hundreds of years from now it will have evolved to be spelled a lot more phonetically than it currently is, and that will make it easier for the whole planet.

We never get to experience the mind's eye of anyone else, but from what I gather we all perceive things differently. To use computer-speak, my mind's eye is pretty much a graphics processor that locks onto and makes sense of images rather than words. My mind's eye struggles with text—with words, and with pages that are full of small black characters. Every page to me looks the same, and therefore I find books visually boring. For me, engaging with pages of text brings about a mild and sometimes strong sense of physical discomfort. I do not feel relaxed when I try to engage with text, it does not feel natural to me. Reading, for me, is a real chore. I go through phases of forcing the discipline of reading into my life because of the obvious benefits. I know that reading is an important way to gain knowledge and understanding, and I have dedicated great chunks of time to it. I also appreciate (and admire) how quickly some people can consume words on the page and recall them later. My wife is a lawyer (and therefore, it seems, a professional reader). The speed at which she can get through documents and the pile of books on her side of the bedroom would almost suggest we are not of the same species.

I never read when I was a kid. When I was nine years old my mum tricked me into reading by buying me a weekly British comic. This introduced a whole new world to me, and through the speech-bubble interaction between characters I was, for the first time in my life, reading consistently. Every week I consumed that comic from cover to cover. It was the only reading I enjoyed, and in hindsight I understand why: there were images and pictures to look at on the page.

When I am trying to spell a word, I engage in a process where I recall an image of the word in my head, or I try to create an image. One word that I never get right and my computer consistently tries to correct is the word *especially*. This is how it came out the other day: espshally. My computer "assistant" offered me the following options: sensually, spyhole, emptily, seashell, asphalt. This was no help at all! (I think Microsoft needs my help to improve their game.)

This is kind of how my mind's eye sees the word when I imagine and try to recall how to spell it: e▬y. Again, this is no help at all. There is a real visual dependency to the way I engage with the world. One advantage of this visual way of seeing the world is that I often notice things other people miss. For example, I will probably notice, on the day it happens, that neighbors three houses away have trimmed their hedge or had a heat pump installed.

My point with all this is to say words, pages of text, books—they are not my natural or easiest way of engaging with the world. And so, the problem for me about the spiritual framework in my Christian culture is that I struggle to find ongoing meaning and sustenance if it relies on engagement with a book! How unlucky am I?

I know the Bible is not a book we worship, though it often feels like it. So much significance is loaded into this single collection of documents. We make such a big deal about the "word": "In the beginning was the Word, and the Word was with God, and the Word was God" (John 1:1 ESV). Try to imagine how uninspiring this idea is to someone not energized by text and reading and words. Fortunately, a redeeming notion can be found a few verses later: "And the Word became flesh and dwelt among us, and we have *seen* his glory" (John 1:14 ESV; italics added). Or as Eugene Peterson put it: "The Word became flesh and blood, and moved into the neighborhood" (MSG).

The Word became visual: it became image. This helps me to imagine not the "word of God," but the "flesh and blood of God" or the "neighborhood God." I can grasp and imagine that kind of God. I have seen him. One of the problems, though, is that we have added some additional text to that verse in John's Gospel: "And the Word became flesh and blood, and moved into the neighborhood[, and it then became word again]." Church communities can seem more focused on the "word of God" than on the "flesh and blood and *neighborhood* of God."

I want to make a brief link now to the *image* of God: "Then God said, 'Let us make [humankind] in our image, according to our likeness'" (Gen 1:26 ESV). What follows is that humans are amazing—because God is amazing. The amazing things humans do are amazing because of God. Of the various building blocks of theology, general revelation shows the works and existence of God in the physical world. It is often expressed as: climb a mountain and look at the view, marvel at a sunset, listen to the sounds of nature. We learn about God from nature, and noticing the beauty around us can help us know of God and of spiritual principles. Unfortunately, these experiences are often limited to fridge magnets with beaches and sunsets. General revelation comes through perceiving God's hand in the external events and things around us and then interpreting our experiences through that lens. That is what I am learning to do as I worship God individually and sometimes corporately. For some people it might be easier to align to artists who create sculptures or paintings depicting biblical moments or themes. But for me the awe I experience when I consider A380s, and the amazing technology, design, engineering, and beauty reflected, talks about our amazing God. Whenever my eyes are opened to this reality it somehow transforms me.

I often find myself connecting with God, and offering myself to God, when I *see* something amazing done by humans. And so, in search of God I go looking for these amazing creations made by humans. I do see a glimpse of God when I watch an A380 fly over. I get a glimpse of God when I see an artist express something never seen before. And these realizations and experiences help me worship God. The amazingness I see in some human works is, to me, a part of creation speaking of God. And it somehow connects me to God and helps me to worship God in a new way. The images in my thirty-four slides, the creativity and genius expressed there, leave me with the sense that I am part of something bigger, more significant, and more amazing than I could ever articulate with words. I see this in images in nature, too: trees and the change in season have a big visual impact on me. A few years ago, I planted seventy-five daffodil bulbs under our lawn. They are now piercing through the ground and starting to flower. Every day from mid-winter through to the end of spring they help me notice God.

Does this make sense to you? Do you relate to any of these experiences? Or do you have thoughts of doubt about me? Can you think of people who might relate to these descriptions as their God experiences and Christian spirituality? Once I realized it is legitimate to find spiritual connection and express worship through visual fueling, rather than through writing, speaking, reading, singing, or physical postures and routines, I discovered a freedom that nourishes growth, security, wonder, challenge, and sustenance. These avenues have now become my spiritual practice. This did not happen on my own or in isolation—various faith communities and individuals have crossed my path over the last twenty-five years and opened new windows for me. In fact, this window analogy is a link back to other Christian traditions where the art of icons opened windows into spiritual contemplation, devotion, and practice, particularly for people who could not read.

How does this spiritual practice actually happen? Practicing a visual spirituality when your faith depends on it sometimes happens by chance. You stumble over the intentional work of an artist who has created something for a public space, or in a similar way you notice the flyover of the A380. But visual spirituality is also something I plan into my life. I am a member of my local art gallery. I watch plane videos on YouTube (planes landing in severe winds always incites wonder). I sometimes sign up for events where faith and the arts combine. A very memorable event of that sort was a ten-day art and spirituality tour where we visited artists and faith communities, galleries, exhibitions, historic and contemporary places of worship. Although this tour was a decade ago it still fuels my imagination. Another experience included my wife and I holidaying in Rome. There was so much to take in, it was an amazing fuel for my eyes that also continues to sustain me. One random memory from that trip was running into a small church building to shelter from the rain and noticing a Caravaggio hanging on the wall. There was so much to look at from a Christian art perspective. I feel I have a lifetime of resources in my mind's eye from that single week. (I have moments of encounter in the Auckland Art Gallery, too, so it's certainly not dependent on overseas travel or spiritual art.)

I could end my chapter here but I want to return to the "normal" church services mentioned at the start. I hardly ever find connection with God or others in our Sunday sing-alongs. This is not worship for me. I personally call the people leading the band song leaders, not worship leaders.

This makes me wonder, what images are offered in our communal worship for people like me that connect with visuals rather than words? Mostly we just have a band to look at. If you have been to an opera, stage show, or ballet, ask yourself where are the musicians or the band? They are in a sunken area below the stage called the pit. You cannot see them. They are not a visual distraction, and they have no visual importance. Church music used to do this. The organist was often out of sight. Why do we now put the musicians up front on a stage? Why do we elevate them as if church meetings were a concert? Perhaps it is because church services, in the kind of churches I am part of, have actually become performances. I have suggested that the band could stand at the back behind us all, or be put behind a curtain, but nobody has taken that suggestion seriously.

If you have the privilege of leading a faith community in worship, I would like you to know that there are people like me who get bored to tears with most church sing-alongs, waiting patiently for it to finish. I am not saying we should stop having sing-alongs or the singing of songs as part of our worship times. I can see that it enables some people to move closer to God in a communal setting, or it at least offers them a euphoric or feel-good experience that sets them up for the week. But the question is whether there are people who are not part of our faith communities *because* of the sing-along? Who is not attending church services because the socialization into sing-along worship has failed to connect them with God? Could it be that our gatherings have been so thin or meaningless that these people have left church without discovering a way of worship that feels authentic to them or connects them spiritually to God and to others? Are there people who have not yet figured out what could help them to worship God and we have not managed to find ways to help them?

I suggest that if we are going to have a thirty-minute sing-along, we also offer thirty minutes of some other form of communal worship or reduce the singing to once a month. We could lead, model, or teach how to spiritually connect and worship God in other ways the rest of the month. Can we broaden our understanding of gathered worship? Why not take worship off the stage and even out of the auditorium? I must add here that there are occasions where I do experience some sort of connection in the sing-along. There are some anthem-type songs with words that are rich in imagery and that I can authentically sing (Hillsong Worship's adaptation of the Apostle's Creed being one example[2]). And I am not against music. I even played second trumpet in the horn section of a Christian ska band that toured the North Island of New Zealand in my twenties, but I am just wanting to offer a different perspective.

Conclusion

Is the spiritual practice I have described here simply "looking with appreciation and wonder"? Some days (or better, most days) I find myself momentarily arrested by something I see that captures my wonder of God. I now describe these situations as moments of spiritual transformation

---

2. Hillsong Worship, "This I Believe (The Creed)."

where I connect with God in worship and experience an increase of motivation to serve and follow Jesus. Other times (which are currently very occasionally) I curate an intentional day where my eyes notice and consume wonders, and this leads to a spiritual presence. These times sometimes feel like luxuries, because these times could be spent being more productive or what other people call "spiritual" (like sitting through a church service or reading the Bible). Other times this sense of awe and wonder appears out of nowhere and can linger in my mind for a long time. Perhaps for some people these moments would be nothing more than good memories, and perhaps that is enough if there is a connection with the Creator.

What sustains me spiritually and deepens my Christian faith? I look for images in the world around me that might be able to represent some aspects or characteristics of the Creator. I see these images every day, and sometimes in exceptional ways. I know that these images are always hopelessly inadequate, but nevertheless they provide windows to look through and take me to new horizons. These windows help me worship God. They sustain me and encourage me to continue my Christian spirituality. When I engage in this practice and share my experience and insights with others, my life becomes part of a more expansive story and I feel connected to something much bigger than myself. This practice also helps me clarify my understanding and adoration of God. Something of my spiritual journey is enhanced by the fueling of my mind's eye with divine images and adding these images to the visual library inside my head. I have come to call this practice a visual spirituality. If this does not describe you, perhaps someone comes to mind who is more like me, and perhaps you, like my mother, could give them the comic book version that affirms another way for them to engage with the gospel and our Triune God.

Bibliography

Crudge, Mike. "Visual Spirituality." https://mikecrudge.com/visual-spirituality.
Hillsong Worship. "This I Believe (The Creed)." Track 1 on *No Other Name*, written by Matt Crocker and Ben Fielding. Sydney, Aus.: Hillsong MP Music, 2014.

19

The Sacred Art of Dancing

JENNY DE LEON

The author of this chapter is a remarkable woman who very early in her life knew that there was a particular calling upon her life. Jenny felt chosen to engage in the sacred art of dancing and dedicated her whole life to this spiritual discipline of dancing for her God and Maker. This chapter is Jenny's story. It describes how she surrendered to this calling and diligently engaged in a prayer-dance practice that ultimately prepares her for the moment when she meets Jesus face-to-face and dances for him in the courts of the Lord. While not many people are called to pursue dancing as Jenny does, there is a lot we can learn from her personal story.

Jenny likens her journey to a pilgrimage that was motivated by her search for a greater fullness of light, a greater fullness of meaning, and a closer relationship with God. Dance, as an embodied, lived, and creative form of spirituality, became her prayer and the way or path for her pilgrimage. It expanded her heart and got her in touch with both the darkness and the light within it. As the method and the way for this pilgrimage, this prayer-dance practice invited her to dance through fear, anxiety, injury, surgical intervention, and the unknown until she eventually came out on the other side. This sacred art of dance has not just been a form of physical movement for Jenny but a means of connecting with God with her whole being and aligning herself to his character and will. May you also experience a sense of your chosenness and belovedness in response to the One who always asks: May I have this dance?

> There is a time for everything, and a season for every activity under the heavens . . . a time to weep and a time to laugh, a time to mourn and a time to dance.
>
> —ECCLESIASTES 3:1, 4

EVER SINCE I WAS very, very young the urge to dance has been within me. Although I was born a so-called heart child with a small hole in my heart and spent much of those early years in the cardiology unit at hospital, I have always felt profoundly connected to dance, art, and music. The desire to move runs through my veins and has held a special place in my heart. Over the years it has grown more and more and become my greatest passion. In my childhood and younger years, I did not have a clear concept of God, or what it means to sense God's call on my life. However, looking back I can see that I was chosen by God and given a special mission—namely, to dance. Now that I am older, I would describe this calling with the following words: my whole life is and has been a rehearsal and a preparation for the moment when, by his grace, I dance in the courts of the Lord—perhaps even before his throne.

My experience as a dancer and performing artist shows that dancing connects me to something that is beyond myself and beyond words. As I dance, I transcend the ordinary world and connect with a reality that is outside of time and space. Dancing is a language that helps me to express myself when there seem to be no words to articulate how I feel. It becomes a prayer that I send to my Creator. My body and the music morph into different shapes and for a moment I leave all earthly things behind until there is nothing left but God and this dance.

This chapter is about dance and the call. It is also an invitation to you, the reader, to consider that dance could be or could become your own new spiritual practice. You might say that dancing is not your thing, or that you are not good at moving your body. Let me encourage you, there is nothing that needs to stop you. Any "limitation" can turn into an opportunity. I know that God can take our physical awkwardness and our stumbling offerings and add the grace, strength, and beauty that are needed to create a beautiful dance, a dance that becomes a prayer, or an act of worship and adoration. God invites you into his courts and, using theatre terms, says, "Ladies and gentlemen, lights up. It is time to dance."

What follows is a summary of my journey and the insights that I have gained throughout the years as a worshipper, choreographer, dancer, and performing artist. Perhaps you too will respond to God who invites you onto the dance floor and is asking you, "May I have this dance?"

Poyema

Some years ago, I set up a small dance company which I called Poyema. The word *poyema* (poiēma) can be found in Eph 2:10 and means God's handiwork. "The cognate verb is used to speak of God's handiwork as a potter works with clay (Isa 29:16, cited in Rom 9:20)."[1] The vision for Poyema was to be a vehicle for making and presenting professional and sacred dances that make spirituality visible. My aim was to talk about our search for meaning, our very diverse but also shared stories, and both the awe and uncertainty that are part of our human experience as we journey through life. Via dance we can weave our individual stories as Christ's disciples and pilgrims on this earth into a much grander God story and thus serve as "Tellers of the Story."

At the beginning, Poyema consisted of professional-level dancers and musicians performing original work. It was the only dance company of its kind in New Zealand during the twenty years of its existence. Through that time, I continued my work as the company's director, choreographer, and performer, either as a solo practitioner or with other dancers and musicians who joined me for a season. My prayer has always been that I reflect God's character as his "handiwork." To describe the essence of Poyema Dance, the words *sacred*, *profane*, *muse*, and *mystery* as well as the following quotation come to mind:

> I find myself balanced—at the eye of the paradox,
> between the contradictions of despite and affirmation,
> unbelief and love.[2]

---

1. Cohick, *Letter to the Ephesians*, 166.
2. Donaldson, *Lord Foul's Bane*, 442.

The words *despite* and *unbelief* here refer to my shadow side or the aspects of my life that I have struggled to accept and pushed down into my unconscious mind. They also relate to the forces that pull me away from my true self or core being, and to all that robs me of love, joy, faith, hope, and the desire to unite with God and pray. On the contrary, the words *affirmation* and *love* describe God's energy that is consistently flowing into my life, encouraging movements of my becoming, and inviting me into the greater dance, a dance where I say yes to new possibilities and all that unfolds before me.

But what does this spiritual practice of dancing for God practically look like and why is it for me a Pilgrimage of Prayer? Like a pilgrimage, this practice describes my journey of personal growth and exploration. It is not an easy path but rather a road full of perplexity, paradox, faith, and surrender. My dance is an embodiment of a prayer that moves through different stages—away from simplicity, through complexity and perplexity, toward synergy and harmony. As I dance, I strive and surrender; I encounter belief and unbelief, current and undertow, stillness and movement. I wrestle with but also interweave all the opposing forces at play.

To illustrate this process further I want to describe a dance work I choreographed in the late eighties called *Whitewave and Undertow*, which is based on Benjamin Britten's compositions called "Dawn" and "Moonlight" from *Four Sea Interludes*.[3] From my earliest memory the dance form that has evolved within me reflects this theme of whitewave and undertow. Whitewave is the Celtic version of my first name, Jennifer. The current that runs counter to the main current is called the undertow or, as the Collins Dictionary describes it, "An undertow is a strong current of water that is moving below the surface current and in a different direction to it."[4] In the great depths of the ocean the wave is formed, then gathers slowly and imperceptibly more and more volume and momentum until it rolls to the shore. This movement is relentless, undeviating, and inexorable. With all its force the wave smashes on the rocks or sand, and then moves back and becomes the undertow. Whitewave and undertow are opposite forces that I bring together in my dance. The visible and passionate outpouring of color, sound, movement, and energy beautifully synergizes with the glorious, smashing, under-the-surface in-gathering.

---

3. See, for example, BBC Music, "Benjamin Britten in 360 Degrees."
4. Collins Dictionary, "Undertow."

This dance work is a metaphor that symbolizes both the energy that gives life and the counter-energy that draws life from me.

Thus to Fling Her Soul

More recently I choreographed a dance work titled *Thus to Fling Her Soul*. This title was inspired by the words of the following poem that describe my current stage:

> An aged thrush, frail, gaunt, and small,
> In blast-beruffled plume,
> Had chosen thus to fling [her] soul
> Upon the growing gloom.[5]

The dance *Thus to Fling Her Soul* has three parts expressing the following notion:

> Part 1: Hunger
> Part 2: A kind of madness
> Part 3: Grace
>
> To give, give my all.
> A kind of endlessness,
> asks all—so give all.

The work is about age, vulnerability, enduring, and grace. It is both a dance work and a prayer. To explain this further let me give you some background to this practice and a description of my daily routine. With dance as my prayer practice, I use my physical body to formulate my prayers. My body has suffered greatly over the years. A congenital heart defect; rheumatic fever; a car accident that killed my mother; a motorbike accident that destroyed my right leg and required knee reconstruction, eight operations (eight years on and off crutches), two full hip replacements, a right shoulder replacement, and foot reconstructive surgery; and now, pervasive, creeping arthritis have been part of my story. It took a lot of effort to regain and maintain my health and develop my skills in this prayer practice further. As part of my daily routine I do hot yoga, practice dance in the studio, swim in the ocean, plus extra sequences of exercise routines throughout the rest of the day. The whole regime takes up between four and five hours per day.

---

5. Hardy, "Darkling Thrush," lines 21–24.

I very often feel challenged beyond what I think I can bear. But there is a deep and profound calling to this work which keeps me going and helps me to persevere. As I grow older, I find that because my will is strong, I can keep going. But is this enough? Will, determination, and perseverance, through their daily iterations, can become jaw-clenching doggedness, a practice dedicated—and enslaved. The weary aching of my body is in constant conversation with my God and this unrelenting call to try again. Therefore, I try again—I will, I must, I will, I must—try again. This whole process is my pilgrimage and prayer—at times a prayer of despair, at other times a prayer of victory and grace.

Although I am frail, gaunt, and small I surrender and avail myself to this practice. I choose "to fling my soul" into God's arms of love and care. This *is* my dance; this *is* my prayer. You might ask what is the incentive, the vision that draws me *on*, through enslavement and despair? Why do I not succumb to the subtle corrosion of age-vulnerability, age-victimhood, the fear of my faculties crumbling? How can anything so ephemeral, unpredictable, precarious as dance possibly enable me to manage my unbelief, hope, and, at times, terror? How shall we, how can we, "fling our souls"?

My response to this is that within this dance-prayer-journey there is a profound, deep, and holistic experience of union with God that comes into existence. It happens without words and feels like a flowing current. It is felt and sensed in the body, expressed in gestures, shapes, and rhythm. There is an inflow and outflow, an initiation (flinging) and a welcoming response.

Choreographing my prayers in the form of a dance is done by consistently working and reworking the dance. It is a process where I empty myself of preconceived ideas and "sensible" interpretations and open myself to inspirations from above. I am receptive and attentive to what emerges, always looking for subtleties of movement, further meanings, and new developments. There is a sense of mystery and wonder. It is a contemplative, organic, miraculous unfolding where I am constantly "led to transcend rational meaning and arrive at some infinitely deeper understanding."[6]

Prayer Themes

In the dance work *Thus to Fling Her Soul*, I use themes which are known to us all—hunger, a kind of madness, and grace. Embedded in these

---

6. Lees, *Mallarmé and Wagner*, 81.

phrases are subtopics such as yearning, vulnerability, aging, the losing and gaining of faith. These themes express the fundamental and inexorable aspects and dynamics of our existence. They contain many layers of meanings and each of us adds to them different views and interpretations.

The process of dancing-choreographing-praying calls us to move beyond the known and preconceived ideas into the unfamiliar and unknown realm. It invites us into a dimension that brings together the spiritual and physical. All becomes one in the movement of surrender, in which mind, body, dance, and faith flow into and through each other.

May I invite you to try this way of prayer? Make it into a wonderful, nonstriving, "transformative experience that cannot be expressed in words,"[7] a prayer where your whole body is aware—your poyema.[8]

Within this dance-prayer I discover that life's muddle and paradox, the hunger, madness, grace, and the call to keep giving when I think I have already given my all are all contained in a deeper dance with its current and undertow. These forces are symbiotic and cannot exist without each other. As I dance, I find this still point that for me is the place where I meet God, beyond space and time, the place where the call, where poyema is birthed, and I am God's handiwork.

Method and Metaphor

Dance is the method, procedure, or process that brings me into communion with God. It is also a beautiful metaphor of how I use the music of my life, express the stirrings in my heart and attune to the One I dance for. Dance, therefore, is an integral part of my prayer practice. But since dance is wordless, experimental, and full of emotions it seems important to find a bridge between dance and words. Sharing my choreographed dances with others and finding words that describe the dance movements can be very healing as hidden messages become visible and conscious.

Dance is an expression of who I am and a prayer practice that is built on total honesty and authenticity. It displays all of me—body, soul, spirit, the personal, the public, and the dancer-choreographer-performer-therapist-academic-mother-crone. I bring all of myself to this prayer practice.

---

7. Chodorow, *Dance Therapy and Depth Psychology*, 196.

8. For inspiration, I suggest Ladinsky's poem "His Choir," in *Love Poems from God*, 121.

Choreographing and teaching myself the steps and processes in which I am taking my body through form, flow, line, rhythm, effort, gesture, nuance, and feeling in order for the dance to emerge and unfold. There is always more fine tuning, development, becoming, angles and curves to explore, rhythms yet to master, nuances to embody further. There are always lighter, deeper, richer, and other ways to approach certain movements. For the observer my dances may appear as a calculated sequence, but it is more, an endlessly complex interrelating of form, motion, impulse, intention, dynamic, time, stillness, emotion, and sensation. Even when I repeat a dance it is never the same as the previous time. This is a prayer that is forever unfolding.

I want to offer you, the reader, some of my learnings on this journey and ideas to ponder. These ideas compare thinking with dancing and show two perspectives that allow us to perceive this notion of embodied prayer:

- Thinking explores the what and the why of thinking.
- Dance takes thought into the felt, sensory, visceral, wordless "knowing."
- Thinking teaches us epistemology.
- Dance enables us to be present—here and now.
- Thinking is interpretation explained in words.
- Dance is interpretation embodied and expressed through movement.
- Thinking can be impersonal.
- Dance is immediate, experiential, and very personal.
- Thinking is the search for explanation.
- Dance is the acceptance of and search for all that is real.
- Thinking uses analysis and tries to categorize and label ideas and concepts.
- Dance weaves everything together and leaves room for ephemeral and liminal dimensions.
- We need thinking to understand what we know.
- We need dance to move into the unconscious and know how we feel.

We are all on a pilgrimage and on our way to our eternal home. We are seekers and travelers who long to connect with the transcendent, our ultimate source and guide. We move upward, inward, and out into the world in search for a place beyond and a destination just ahead. This earthly life and my dance combine in prayer and express my longing and hunger, a kind of madness, and my profound experience of grace. And as I choreograph the steps of my next dance, the next movement on my pilgrimage, I am aware how much it is both hard work and total surrender, a disciplined life and willingness to let the master choreographer inspire me, work through me, and shape this dance. The following Scriptures reflect these thoughts: "For it is God who works in you to will and to act in order to fulfill his good purpose" (Phil 2:13); and "Run in such a way as to get the prize . . . a crown that will last forever" (1 Cor 9:24–25).

It is an unmitigated paradox! I work out the particularities of the dance, the minutia, the subtleties, and endless variations, and respond to new insights that come my way through life, the passing of time, and experience. And at the same time, I let go of my ideas, I surrender, and say my wholehearted yes to God as my guide and to life, which is always relational, a flow, the creation of a dance.

As God's poyema, his handiwork, I know that our dancing bodies are symbols of prayer. They are vehicles for "unspeakable human truths, which, because they are unspeakable, leave us little to say. For the dance remains an ephemeral event whose immediacy cannot be captured in words, too fragile and too fleeting for comment."[9]

A Scripture that has encouraged me to keep going in this prayer practice is Rom 8:26–27:

> In the same way, the Spirit helps us in our weakness. We do not know what we ought to pray for, but the Spirit himself intercedes for us through wordless groans. And he who searches our hearts knows the mind of the Spirit, because the Spirit intercedes for God's people.

And if God's Spirit is truly working in me and interceding for me so that I can act in accordance to God's good purposes, then this prayer practice of movement-and-words, written, but also fluid, integrative, holistic, ambiguous, and transcendent is truly the vision and prayer that lead me on.

    Surrender and Receptivity
    Always
    Both . . . and

---

9. Foster, *Reading Dancing*, xvi.

Paradoxical Turns

There are many paradoxes in life and as I get older, I learn to hold them in my heart as an unsolvable reality and know that there is a lot I will never fully understand. I seek God in this prayer practice, but I realize I cannot find God unless he shows himself to me; yet, God would not have inspired me to seek him in the dance unless I had already found him there. That is to say, dance as a prayer practice requires an acceptance of all that is unknown and not fully understood yet. However, as I pursue the questions, as I draw closer to God and seek him with my whole heart, as I diligently engage in this spiritual discipline and practice, I experience that God also draws closer to me and that new possibilities and meanings open to me. I slowly move into a deeper understanding of God, myself, the dance, and life, and in this way get closer to the answers to my questions.

I have used many words to describe this prayer practice. However, the imagination, reflection, contemplation, daring, and faith that are all part of this process of traversing liminal boundaries and uniting with God are experiences that are beyond words and utterly beautiful. Since "every day there are new interpretations because every day God renews the work of creation,"[10] I partner with God and welcome each day as an opportunity for further growth, renewed practice and prayer, which leads to a renewed sense of self and being.

Prayer-dance, therefore, is to me "the means through which we may connect ourselves to a higher truth. Its deepest aim, if we will allow ourselves to surrender, is to transform us, so that we will leave behind 'the weary weight of the unintelligible world,' and become what we are meant to be: 'a living soul'. It allows us to imagine ourselves anew, if we will permit it to do so."[11]

While this practice on one side is extravagant, meaning-making, and replete with God, it is also a practice through which I am confronted with my impermanence, fragility, inadequacy, and realization that I might dare too much. I therefore adopt David's thoughts and make them my prayer: "My heart is not proud, O Lord, my eyes are not haughty; I do not concern myself with great matters or things too wonderful for me" (Ps 131:1).

By writing this chapter I endeavored to capture the essence of my dance prayer practice in words. I would like to invite you, as the reader, into the experience of this practice and pray that as you use your body

---

10. Rabbi Zadok haCohen cited in Sacks, *Great Partnership*, 368.
11. Hadlow, *Other Bennet Sister*, 375.

to formulate your prayer you will feel God's presence and affirming gaze and know that you are God's handiwork and poyema. May my story of giving my all and "flinging my soul" into the arms of my Creator encourage and touch you.

Bibliography

BBC Music. "Benjamin Britten in 360 Degrees: 'Dawn—Four Sea Interludes' Performed by the BBC Philharmonic." YouTube, Jan. 10, 2019. https://www.youtube.com/watch?v=c80QuZJkcR4.

Chodorow, Joan. *Dance Therapy and Depth Psychology: The Moving Imagination.* London: Routledge, 1991.

Cohick, Lynn H. *The Letter to the Ephesians.* New International Commentary on the New Testament. Grand Rapids: Eerdmans, 2020.

Collins Dictionary. "Undertow." https://www.collinsdictionary.com/dictionary/english/undertow.

Donaldson, Stephen R. *Lord Foul's Bane.* Book 1 of *The Chronicles of Thomas Covenant, the Unbeliever.* New York: Holt, Rinehart and Winston, 1977.

Foster, Susan Leigh. *Reading Dancing: Bodies and Subjects in Contemporary American Dance.* Los Angeles: University of California Press, 1986.

Hadlow, Janice. *The Other Bennet Sister.* New York: Holt, 2020.

Hardy, Thomas. "The Darkling Thrush." Poetry Foundation. https://www.poetryfoundation.org/poems/44325/the-darkling-thrush.

Ladinsky, Daniel. *Love Poems from God: Twelve Sacred Voices from the East and West.* New York: Penguin Compass, 2002.

Lees, Heath. *Mallarmé and Wagner: Music and Poetic Language.* London: Ashgate, 2007.

Sacks, Jonathan. *The Great Partnership: God, Science and the Search for Meaning.* London: Hodder & Stoughton, 2012.

Index

Note: Locators followed by "n" refer to footnotes.

Abraham (prophet), 170
    bargaining with God, 203
    two-way encounters with God, 204
Altmann, Peter, 169
Antonaccio, Maria, 135
Aronson, Elliot, 105
art and spirituality. *See* visual spirituality
The Artists Way (Cameron), 97
asceticism practices, 131, 133
    ascetic life, 138–39
    and consumerism, 136–37
    desire reorienting, 133–36
    spiritual space creation, 137–38
As One Without Authority (Craddock), 37
attention restoration theory, 79
awe, 80–81, 83

Baab, Lynne M., 37, 128n12
Bakke, Jeanette, 208
Balthasar, Hans Urs von, 41, 233, 237
Barry, Don, 212, 213n9
Barry, William, 27–29
Baxter, Richard, 41
    about meditating on Scripture, 48
    about reasoning/preaching with/to ourselves, 44
    about self-talk, 41–42
Being Christian (Williams), 205
being psychology vs. deprivation psychology, 11
Benner, David, 14
Berry, Thomas, 100
Berry, Wendell, 100
Bible memorization, 50–59. *See also* reading of Bible missionally
    C. S. Lewis's case, 53–54
    and humility, 57
    marketing analogies, 51–52
    SPIN cycle analogy, 54
    "Topic, Reference, Verse, Reference" process, 55–56
    and wisdom, 58
Bible Society of New Zealand, 36
Bonhoeffer, Dietrich, 144, 145, 149, 150
Book of Common Prayer (BCP), 187, 190
    in Māori Christianity, 190–92
    memorization and recitation, 194–96
    missional impact and potential, 196–97
    translation of Morning and Evening Prayer services, 193
Bourgeault, Cynthia, 17–18
Browning, Elizabeth Barrett, 87
Buechner, Frederick, 236
Burghardt, Walter, 87–88
burnout, 104–6
    gardening effect on, 108–9. *See also* contemplative gardening
    as a God-sent intervention, 109–10
    stages of, 106–8
Burrows, Sam. *See* prayer and near death-experiences

Cain, Paul, 228
Calvin, John, 46
Cameron, Julia, 97
Capon, Robert Farrar, 169, 171, 176
Cassian, John, 81, 205
charismatic renewal movement, 4
Chase, Stephen, 100
Chesterton, G. K., 34
Christ-centered prayer approach, 4
Clare of Assisi, 131–32, 137–38
    Clare's Rule, 134–35, 139
Coakley, Sarah, 135
Coleman, Strahan, 111
Collins, Bronwyn, 54
Collins, Tim, 50–51. *See also* Bible memorization
Comer, John Mark, 75
compassion, 2, 8, 80
    fatigue, 104–6. *See also* burnout
confession, 150–52
consumerism, 136–37
contemplation, 5, 38, 45–46
    Burghardt's description of, 87–88
    and spirituality, 4–5
contemplative gardening, 103–4, 111. *See also* burnout
    grander narrative, 111–12, 116
    gratefulness, 112, 116
    innocence and goodness, 112–13, 116
    presentness, 111, 116
    seeds as hope symbol, 114–16
    surrendering to God, 113–14, 116
counting down our days practice, 121–23, 129–30
    benefits, 124–29
Craddock, Fred, 37
Crudge, Michael. *See* visual spirituality

dancing as spiritual practice, 255–60
    as method and metaphor, 261–63
    Poyema dance company, 257–60
    paradox of, 164–65
    prayer and, 255–56, 260–61, 264
death. *See* counting down our days practice
De Leon, Jennifer. *See* dancing as spiritual practice
Delio, Sister Ilia, 100

Department of Conservation (DOC), 75
deprivation psychology vs. being psychology, 11
desire reorienting
    askesis practice, 133, 133n3
    flourishing self, 136
    fullness of life, 135–36
    privilege of poverty, 134, 134n8
    self-denial, 133–34
Deuteronomy, 35, 57, 170–71, 173
diaries. *See* journaling
discernment of spiritual experiences, 216–17, 223–24, 229–30. *See also* prophetic listening
    in church history, 224–26
    framing of, 227–28
    Kim's perspective of, 228–29
    The Divine Dance (Rohr), 92
Donoghue, Denis, 44
Drake, Lyndon. *See* prayers in Māori communities
Duhigg, Charles, 56
Duncan, Mick. *See* prayer

eco-spirituality, 100
Edwards, Jonathan, 225
ego, 15–16
    boundaries, 12–13
    transformation, 17–18
Elrod, Hal, 10–11
Eriugena, John Scotus, 108
eternity, 121–22
Every Moment Holy, 177

faith in spiritual practices
    engagement with spiritual practices, 3
    participation in church communities or faith traditions, 3, 4–5
    psychological development, 3–4
false self, 17
fast fashion, 136
feast(ing), 168–70
    and Christian calendar, 178–79
    at home, 176–78
    at Lord's Supper, 180–81
    in Old Testament, 170–75
    today, 176–81
    in Torah, 172–74

Feast of Ascension, 178
Feast of Epiphany, 178, 179
Fee, Gordon, 221
fellowship, 143–46, 152
    benefits of, 147–52
    face-to-face encounters, 146–47
Ferrer, Vincent, 224
Fight Club (Palahniuk), 233–34
Fitzmaurice, Simon, 127
Ford, Henry, 248
forest bathing, 80
Four Sea Interludes dance, 258
Fowler, James, 25–26
Fox, Matthew, 90, 91, 100
Francis of Assisi (St.), 91, 99–100, 224
Francis of Paola, 224
Freudenberger, Herbert, 105
Freud, Sigmund, 113
friendship. See fellowship
Fu, Janling, 169
fullness of life, 132, 135–36

Galli, Mark, 201
Gandhi, Mohandas Karamchand (Mahatma), 104
gardening as spiritual practice. See contemplative gardening
Garland, David, 223
Garofalo, Michael P., 112
Garrett, Susan R., 133, 136
George, Santhosh. See hiking
Gerard (Father), 26–30
Goldingay, John, 125, 203n5
Gonzalez, Michelle, 136, 137, 137n23
Graham, Billy, 129n13, 204–5
Greene, Graham, 105
Green, Gene L., 162
Green, Julian, 45
Gregg, Douglas, 145, 147, 150
Gregory IX (Pope), 134
Gregory of Nyssa, 81
Grudem, Wayne, 224
Guigo the Second, 38. See also *lectio divina* (sacred reading)
Guinness, Os, 36
Guyon, Jeanne Marie, 40

Halstead, Angelika. See contemplative gardening; transformation through spiritual practices
Halstead, Philip. See counting down our days practice; land
Hari, Johann, 126
Harris, Dan, 131
Hartman, Laura M., 137
having less, 131–33
    and asceticism, 138–39
    consumerism critique, 136–37
    desire reorientation, 133–36
    spiritual spaces creation, 137–38
Hawker, Paul, 100
hearing God's voice, 210–12. See also discernment of spiritual experiences; prophetic listening
hiking, 73–75, 83
    awe and wonder effect, 80–81, 83
    effect of being in nature, 79–80, 83
    hardship effect, 82–83
    simplicity, 81–82
    withdrawing, 75–79, 83
Hildegard of Bingen (St.), 90–91, 99–100
Hoarders (reality TV show), 136, 136n19
"home" concept, 11–13
Holy Invitations (Bakke), 208
Holy Spirit, 12, 28, 57, 200
    availability of gifts, 4
    in Bible origins, 64
    Christ-centered prayer approach, 4
    guidance, 227
    supernatural activity, 229
    transforming work evidence, 225
Hooper, Walter, 53–54
Hopkins, Gerard Manley, 80

Ignatius of Loyola spiritual exercises, 23–24
    Barry's theological framing, 27–29
    personal journey, 24–27, 29–32
    rhythm of prayer and journaling, 27
imagination engagement, 40–41, 42–43, 47
Interactive Drawing Therapy (IDT), 89n8
interconnectedness, 90–91

Isaac, Munther, 161
Israel/Israelites
　Feast of Unleavened Bread, 172–73
　formative practice of feasting, 170–72, 171n6
It's Not Yet Dark (Fitzmaurice), 127

Jamieson, Alan. *See* Ignatius of Loyola spiritual exercises
The Jesuit Guide to (Almost) Everything (Martin), 32
Jesuits, 24, 25
Jesus Christ, 200
　and feasting, 175
　Matthew on transfiguration of, 239–40
　and nature, 155
　on prayer, 206
　on prophets, 220
　on simplicity, 81, 135–36
　and transformation, 13
　and withdrawing, 9, 75, 79
　and word of God, 35–36, 38
Joel (prophet), 221–22
Johnson, Darrell, 35
Jonah (prophet)
　expressive prayer, 202–3
　two-way encounters with God, 204
journaling, 207–9, 212–14
　hearing voice of God, 210–12
　steps, 209–10
Julian of Norwich, 91, 100
Jung, Carl Gustav, 1
　about psyche, 14, 92n20
　about ego structure, 16
　Self, 1, 15
　shadow, 15, 16
Jung, Shannon L., 172

Kaa, Hirini, 191
karakia. *See* prayer in Māori communities
Keating, Thomas, 5
Kicker, Lydia, 151
Kilmer, Joyce, 79
Kim, Kirsteen, 227, 228, 229
King, Martin Luther, Jr., 228
Kondo, Marie, 82, 82n31, 132–33, 136
KonMari method, 133

Lane, Belden, 82–83
land, 154–56
　benefits, 164–65
　homelessness, 162–63
　role of land, 156–62
Laudato si' (Pope Francis), 100
lectio divina (sacred reading), 33–34, 38
　contemplatio (living out), 45–48
　lectio (reading), 39–40
　meditatio (meditating), 40–44
　oratio (prayer), 44–45
　pattern for, 38
　priority of, 34–36
　problem of, 36–38
Lee Kuan Yew, 79
Lewis, C. S., 53, 55, 76, 146
The Life-Changing Magic of Tidying Up (Kondo), 132–33
Life Lessons Learned Lecture (LLLL), 127–28
liminal space, 6
Lloyd, Kasey, 137
"Loneliness" poem (Oliver), 92
loneliness to solitude transition, 77–79, 83
A Long Obedience in the Same Direction (Peterson), 159
Loorz, Victoria, 96, 100
Lord's Supper, 175, 180–81. *See also* feast(ing)
love of God, 28, 31, 90–91, 237
　love, language of, 12–13
Low, Mary, 155
Lucado, Max, 148

Makant, Mindy, 137
　Manakinui Te Kahu (land). *See* land
Māori culture and language, 100. *See also* land; prayer in Māori communities
　Mana Atua (God), 160–61
　Mana Tāngata (humanity), 160, 161
　Mana Whenua (the land), 160, 161
　marae (meeting place), 160
　te reo (Māori language), 155, 188
　tētahi ki tētahi (fellowship), 144, 149, 152
　whānau (extended family), 91, 147, 155, 159

whare karakia (church), 160
whare tipuna (house of ancestors), 160
urupā (cemetery/burial site), 159–60
Māori wholistic worldview (*te ao*), 158
    burial of placenta in, 163
    spiritual concepts in, 160–61
Marsden, Samuel, 188
Martin, James, 32
Maslach Burnout Inventory, 105
Maslach, Christina, 105
Maslow, Abraham, 11, 13
Mathis, David, 144, 148, 152
Maximilla, 224
McFague, Sallie, 136
meditation on Scripture, 6, 38, 40–44
    attention role, 40, 41, 47
    context role, 40, 41
    imagination role, 40–41, 42–43, 47
    self-preaching/reasoning, 43–44
    self-talk, 41–42, 44
Mellar-Smith, Robyn. *See* journaling
Merton, Thomas, 12, 110, 232
metamorphosis, 52
Metge, Joan, 195
Minimalism (film), 131
minimalism, 132, 134, 138. *See also* having less
The Minimalists, 138
The Miracle Morning (Elrod), 10–11
missional hermeneutics, 60
Moetara, Simon. *See* fellowship
monasticism, 134
Montanus, 224
Moo, Douglas, 100
Moo, Jonathan, 100
Moses, 125
    expressive prayer, 202, 203
    two-way encounters with God, 204
Mother Earth, 92, 93, 95–96
Mount Pirongia, New Zealand, 74, 82, 83
    movements of spiritual transformation
        inward, 6–8
        outward, 10–11
        upward, 8–9
Muir, John, 98n30, 109
mystical experience, 86, 86n1

nature therapeutic effects, 79–80. *See also* contemplative gardening
nature-gazing practice, 85–87
    origins, 89–92
    personal encounters with nature, 93–94
    practical guidelines, 97–100
    as spiritual routine, 87–89
    transformational potential, 95–96
near-death experiences. *See* prayer and near death-experiences
neuroplasticity, 50–51
New Seeds of Contemplation (Merton), 232
New Testament, 35
    minimalist movements in, 134
    Passover celebration, 176n19
    pastoral ministry in, 37
    pattern of reading words of God, 47
    prophecy in, 220, 221
New Zealand (Aotearoa), 155–56. *See also* Māori culture and language
    Christianity in, 189–90, 196
noise to silence transition, 76, 83
Nouwen, Henri, 78–79, 238

obedience, 46, 133, 135, 138
O'Brien, Kevin, 30–31
O'Donohue, John, 111, 143
Old Testament, 35, 36
    feasting in, 175, 179
    prophecy in, 220
Oliver, Mary, 92, 100

Palahniuk, Chuck, 233–34
Palmer, Tim. *See* discernment of spiritual experiences; prophetic listening
Passover, 177, 176n19
    Feast, 173, 173n14
pastoral ministry, 37
Paul the Apostle, 220–23
    about encouragement, 147
    expressive prayer, 202
    about transformation of mind, 52
    two-way encounters with God, 204
Pennington, William, 137
perception, 17

INDEX

Peterson, Eugene, 34, 159
   about contemplation, 45–46
   about conversations with God, 44
   about meditation on Scripture, 40
   about reasons for human failure, 39
   about writings of Psalms, 45
Peter the Apostle, 144, 213, 239
philosophical pluralism, 37
Pines, Ayala, 105
Piper, John, 53
playfulness, 13, 99
Poor Sisters, 134–35
possessions, 2, 24, 81. *See also* having less
poverty, 134, 134n8
The Power of Habit (Duhigg), 56
Poyema dance company, 257–58
   Four Sea Interludes, 258
   Thus to Fling Her Soul, 259–60
   Whitewave and Undertow, 258
Prayer (Balthasar), 237
prayer, 198–200
   expressive, 202–4
   intimate, 200–202, 205–6
   two-way, 204–5
prayer and near death-experiences, 232–34, 240–41
   COVID experience, 234–39
   Matthew's transfiguration of Jesus, 239–40
prayer in Māori communities, 163–64, 187, 190
   contemporary use, 192
   memorization and recitation, 194–96
   missional impact and potential, 196–97
   Morning and Evening Prayer, 188–89, 193, 196
   Te Haahi Mihingare (Māori Anglican Church), 188
presentness, 111
Priscilla, 224
Pritchard, Sheila, 89, 95
Prophetic Etiquette (Sullivant), 225
prophetic listening, 216–18, 229–30. *See also* discernment of spiritual experiences
   in 1 Corinthians, 221–22, 223
   exercises, 218–19, 222–23, 226–27, 228–29
   prophecy definition, 219–20
psyche, 14

quality time with God, 75

Rāwiri (Prayer Book). *See* Book of Common Prayer (BCP)
reading of Bible missionally, 60–62. *See also lectio divina* (sacred reading)
   aspects of, 62–64
   book of Acts example, 64–67
   practicing, 67–69
Rhodes, Michael J., *See* feast(ing)
Rhodes, R. H., 191
righteousness, 169
Robeck, C. M. Jr., 220
Rohr, Richard, 4, 18, 92, 98
Roosevelt, Theodore, 82
Ross, Michael, 37
Rublev, Andrei, 91
The Ruthless Elimination of Hurry (Comer), 75
Ryle, James, 225

Sacks, Oliver, 104, 108
Sacks, Rabbi Jonathan, 146
sacred moments, 5–6
The Saints' Everlasting Rest (Baxter), 41
Sanford, Agnes, 157
The Screwtape Letters (Lewis), 76
self-sufficiency, 13
self-talk practice, 41–42, 44
silence, 76, 78, 83
Silence, Affirmations, Visualization, Exercise, Reading, and Scribing (SAVERS), 11
simplicity, 13. *See also* having less
   ascetic vision of, 136
   and community, 115
   in Christian spiritualities, 131, 133
   and Jesus's, 135
   spiritual discipline of, 81–82
Sione, Ricky, 152
Sister Patricia, 208, 209, 211
Socrates, 7
solitude, 77–79, 90, 98

soul
    freedom of, 134–35, 138
    in Jungian psychology, 14–15
spiritual awakening, 232
spiritual direction, 90, 90n9, 208
Spiritual Directors' Formation
    Programme (SDFP), 90–92
Spiritual Exercises (Ignatius), 26n4
spiritual fruit, 56–57
spiritual space creation, 137–38
Stace, Arthur, 121
Sternberg, Esther, 112
Stoics, 133
submission, 150–51. *See also* fellowship
Sullivant, Michael, 225
The Supper of the Lamb (Capon), 176

Tan, Siang Yang, 145, 147, 150
Teach Yourself Judo (Dominy), 30
Teilhard de Chardin, Pierre, 100
Theologies of Land (Yeo and Green), 162
Thompson's Guide to Practical Ship Building, 34
Tidying Up (Kondo), 132, 136
Tolkien, J. R. R., 80
"Topic, Reference, Verse, Reference" process, 55–56
Torah
    commands to rejoice, 170, 171n7
    feasting in, 170, 172–74
Tozer, A. W., 241
transformation through spiritual
    practices, 1–3, 11–17
    deepening relationship with God, 8–9
    inward journey, 6–8
    Jesus's belief in, 13–14
    modern challenges to, 2
    psycho-spiritual transformation, 2, 14, 16
    social component of, 10–11
    stages of faith, 3–6
    as operating system change, 17–18

Trinity, 217, 238

Trinity icon (Rublev), 91
Tucker, John. *See lectio divina* (sacred reading)
Tulip, Katrina. *See* nature-gazing practice
Turner, Max, 228
Twain, Mark, 81

unconsciousness/unconscious thoughts, 7
    memories in, 6
    personal, 15, 16

van Gemerden, Jaimee. *See* having less
Vanhoozer, Kevin, 239
visio divina, 99
visual spirituality, 245–54
    in Bible's words, 250–51
    inclusive worship model, 252–53
    visual way of seeing world, 249–50
Voil, Simon de, 91

Wells, David, 36
Wesley, John, 144
Whitewave and Undertow dance, 258
Whittier, John Greenleaf, 126
wholeness, 13, 58
Wieland, George M. *See* reading of Bible missionally
Willard, Dallas, 145, 150–51
Williamson, Paul, 162
Williams, Rowan, 205
wisdom through conflict, 58
withdrawing, 75–76
    from loneliness to solitude, 77–79, 83
    from noise to silence, 76, 83
    from work to rest, 76–77, 83
wonder, 80–81, 83
Woodley, Randy, 162
Wordsworth, William, 104
work to rest transition, 76–77, 83
Wright, Nigel, 227

Yancey, Philip, 149
Yeo, K. K., 162

www.ingramcontent.com/pod-product-compliance
Lightning Source LLC
Chambersburg PA
CBHW050840230426
43667CB00012B/2078